WITHDRAWN

the series on school reform

Patricia A. Wasley
Bank Street College of Education

Ann Lieberman
NCREST

Joseph P. McDonald
New York University

SERIES EDITORS

Good Schools/Real Schools: Why School Reform Doesn't Last
DEAN FINK

Beyond Formulas in Mathematics and Teaching: Dynamics of the High School Algebra Classroom
DANIEL CHAZAN

School Reform Behind the Scenes
JOSEPH P. McDONALD, THOMAS HATCH, EDWARD KIRBY, NANCY AMES, NORRIS M. HAYNES, AND EDWARD T. JOYNER

Looking Together at Student Work: A Companion Guide to *Assessing Student Learning*
TINA BLYTHE, DAVID ALLEN, AND BARBARA SHIEFFELIN POWELL

Teachers—Transforming Their World and Their Work
ANN LIEBERMAN AND LYNNE MILLER

Teaching in Common: Challenges to Joint Work in Classrooms and Schools
ANNE DIPARDO

Charter Schools: Another Flawed Educational Reform?
SEYMOUR B. SARASON

Assessing Student Learning: From Grading to Understanding
DAVID ALLEN, EDITOR

Racing with the Clock: Making Time for Teaching and Learning in School Reform
NANCY E. ADELMAN, KAREN PANTON WALKING EAGLE, AND ANDY HARGREAVES, EDITORS

The Role of State Departments of Education in Complex School Reform
SUSAN FOLLETT LUSI

Making Professional Development Schools Work: Politics, Practice, and Policy
MARSHA LEVINE AND ROBERTA TRACHTMAN, EDITORS

How It Works—Inside a School–College Collaboration
SIDNEY TRUBOWITZ AND PAUL LONGO

Surviving School Reform: A Year in the Life of One School
LARAINE K. HONG

Eyes on the Child: Three Portfolio Stories
KATHE JERVIS

Revisiting "The Culture of the School and the Problem of Change"
SEYMOUR B. SARASON

Teacher Learning: New Policies, New Practices
MILBREY W. McLAUGHLIN AND IDA OBERMAN, EDITORS

What's Happening in Math Class?: Envisioning New Practices Through Teacher Narratives (Volume 1)
DEBORAH SCHIFTER, EDITOR

What's Happening in Math Class?: Reconstructing Professional Identities (Volume 2)
DEBORAH SCHIFTER, EDITOR

Reaching for a Better Standard: English School Inspection and the Dilemma of Accountability for American Public Schools
THOMAS A. WILSON

Restructuring Urban Schools: A Chicago Perspective
G. ALFRED HESS, JR.

The Subjects in Question: Departmental Organization and the High School
LESLIE SANTEE SISKIN AND JUDITH WARREN LITTLE, EDITORS

Authentic Assessment in Action: Studies of Schools and Students at Work
LINDA DARLING-HAMMOND, JACQUELINE ANCESS, AND BEVERLY FALK

School Work: Gender and the Cultural Construction of Teaching
SARI KNOPP BIKLEN

School Change: The Personal Development of a Point of View
SEYMOUR B. SARASON

The Work of Restructuring Schools: Building from the Groun Up
ANN LIEBERMAN, EDITOR

Stirring the Chalkdust: Tales of Teachers Changing Classroom Practice
PATRICIA A. WASLEY

This series also incorporates earlier titles in the Professional Development and Practice Series

GOOD SCHOOLS/REAL SCHOOLS

Why School Reform Doesn't Last

DEAN FINK

Teachers College, Columbia University
New York and London

Published by Teachers College Press, 1234 Amsterdam Avenue, New York, NY 10027

Library of Congress Cataloging-in-Publication Data

Fink, Dean, 1936–
Good schools/real schools : why school reform doesn't last / Dean Fink.
p. cm.—(The series on school reform)
Includes bibliographical references and index.
ISBN 0-8077-3945-6 (cloth)—ISBN 0-8077-3944-8 (pbk.)
1. Lord Byron High School. 2. School improvement programs—Canada—Ontario—Case studies. 3. School management and organization—Canada—Ontario—Case studies. 4. Schools—Canada—Ontario—Sociological aspects—Case studies. I. Series.

LB2822.84.C2 F56 2000
373.713—dc21

99-088477

ISBN 0-8077-3944-8 (paper)
ISBN 0-8077-3945-6 (cloth)

Printed on acid-free paper

Manufactured in the United States of America

07 06 05 04 03 02 01 00 8 7 6 5 4 3 2 1

To my parents, my mother, Marjorie, and my late father, Roy, for believing that my education was important, and for making it possible.

To my wife, Ramona, who makes the continuing pursuit of my dreams possible.

Contents

Acknowledgments

This book and the Ph.D. thesis from which it has been derived has represented a major slice of my life. Its completion is directly attributable to my wonderful family, friends, and colleagues. I would like to acknowledge the following:

- to my friend, partner and mentor, Andy Hargreaves, words cannot express my appreciation for his support, scholarship, and encouragement in all phases of this effort;
- to Bob Moon, for taking a risk on an unknown Canadian, and supporting his lifelong ambitions to undertake a doctoral program;
- to my friend and writing and consulting partner Louise Stoll for her advice, scholarship, encouragement, and help in this and many other projects over the past 10 years;
- to my friend Corrie Giles for his scholarly critique, willingness to share resources, and sympathetic understanding of what I was experiencing;
- to my former colleague Kit Rankin for taking the time to proof this effort in the midst of her ridiculously heavy workload;
- to the many people who have assisted me in my "Third Age": Vladimir Briller, Brent Davies, Peter Daly, Pat Diggins, Lorna Earl, Michael Fullan, Peter Mortimore, John Gardner, Jenny Lewis, Dale Mann, John Novak, John Retallick, John Rowe, Betty Seigel, Paul Shaw, Harry Turner, John West-Burnham, to mention only a few;
- to the staff, present and past, of Lord Byron High School who gave so willingly of their time to help me with this project;
- to the many former colleagues with the South Board of Education who willingly and candidly offered their perspectives on the Lord Byron story;
- to Brian Ellerbeck of Teachers College Press for his guidance in all phases of this effort;
- to Ann Lieberman for her encouragement and support from the beginning of this effort;
- to my children, Danielle, Tracy and her husband Glenn, and my

grandsons, Zachary and Riley, for their love and encouragement and their tolerance of my addiction to the completion of this project;

- to my mother, Marjorie, for over half a century of love and encouragement, and my mother-in-law, Mona, for over a quarter of a century of support;
- to my wife, Ramona, for her love, encouragement, and assuming responsibility for the daily pressures of life so that I could complete this project.

Introduction

Throughout the Western world, there appears to be a consensus among policymakers and influential elements of society that schools as we know them have failed to prepare children for the challenges of the emerging information age. National and state governments have spent large sums of money to "reform" allegedly fatally flawed educational systems. Their solutions are amazingly similar. Important decisions about students' learning, such as what they are to learn, when they are to learn it, and how students are to demonstrate their learning, have been removed from local settings and assumed by bureaucrats in offices far removed from schools and classrooms. Conversely, resources have been devolved directly to schools to make local "site-based" decisions, usually accompanied by a reduction in government support. In most situations, increased parental involvement in substantive school policy issues has been mandated in the form of school governors or school councils. While inconclusive, there is a building body of evidence that suggests that these ambitious reform and restructuring efforts are making little positive impact on classrooms. In fact one might well argue that many marginalized students are worse off than before (Cohen, 1995; Elmore, 1995; Newmann & Wehlage, 1995; Robertson, 1996; Whitty, 1997; Whitty, Power, & Halpin, 1998). These efforts do, however, seem to prove the old adage that "for every complex problem there is a simple answer and it's usually wrong."

Increasingly, the inability of these reforms to produce revolutionary transformations in schools and improved educational quality has produced a feeling among some policymakers that if somehow society could just eliminate the existing schools and school systems and start over again, then, magically, all the educational problems would disappear. In the United States, for example, a great deal of money and energy have been poured into the New American Schools initiative (Odden, 1996; Stringfield, Ross, & Smith, 1996). Charter schools in North America, selective schools in the United Kingdom, and an expanding private school sector in New Zealand and Australia are symptomatic of this search for new alternatives to conventional schooling. In the

United Kingdom and more recently the United States, threats to close failing schools and reopen them as new schools with "heroic" heads (principals) and new teaching staffs capture headlines in the daily press (Barber, 1995). This hope, of course, is not just a recent phenomenon. Over the years new schools have been built annually. Virtually every new school is proclaimed or declares itself to be "innovative," or a "break-the-mold" or "lighthouse" school. Very little is heard from them after the initial "honeymoon" ends (Doremus, 1981a, 1981b, 1981c, 1982). Some of these schools join the educational "mainstream," while others experience ongoing turmoil and in extreme cases closure (Doremus, 1981a; Fletcher, Caron, & Williams, 1985; Riley, 1998). It is this process that this book calls the "attrition of change" and it is this phenomenon that is at the heart of this investigation.

This is a reworked version of a study that helped me to get a Ph.D. Before you reject it as a typically turgid, esoteric work of little practical significance in real schools with real teachers and students, I would hasten to suggest that this is different. First, I am not your typical newly minted Ph.D. I am now enjoying what Handy (1995a) has called the "Third Age"—the post-career phase of life. Unlike most people who complete graduate work to advance a career in progress, I can look back on one that has been lengthy and varied. In some ways this book is autobiographical because I have not only studied the events described, but I participated in many. Second, as a former teacher, and principal, and senior official in a school district, I have always abhorred the exclusionary pseudo-academic language of most educational studies; therefore, I have made every effort to write this book in an accessible but scholarly style that will make it useful to all who want to understand change in schools over time.

Each year of my 34 years as a public educator brought its challenges and rewards, but the three years 1970 to 1973, as a department head and original staff member of Lord Byron High School, remain in my memory as being among the most exciting and influential in my career.[1] As a result, when I began my search for a meaningful topic for a thesis, and ultimately for this book, my mind moved rather quickly to this significant educational experience. The book, therefore, is a study of the 25-year history of a new and purposefully innovative school, Lord Byron High School.[2] It opened in 1970, and quickly gained a reputation as one of Canada's most innovative schools. In its first 3 years of operation, it hosted thousands of visitors, many from outside of Ontario. Gradually, however, the school lost much of its innovative zeal. Lord Byron High School today looks very much like a regular Ontario secondary school. The emphasis on creativity and experimentation in the 1970s has been replaced by a focus on survival and continuity in the late 1990s and into the new millennium. This pattern raises the question of why a school that started out with more advantages than virtually any other secondary school in Canada lost its innovative momentum and experienced an "attrition of change." An examination of this essential question can provide insight into the complex and often paradoxical forces that impact on a school and affect its ability to sustain an innovative culture over time. Answers to this question cross national boundaries. Since my Third Age has involved consulting work in over 27 different countries around the world, I can assure the reader that even though Lord Byron is located in Ontario, Canada, the study of its attrition of change is relevant whether you live in Cleveland, Calgary, Bury in the United Kingdom, Palmerston North in New Zealand, or Wagga Wagga in Australia.

Over my career, I have been associated with a number of new and innovative schools. They all appeared to me to have started out similarly, as places of hope, enthusiasm, energy, and creativity. Within a relatively short time these schools, like Byron, seem to have become rather conventional schools. Just as Huberman (1993), Sikes (1985), and others have described teacher life cycles, there appears to be a life cycle for schools, as there is for other organizations. Kanter (1983), for example, describes some business organizations as experiencing "cultures of age" and others, "cultures of youth," and also some that live with the mistaken belief of "organizational immortality" (p. 349). This organizational literature as well as my own observations led me to wonder: Is there a "life cycle" to new and innovative schools that contributes to the attrition of change? If such a life cycle exists within such schools, what are its stages and characteristics?

If there are life-cycle patterns, then logically it becomes useful to know what events and forces contributed to shifts in the directions the school took over time. Increasingly, scholars are recognizing that schools are extremely complex and nonlinear structures (Gunter, 1995; Wheatley, 1994) that must be looked at through multiple frames (Telford, 1996). To determine the interrelationships and interconnections among events and forces that helped to shape the school, I sought answers to this question: Are there identifiable danger points and forces, internal and external to the school, that contribute to the attrition of change within it?

As indicated at the beginning of this Introduction, a related intention for creating "model" schools or "new" schools appears to be to use these "innovative" schools to influence other schools in the larger system to adopt similar reforms (Fletcher et al., 1985; Fullan, Eastabrook, Spinner, & Loubser, 1972; Gold & Miles, 1981; Stringfield et al., 1996). The existing evidence, however, suggests that this "scaling up" is a questionable strategy, at least in the short term (Lortie, 1975; Sarason, 1971). Instead of contributing to change, such schools often create animosity and resistance to change in other schools (Gold & Miles, 1981; A. Hargreaves, 1984; Smith, Dwyer, Prunty, & Kleine, 1987). Does an innovative school, therefore, merely provide an excuse for other schools in the system to resist innovation and change as these studies suggest or, over time, does it exert significant impact beyond its own walls through the rule-breaking precedents it sets that open up opportunities for others? Are they indeed break-the-mold schools? These issues beg the more comprehensive question: How appropriate is the establishment of an innovative or "lighthouse" school in promoting change in a school system?

There is an increasingly rich change literature that analyzes the complexities of change (Fullan, 1991; A. Hargreaves, 1994; Hopkins, Aincow, & West, 1994). Various researchers, for example, have shown the relationship between change and organizational meaning (Fullan, 1993; Sergiovanni, 1992a), change and micro-politics (Ball, 1987; Blase, 1988); change and organizational cultures (A. Hargreaves, 1994; Little, 1987; Nias, Southworth, & Yeomans, 1989; Rosenholtz, 1989), change and professional learning (Barth, 1990; Lieberman & Grolnick, 1998; Senge, 1990), change and leadership (Block, 1993; Crump, 1993; Leithwood, 1992, 1993; Starratt, 1993; Telford, 1996). Similarly there is no shortage of advice to school leaders on helping schools to improve (Fullan, 1991; Hopkins et al., 1994; Stoll & Fink, 1996). In spite of this extensive and varied literature on change, and the accepted principle that lasting change takes a very long time to establish (Fullan, 1991; Louis & Miles, 1990), there are very few recent in-depth studies of how schools develop and change over time. There are even fewer long-term studies of new, innovative schools, especially secondary schools. It is therefore anticipated that this book will contribute to an understanding of why new schools almost invariably start with great potential and notoriety but eventually become rather conventional institutions, like most other schools. Moreover, unlike much of the change literature that focuses on how schools can improve, this book gives insight into the pathology of "failing" (Stoll & Myers, 1998) and "cruising" or mediocre schools (Stoll & Fink, 1996). The warning signs of deteriorating conditions described in this study, therefore, will help school leaders to assist successful schools to "stay the course." On a more hopeful note, however, this effort also provides evidence to support the concept that, under certain circumstances, innovative schools can indeed be a catalyst for change.

METHODOLOGY

As an educational practitioner for all of my working life, I seldom read the methodology section of research reports. I assumed the academic community would assure intellectual honesty. Now that I am part of this community, I review methodology sections with a much more inquiring and skeptical eye. The research approach taken in this book is presented in detail elsewhere for those who find such discussions of interest (Fink, 1997). To assure the general reader that the procedures used in this study are intellectually and conceptually sound I will briefly outline my approach. The retrospective nature of the topic and its "boundedness" necessitated a qualitative case study. Since the researcher is the key methodological instrument in qualitative studies (Anderson & Stiegelbauer, 1990; Woods, 1986), I have avoided what Goetz (1988) has called the "pseudo-objectivity" of using the third person in science writing by using a first-person, "researcher as instrument" (Ball, 1993, p. 46) stance. To investigate the case in some depth required methodologies from three research traditions. The historical aspect of the case led to a search of relevant documents from the province of Ontario, the South Board of Education (of which Lord Byron was a part), and the school itself. An ethnographic approach was used to search for factors that led to the attrition of change. To this end, I interviewed over 70 present and past Lord Byron staff members as well as key respondents from the South system. The vast majority of these interviews were conducted with people who were teachers at Lord Byron at various junctures in its evolution.

I selected a sample of interview respondents from among staff members from three different eras. To this end I randomly selected names from the staff lists for Lord Byron from 1975, 1984, and 1993. This provided me with a minimum of 15 subjects in each of the 3 years.

Although this was not a random sample in the statistical sense, it was what Ball (1984) would call "naturalistic coverage" (p. 75) because it approximated the diversity of people who were involved in Byron over the years. I contacted each selected potential respondent and requested an opportunity to conduct a one-hour interview. No one declined my request (see Fink, 1997, for the interview protocol). In addition, all principals were interviewed in depth. I also contacted senior system administrators who had expert information related to the politics of the South Board and the province.

The third source of data was my investigation of the relationship of Lord Byron to the professional and personal lives of the respondents. My review of the change literature convinced me of the importance of investigating teachers' work and lives as part of the larger conceptual framework (Ball & Goodson, 1985; Goodson, 1992; Goodson & Walker, 1991). I therefore augmented my scripted interview questions with in-depth probes into the question of Byron's relationship to respondents' professional and personal lives.

Another important source of data and "triangulation" was my personal involvement in events at the school. It has become increasingly accepted in the research community that the researcher's subjectivity operates during a research project. Woods (1986) argues that positivistic approaches that attempt to eliminate the effects of the researcher from the data and naturalistic qualitative methods in which the researcher becomes "a neutral vessel of cultural experience" (p. 14) are futile. His resolution is for the researcher "to recognise the reflexive character of social research that is, to recognize that we are part of the social world we study" (p. 14). To understand my relationship to the "social world" of Lord Byron I have attempted, throughout the book, to intersperse sufficient detail of my personal involvement as a researcher and participant in the Lord Byron case to assist the reader to decide on its usefulness, while attempting to avoid becoming too self-indulgent.

I played many different roles in my association with Lord Byron High School. At various times, I was a very active and accepted "insider."[3] In a sense, I was a participant observer, but not a "participant observer" in the research sense of someone who interacts, takes careful field notes, and conducts unstructured interviews to arrive at some understanding of the school's culture. My observations based on participation are in hindsight. As an insider and an original member of the Lord Byron staff, I had relatively easy entry into the school and access to interview subjects. Since I had shared the Byron experience, particularly in the early years, I was seen by many as part of the Byron alumni, and therefore perceived to have an insider's understanding of what the school was about. For most of Byron's history, however, I was an outsider who was able to observe Byron from various vantage points in the school district. In combination, therefore, my unique "inside-outside" observations and the historic, ethnographic, and life-history data provided a comprehensive picture of Byron over its 25-year history.

ORGANIZATION

It is my intent that this book prove useful to scholars and students, but of equal if not more importance, is my desire to assist people who work in schools and school districts. This book can be read in two ways. The more obvious is from cover to cover. For this reason I have organized the chapters in a way that they unfold logically and, I hope, seamlessly. Chapter 1 provides a contextual basis for a study of change and introduces the conceptual framework for the study. Chapter 2 briefly outlines the history of Lord Byron High School as a point of reference for the analytical chapters that follow. Each of the next six chapters (Chapters 3 through 8) develops one of the conceptual structures I used to collect, analyze, and record the results of my study—context, meaning, leadership, structure, culture, and the lives and work of teachers. The reader can peruse each of the first eight chapters as a "stand-alone" and "dip" into their contents as interest directs. The final chapter provides a summary of the findings of this study and suggests its implications for policy and research.

Lord Byron, like all schools, was and is a complex, diverse, and nonlinear organization. What you see is not necessarily what you get. As with an iceberg, much is hidden from casual observation. One may see structures such as the use of time and space, and charts of roles and responsibilities and intended curricula and lessons in session, but an understanding of the heart and soul of a school requires living the experience. It is the values, beliefs, meanings, and emotions that people bring to organizations that determine the effectiveness of structures and whether organizations will embrace or reject change. A study, therefore, that looked at a school through only one perceptual lens would be "incomplete, biased and potentially misleading" (Morgan, 1997, p. 5). Chapter 1 places this study in the context of the change literature and introduces the multiple frames (Boleman & Deal, 1997), images (Morgan, 1997), or lenses through which I attempted to understand the rich complexity of Lord Byron High School. For change agents, this approach will provide a useful model to "frame" change in their own environments.

CHAPTER 1

Multidimensionality of Change

As I indicated in the Introduction to this book, I am now in my Third Age—the post-career phase of life. My First Age was my preparation for a career, my Second Age was 34 years spent as a teacher, principal, and senior school district administrator in Ontario, Canada, and now in my Third Age I have been fortunate enough to travel widely and share my experiences with—and learn from—colleagues internationally. This Third Age, however, has its downside—one has to get old to qualify, and rainy days make my arthritic knees ache; it also has its upside, not the least of which is the ability to place contemporary affairs into a historical context. As my 90-year-old mother commented after she saw the movie *Titanic,* she was one of the few people in the theater for whom the disaster depicted was once a current event. In looking at the evolution of our knowledge of educational change over the past 40 years I am in somewhat the same situation. I have seen our understanding of change in complex organizations, in general, and change in schools, in particular, grow from simple input-output systems into fairly sophisticated models that examine change from multiple dimensions. This chapter briefly reviews this evolution, and introduces the dimensions that were used to study change at Lord Byron over time.

CHANGING CONCEPTIONS OF CHANGE

While it is difficult to generalize across nations, one can identify five very broad patterns of change theory over time: its early, rather simplistic phase in the 1960s and 1970s; the more sophisticated yet uncomplicated notions of the 1980s; the increasingly more complex school-improvement focus of the 1980s and 1990s; the concurrent school effectiveness movement; and present-day conceptions, which build on past research and view educational change as a complex, multidimensional phenomenon.

Conceptions of Change in the 1960s and 1970s

The 1960s in both North America and the United Kingdom was an era of tremendous creativity and innovation. It was an age in education that assumed that change was good, and that once a school's staff understood an innovation, wonderful things would happen. In retrospect one could well argue that it was a time of change for the sake of change. Change was believed to have occurred once an "innovation" had been adopted. Implementation often was seen to coincide with a delivery date. The model of change was simple, straightforward, and quite linear:

Input ⟶ Process ⟶ Output

This figure indicates that when an input—for example, a new curriculum—was delivered by experts, usually through some form of in-service, schools would then process the information and, it was assumed, new outputs in terms of pupil achievement would occur. The school, however, was something of a "black box." The research community had little idea of what actually went on after an innovation was adopted by a school.

Clark and Guba provided a more detailed version of this model (in House, 1979):

Research—to advance knowledge to serve as a basis for development;
Development—to invent and build a solution to an operating problem;
Diffusion—to introduce the innovation to practitioners;
Adoption—to incorporate innovation into the school.

In addition to its linearity, and the assumption that adoption of an innovation solved all problems, this model presupposed, somewhat arrogantly, that change was something that experts invented and initiated outside the school, and once teachers understood the inherent wisdom of the change, they would leap at the opportunity to behave as intended. Unfortunately (or in many cases, fortunately), most of the innovations of the 1960s withered and died. Some proved impractical and others inappropriate in some communities (Fullan, 1991). Teachers who usually subscribe to a "practicality ethic" (Doyle & Ponder, 1977) found difficulty adjusting to innovations such as open school architecture, inquiry approaches to curriculum, and discovery learning. These failures led researchers to go inside the black box of the school to try to discover why innovations were working or, in most cases, not working (Sarason, 1971, 1972; Smith & Keith, 1971).

Conceptions of Change in the 1980s and 1990s

Perhaps the most detailed investigation of implementation was the American Rand study of a number of large-scale change projects funded by the American government (McLaughlin, 1990). "The Change Agent study concluded that the net return to the general investment was the adoption of many innovations, the successful implementation of a few, and the long-run continuation of still fewer" (p. 12). The Rand researchers further concluded that "adoption" was only a beginning and did not ensure implementation. Moreover, they found that the funding level of the project alone did not mean success. Factors that did contribute to the few successes included the active commitment of district leadership, locally selected implementation strategies, and timely support for teachers as they tried to implement changes. Most important, the Rand researchers concluded that "policy cannot mandate what matters" (p. 12). Simply stated, policymakers who try to change schools without considering the dynamics of change within schools, and the unique contexts of school, are wasting a lot of peoples' time and energy, to say nothing of money. It is ironic that in the late 1990s, policymakers still view teachers in mechanistic, instrumental ways (Morgan, 1997) and try to force change through what George Bernard Shaw called "brute sanity" (quoted in Fullan, 1991). While somewhat simplified, the model that eventually evolved in the 1980s reflected the implementation failures of the 1970s (Fullan, 1982):

Initiation ⟷ Implementation ⟷ Continuation ⟷ Outcome

Initiation or adoption in this emerging approach became the beginning stage. Implementation referred to processes of application of the innovation(s) within the school, and continuation included those processes required to institutionalize the change beyond its early years, which then would lead, one would hope, to desired outcomes for pupils. The two-way arrows suggest that the process is not totally linear, and that implementation and continuation are the important phases of the process. In more recent times scholars have tended to use the word *institutionalization* instead of continuation. "Institutionalization means a change is taken as a normal, taken for granted part of organizational life; and has unquestioned resources of time, personnel and money available" (Miles, 1998, p. 59). But the question remains:

What goes on in schools when staff members are "implementing" and "continuing or institutionalizing"? The past 20 years have produced a plethora of scholarly work to help us to answer this question and to understand the change process within schools. Fullan (1998) has described the past 10 years as the "decade of change capacity" because of our rapidly increasing understanding of educational change.

Since the publication of Fullan's germinal book *The Meaning of Educational Change* in 1982, there has been a considerable body of international research on the process of educational change (Fullan, 1991, 1993; A. Hargreaves, 1994; Hargreaves, Earl, & Ryan, 1996; Hopkins et al., 1994; Sarason, 1996; Stoll & Fink, 1996; van Velzen, Miles, Ekholm, Hameyer, & Robin, 1985). An important British contribution to this literature has been the in-depth ethnographic examination of change processes within individual schools (Ball, 1981; Burgess, 1983; A. Hargreaves, 1986; D. H. Hargreaves, 1967; Lacey, 1970; Woods, 1979). Miles and Huberman (1984), Smith and his colleagues (1987) and Louis and Miles (1990) provided important insights into change processes in American schools. In effect these scholars on both sides of the Atlantic began to reveal some of the mysteries of the black box. In addition, studies on teachers' lives have contributed to our understanding of how teachers respond to change (Bishop & Mulford, 1996; Goodson & Walker, 1991; Grant, 1988; Lortie, 1975; Louden, 1991; Sikes, 1985; Woods, 1979). Rudduck (1997) and her colleagues give us insight into how pupils deal with change (1996). Brouilette (1996) provides a perceptive look into a community's response to change. She examined changes in an American school district and how different segments of the population adopted very different and often conflicting perspectives on change. More recently Riley's *Whose School Is It Anyway?* (1998) examines contextual factors that affect contemporary British educational policies.

This explosion of interest in change fueled the school-improvement movement in the 1980s, and particularly the 1990s. In the mid-1980s, van Velzen and colleagues defined school improvement as "a systematic, sustained effort aimed at change in learning conditions and other related internal conditions in one or more schools, with the ultimate aim of accomplishing educational goals more effectively" (1985, p. 48).

School-improvement efforts, particularly large-scale government-initiated change projects, have tended to reflect this definition's focus on changing structures to achieve educational goals. Elsewhere, Louise Stoll and I have provided an in-depth critique of traditional approaches to school improvement (Fink & Stoll, 1998). In brief, our concern with the early school-improvement literature is that it says very little about the purposes of school improvement. It gives the impression that people who resist innovation are just perverse or worse. All innovations are not created equal; some require enthusiastic support, and some are worth fighting against with all one's might, or at least subverting. Moreover, practical applications of school improvement have tended to lead to school development plans and site-based management. While each of these structures can contribute to enhanced learning conditions for pupils, there is little evidence to suggest that these structures alone improve schools. Indeed, there is an increasing body of evidence suggesting that they have become strategies to colonize teachers to conform to the dictates of policymakers (Bishop & Mulford, 1996; Robertson, 1996; Whitty, 1997; Whitty et al., 1998). In the 1990s, however, the school-improvement literature has begun to tackle questions of purpose (Fullan, 1993; A. Hargreaves, 1994; Hargreaves & Fullan, 1998; Hopkins et al., 1994; Stoll & Fink, 1996). In addition, these authors and others have suggested that school improvement is much more complex than early proponents have suggested. Fullan (1990) captured this complexity when he stated:

> Our attention in policy, practice and research has shifted in recent years, away from preoccupation with single innovations toward more basic, integrative, and systematic reform. Changes in the culture of schools, in the roles and relationships of schools, districts, universities and states, and in integrating teacher development, school improvement, leadership and curriculum toward more engaging learning experiences for students and teachers, dominate the current scene and will continue to do so for the rest of the decade. (p. 137)

In their definition of school improvement, van Velzen and his colleagues (1985) described the outcome of school improvement as "effective" achievement of school goals. This reflects the influence of the school-effectiveness approach to educational change, which has paralleled the school-improvement movement. School-effectiveness researchers in the 1980s and 1990s have not only demonstrated that schools make a difference to pupils regardless of their socioeconomic background, but also identified factors or characteristics that differentiated effective from less effective schools (Mortimore, 1995; Reynolds, 1996; Reynolds & Packer, 1992). Influenced by the international research community, many British educational authorities and school districts in North America initiated school-effectiveness projects. Most projects, including a project Louise Stoll and I led, tried to implement the characteristics of school effectiveness as a vehicle for school change. We found out that just knowing what made a school effective was not sufficient to facilitate positive change in a school (Stoll & Fink, 1994). It was not until we, and others, linked school effectiveness to school-improvement strategies that we began to see schools implementing and institutionalizing change strategies that made a difference for their pupils (Reynolds, Hopkins, & Stoll, 1993; Stoll & Fink, 1996). It was within this context of a rapidly developing field of scholarly investigation that I undertook to look at the withering away of change processes in an innovative school, Lord Byron.

FRAMING CHANGE

Rather typical of the rapidly moving field of educational change, researchers are looking beyond the traditional school-improvement agenda to consider the variables that affect a school's capacity to deal with change (Louis, Toole, & Hargreaves, 1998). In a sense one could describe these variables as "lenses," "images," or "frames" through which to view and therefore open up to scrutiny the black box of the school (Boleman & Deal, 1997; Morgan, 1997). For researchers and practitioners alike, the idea of "framing change" enables change agents to understand the multidimensionality and therefore the complexity of change in schools.

When I initiated the Lord Byron study, I originally identified the concepts of change, context, culture, teachers' work, and teachers' lives as the components of my conceptual framework. These were constructs identified as core conceptual themes in a meeting of international scholars to initiate a study of professional teacher cultures (Report of meeting from Professional Cultures of Teachers, San Francisco, CA, April 18–19, 1992). My own background, reading, and experience convinced me that leadership is crucial to change in schools and should also be a distinct category for analysis (Fink, 1992a, 1992b; Fullan, 1993; Stoll & Fink, 1996). Moreover, after the first few interviews with former Byron teachers and principals, it became obvious that the structure of the school and the school's meaning and purposes were key constructs that required elaboration. It became equally apparent that it was virtually impossible to separate teachers' work from teachers' lives (A. Hargreaves, 1991a). Since change is a concept that runs throughout this analysis, I concluded that it should be integrated into each category. I finally settled on six interrelated lenses or frames through which to view Lord Byron High School context: meaning, leadership, structure, culture, and teachers' work and lives. The following discussion, therefore, briefly introduces each of these constructs to provide a foundation for the in-depth analysis of each in Chapters 3 through 8.

Context

Change efforts that fail to consider schools' contexts and teachers' contexts have little chance for success (Cohen, 1995; Elmore, 1995; McLaughlin, 1990). Context may be defined as "the whole situation, background, or environment relevant to some happening" (Grossman & Stodolsky, 1994, p. 181). Internal context includes the pupils, subjects and departments, and the school itself; external context encompasses, among other influences, the district or local education authority of which the school is a part, the school's parent and neighboring community, the teachers' union, and the state and the government of the day. While it is beyond the scope of this study, one could add the international context as well. Educational policies have clearly become international and are therefore affected by changing international conditions.

The research evidence is fairly clear that schools can be understood only in their context (Hallinger & Murphy, 1986; Teddlie & Stringfield, 1993). Attempts to determine effectiveness from one country to another, for example, have for the most part been unsuccessful (Reynolds et al., 1994). Broadly based restructuring efforts have made little difference in classrooms (Cohen, 1995; Elmore, 1995; Gewirtz, Ball, & Bowe, 1995) because different contexts bring diverse and often contradictory values, beliefs, and purposes for education. Approaches to "initiation," "implementation," and "continuation" or "institutionalization" of change, therefore, depend heavily on the multiple internal and external contexts into which change is introduced. This theme is introduced in detail in Chapter 3.

Meaning

The importance of "shared meaning" is well documented in the literature (Fullan, 1993; Joyce & Showers, 1988; Louis & Miles, 1990; Rosenholtz, 1989; Sammons, Mortimore, & Hillman, 1995). Too many purposes, unclear purposes, and lack of purpose condemn many projects to an early demise. Similarly, change within schools suffers when strongly held but divergent purposes conflict (Ball, 1981; Grant, 1988; Woods, 1979). In any change effort, teachers and schools should know where they are going and, broadly speaking, they should be agreed on where they are headed. Purposes matter a lot in teaching. Yet teachers cannot be given a purpose: Purposes must come from within. Pursuing their own inspiring mission together is what can most help teachers turn their school around (A. Hargreaves, 1997). The meaning lens or frame is developed in detail in Chapter 4.

Leadership

Efforts to effect change suggest that effective leadership is a key determinant in deciding whether anything positive happens in a school or a school system (Fullan, 1993; Leithwood, 1992; Sergiovanni, 1992a). The leadership frame is concerned with both the formal and informal leaders who must foster organizational development and learning, and also preserve and encourage the kinds of relationships within a school that promote the capacity to respond to change. While an argument can be made that micro-politics is a separate lens through which to view school change (Ball, 1987; Blase, 1988, 1998), for purposes of this study I have tied the topic to leadership. The formal leaders, usually the school principals, determine whether power relationships in a school are "power over" or "power with." The power-with paradigm is a difficult one to maintain in light of leadership structures that create power over (Blase, 1998). Innovative schools usually attempt to alter power relationships (Fletcher et al., 1985; Fullan et al., 1972; Watts, 1977) and share both formal and informal leadership among staff members. Since these relationships threaten people with power over subordinates, power-with structures are subjected to destructive pressures. I look at Byron through this leadership lens in Chapter 5.

Structure

Many of the reform movements that have taken place over the past years have concentrated on changing structures as ways to effect behavioral change among teachers and pupils. Structure is about the use of time and space and the definition and arrangement of roles and responsibilities in schools. Many contemporary change efforts focus almost totally on changing structures, for example, lengthening the school day or school year, altering the timetables of schools, establishing charter schools, or changing the jobs and role descriptions of principals and department heads. In some ways this rational, linear fixation on changing structures is akin to "shuffling the deck chairs on the *Titanic*." Chapter 6 not only shows how the structures that made Lord Byron unique changed over time; it also reveals how these structures helped to change the school's culture from an innovative culture to a "struggling" culture (Stoll & Fink, 1996).

Elmore (1995) has concluded that changes "in structure are weakly related to changes in teaching practice, and therefore structural change does not necessarily lead to changes in teaching, learning, and student performance" (p. 25). He suggests that the relationship of structure to teaching practice is mediated by "relatively powerful forces such as the shared norms, knowledge and skills of teachers" (p. 26). In effect, nonrational factors such as school culture must be attended to before altering structures. While there is little evidence to suggest that structural changes alone make a significant difference to the change process, structural changes are important to provide opportunities for cultural changes (A. Hargreaves, 1994; Louis & Miles, 1990; Miles & Huberman, 1984).

Culture

Structure and culture are inextricably intertwined, and successful changes in both tend to be concurrent. Culture is not easily defined because it is largely implicit and unseen. A newcomer to a school usually discovers the school culture when he or she breaks one of the cultural norms. Schein (1985) identifies various interpretations of the content and forms of culture. Among these are observed behavioral regularities, including language and rituals, norms that evolve in working groups; dominant values espoused by an organization; the philosophy that guides an organization's policy; and the feeling or climate conveyed in an organization. I prefer Deal and Kennedy's (1983) definition of organizational culture as "the way we do things around here" (p. 4). The changing nature of Byron's culture over time is analyzed in Chapter 7.

Teachers' Work and Teachers' Lives

Most change initiatives require teachers to change their practices. As Andy Hargreaves suggests, however, "To change the teacher is to change the person the teacher is" (A. Hargreaves, 1991a, pp. 255–256). A level of analysis that until recently has been overlooked in discussions about change has been the personal and biographical factors of teachers. As Goodson (1992) has argued, from teachers' point of view, "it would seem that professional practices are embedded in wider life concerns. We need to listen closely to their views on the relationship between 'school life' and 'whole life' for in that dialectic crucial tales about careers and commitments will be told" (p. 16). This lens is described and applied to Lord Byron in Chapter 8.

History is a crucial lens through which to view change processes in schools. It explains a great deal about the structure and culture of a school. It provides the meanings people bring to change. It defines the lives and work of teachers, and influences leadership structures, values, and styles. Moreover history, or lack of it, is perhaps one of the most significant factors affecting the context of new and innovative schools. In the beginning, these schools have a very limited history; over time, history tends to dominate change processes. With this notion of history as context in mind, the next chapter outlines the "life cycle" of Lord Byron High School.

CHAPTER 2

The Life Cycle of an Innovative School

The early 1970s was a unique era in the educational history of Ontario and the South Board of Education (school district or local education authority). For those of us who joined the staff of Lord Byron with a view to effecting change in the "deep structures" of Ontario schooling, the times could not have been more propitious. Ontario was in the midst of a progressive era in education that created a context for the South Board and its reform-minded director (Chief Executive Officer) to initiate Lord Byron as an experimental "lighthouse" school. As a teacher with 11 years of experience, I was ready for "experimentation and activism" (Sikes, 1985). Little did I or my colleagues realize the uniqueness of our opportunity. In this chapter, I describe the history of Lord Byron.

This history divides itself into three distinct but overlapping eras. The first was the period of creativity and experimentation that lasted for about 8 years from the school's origins to approximately 1978. Beginning in the middle 1970s was an era of "overreaching" (Miles & Huberman, 1984) in which the school took on so many innovations the staff had difficulty dealing with their complexity, and the school began a process of outstripping its community's ability to understand and support the school. Almost concurrently, signs of "entropy" began to emerge, which resulted in the school's reaching its lowest point in the mid-1980s. The final era is one of survival and continuity in which the school endured by joining the mainstream of secondary schooling in the district and the province. To ensure a comprehensive view of each period I have adopted a layered approach that connects the history of Ontario, the South Board, Lord Byron High School, and my own involvement in key events.

HISTORY AS CONTEXT

"Social forces are human energies which, originating in individual motivations, coalesce into collective manifestations of power" (Gustavson, 1955, p. 28). Economic forces, technological forces, and political forces, among others, shape our daily existence. At certain points in history, such as the late 18th century, combinations of forces merge to produce dramatic—indeed, revolutionary—social changes. Most societal changes, however, occur almost imperceptibly and are scarcely visible from year to year and may not become obvious for decades. To identify when the changes occurred, however, is difficult. Much of human history and particularly institutional history, therefore, seems to be more about continuity than about change. Most people operate on the premise that what has happened in the past will continue into the future. This kind of thinking makes life seem more predictable, stable, and comfortable. This general historical inertia, when combined with contextual factors such as teachers' resistance (Fink & Stoll, 1998), bureaucratic conservatism (Louis & Miles, 1990), community wariness (Fletcher et al., 1985), and students' reluctance (Rudduck, 1991), helps to explains why the "deep structures" (Cuban, 1988) of schooling in most secondary schools have changed very little in the past 25 years.

Lord Byron High School opened with the express purpose of challenging not only the structures of secondary education in Ontario, but also the curriculum, the teaching, and the student assessment methods. Perhaps what was most innovative for the times was the philosophy espoused by its first principal, and in large measure adopted by the original staff. In a formal document of the period, the philosophy was stated thus:

> Our aspirations for Lord Byron are the development of a humane educational environment for students: a situation in which conduct and growth will develop from *reason* and *mutual respect* and *trust.* Only through an appreciation of these basic and individual needs can we achieve an educational experience which will enable students to realize their optimum potential. This experience, it is hoped, will be characterized by an atmosphere of continuous self-evaluation and improvement.

While the climate of progressivism was current in Ontario in the early 1970s, the forces for continuity were mobilizing to blunt if not expunge the influence of a movement that called for more student-centered secondary schools. Teacher organizations saw a threat to teachers' traditional authority, principals decried a lack of order and control, parents expressed fears that new approaches might hurt their children's chances for success, and politicians and the press reflected these growing doubts. In the context of Ontario, the South Board of Education, and even the local community, the pedagogical, curricular, organizational, and structural innovations introduced at Lord Byron were revolutionary and intimidating to groups who sought to preserve continuity in the educational system. In many ways this study is about the interplay of change (as represented by the progressive philosophy and innovative practices of the school) and continuity (as expressed by the teachers' union, teachers in other secondary schools, some school board members, and some community representatives).

CREATIVITY AND EXPERIMENTATION: THE HISTORY TO THE MID-1970s

To understand the history of a school, it must be seen within its larger system. In the description of these external connections and relationships as well as internal school events over 25 years, major historical trends will become evident. The analysis of these events provides the substance of Chapters 3 to 8.

Ontario to the Mid-1970s

Throughout the 1950s, change in education in Ontario had occurred at a glacial pace. Secondary schools focused on academic learning. For the most part students took a standard program. There was little effort to accommodate individual differences and dropout rates were well over 50%. Students had to fit the structure of the school or fail. Fortunately, throughout the 1950s and 1960s employment opportunities for unskilled labor were plentiful in Ontario. The postwar years had been ones of unparalleled economic growth in Canada and in Ontario in particular. In the 1960s, not only were public schools built or modified, but universities expanded, new universities were constructed, and colleges of applied arts and technology mushroomed across the province. The economic changing times opened the doors of Ontario's educational thought to ideas that had been dormant for 30 years.

> The rapid growth of the 1960s made education for employment seem less urgent, and student activism created a demand for liberalized and "relevant" education. The progressive education movement insisted that school courses be tailored to the needs and interests of individuals and that students be allowed to learn cooperatively in groups. (Curtis, Livingstone, & Smaller, 1992, p. 48)

Recognizing that the Ontario system was out of step with the times, the Ontario cabinet authorized a Royal Commission to look into the educational system. The result was a revolutionary report entitled *Living and Learning* (Ontario Department of Education, 1968), more commonly known as the Hall-Dennis Report after its co-chairmen. From its opening clause, "the truth shall make you free" (p. 9), to its concluding sentence, "truth will make all men free" (p. 175), the report advocated a radical rethinking of education in Ontario. The report savaged the rigidity and sterility of the prevailing system. Drawing on the plethora of progressive experiments in the United States and the widespread publicity in Canada on the *Plowden Report* (Central Council for Advisory Education, 1967) in Britain, the committee clearly and unequivocally articulated a more liberal direction for Ontario schools.

In the Hall-Dennis world, teaching strategies would be more child-centered, curriculum less subject-centered. The report challenged just about every structure in existing schools. It opposed corporal punishment and criticized grades and percentages and other reporting procedures. Instead, the report advocated schools that were positive, supportive, and noncompetitive, and that communicated with students and parents in a spirit of openness and mutual support. Failure would disappear, it was claimed, as students proceeded at their own rates through a curriculum determined by their personal needs and interests. For a brief time, the Hall-Dennis Report captured the imaginations of educators and policymakers. While skeptical, the business community, universities, and the more conservative press were reserved in their criticism.

To many of today's critics, the alleged decline of Ontario's education system began with Hall-Dennis. (Ontario Department of Education, 1968) The irony, however, is that its popularity was so short-lived that much of its approach never impacted teaching and learning, particularly in secondary schools (Hargreaves, Fullan, Wignall, Stager, & Macmillan, 1992). Hall-Dennis recommended a diversity of courses, student choice of programs, concern for racial and ethnic minorities, and more school-based decision-making. It resulted in a document called *High School 1* (H.S. 1), which introduced an individualized credit system (Ontario Department of Education, 1971). Students were required to take very few compulsory subjects. This was quite a contrast to previous requirements. The document left considerable scope for school districts and schools to organize in different ways and to offer a variety of courses to engage students in their learning. The shift from tightly structured, narrowly academic, inflexible curricula to progressive, open-ended, totally flexible curricula resulted in many exciting and imaginative programs for students, as well as some courses that were unchallenging, anti-intellectual, and of questionable rigor and utility, such as self-esteem courses.

Increasingly, however, taxpayers objected to rising costs for education, and secondary school teachers and their union complained that the credit system had produced permissiveness, reduced time for the basics, and created timetabling inflexibility (Crittenden, 1969). The press, university registrars, chambers of commerce, and other groups and individuals lobbied for a return to greater uniformity in curricula, more academic rigor, and external testing. By the mid-1970s the government responded to both political and economic pressures by tightening the curriculum and dramatically reducing the flexibility enjoyed by schools and their districts.

The South Board to the Mid-1970s

The South Board of Education was one of the newly established school boards (school districts) created by provincial fiat in 1969. The 10 smaller school boards that had administered public education in South County were now consolidated into one larger and presumably more cost-efficient school board. Each board was required by legislation to hire a director of education. South Board's choice was the former city of Middleton director Jim Sizemore. Sizemore's initial challenge was to amalgamate 10 different ways of doing things into one coherent set of policies and procedures. At the same time, he had to work toward some degree of equity in facilities, leadership, and programs for students across a large and diverse geographic area. Sizemore was something of a benevolent autocrat. He had a very clear conception of educational change, a no-nonsense approach to achieving his goals, and the confidence to invite creativity and experimentation.

A former army officer, Sizemore tended to operate from a military stance. He created a formidable bureaucracy that included a large cadre of staff people to support schools, principals, and teachers. Curriculum, for example, was initiated at the central office and delivered by subject coordinators to the schools. Compliance was assured through a number of assistant superintendents (inspectors) who had the job of inspecting principals and teachers. Change, therefore, was initiated at the board office, developed into policy by a supportive school board, and delivered to the schools by the bureaucracy.

The director modeled his belief in hard work, innovation, intellectual rigor, and goal achievement. Sizemore initiated system-led professional-development programs at a time when staff development was episodic in most jurisdictions, if it existed at all. His belief in the importance of leadership resulted in the creation of a leadership program that continues to the present. Sizemore believed that a school system and its schools should be constantly looking for better ways to educate students. To this end, he created the Innovations Committee in 1969. With a new secondary school required to accommodate growth in the east end of Middleton, members of the committee were funded to visit innovative schools throughout North America. The committee included the principal designate of Lord Byron, Ward Bond. He was appointed a year before the scheduled opening to participate in the Innovations Committee and to turn its findings into practice. As a result, in September 1970 Lord Byron opened as South's school of the future, the "lighthouse" school. Sizemore's influence on the Lord Byron concept was described by its first principal.

> It has been a long time since Jim departed but you can still remember the things he said, "Innovation was something that you did instead of, not added on." Jim Sizemore was the guy who initiated the committee for the purpose of looking into the physical design but it wasn't limited to that. It was really educational design. He constantly encouraged growth and trying and seeing new things. Whenever you saw Jim, you could count on being asked where have you been, who have you been talking to and what have you been reading. It was that attitude that made Lord Byron possible and I didn't see it anywhere else in the province. He was so in control of what he was doing as director that he was able to direct. He didn't have to spend his time "covering his ass." He could be a leader in the sense of encouraging growth of people, new ideas, and trying things, more supportive.[1]

Lord Byron to the Mid-1970s

Lord Byron was built a mile and a half from Roxborough High School. Roxborough was an established and well-regarded school in the community. This reputation persists to the present. In 1969, it was the prototypical school of the times. Slow to innovate, skeptical of change, Roxborough has always tended to embrace innovations only when they have been proven elsewhere. This strategy has worked well. Its affluent middle- to upper-middle-class community likes it this way (Hargreaves et al., 1992). The contrast of philosophies between the two neighboring schools created deep divisions between their staffs and has tended to divide contiguous communities.

Lord Byron's innovations reflected the Hall-Dennis Report and many of the ideas current in 1970. Byron was the first semestered school in Ontario. Instead of a student following the traditional pattern of eight courses, 40 minutes each per day, for the entire 10-month school year, Byron's program required a student to take four courses in each of two five-month semesters. Students at Lord Byron were required to complete 32 90-hour courses or credits to receive a Secondary School Graduation Diploma, whereas H. S. 1 (the Ontario Secondary School Program) obliged students to complete 27 courses or credits of 110 hours, but the Department of Education allowed experiments.[2] The Byron program enabled students to choose from a wider diversity of courses than students in other Ontario schools. The school day at Byron was divided into six 60-minute periods. Each student was required to be registered in four courses, and therefore had one free period plus a lunch period. Each teacher had a similar timetable, four classes per semester and one free period plus one hour for lunch. The 10 department chairs taught two periods per day and the other four periods were available for them to support their departments.

This organization was designed to allow students to broaden and deepen their programs. The intention of the free periods for students was to provide them with the opportunity to learn to exercise responsibility by managing time. For students who had difficulty, extra counselors were allocated. The free period was certainly the most controversial innovation. The semestered organization also allowed students to accelerate their programs to complete high school earlier than in a traditional organization or, conversely, to repeat courses they may have failed without delaying their opportunity to graduate on time.

The longer period enabled teachers to use a variety of teaching strategies to engage students. Since classes were heterogeneous for the most part, unlike most other schools in which students were rigorously tracked, the longer period gave secondary teachers the time to use grouping and other inclusive strategies that were common in elementary schools. Since most teachers (myself included) were not experienced in these approaches, considerable staff development was required. Teachers at Byron were usually required to prepare only two courses on a daily basis compared with three and four in more conventional schools. The Byron teachers, however, spent more time with classes than did teachers in other schools. Byron teachers taught eight classes in a year, four per semester, whereas teachers in other schools covered six classes in a year. Forty-eight Byron classes could be covered by six teachers compared with eight teachers at a school like Roxborough. This realized a savings in teacher allocation at Byron. In other words, whereas a school of 1,000 might require 60 teachers, Byron could cover all of its classes with 15 fewer teachers. Some of this saving was allocated for extra counselors or to provide time for chairpersons. If, for example, the saving in teacher allocation was the equivalent of nine teachers, the average salary of six not allocated was given to the school to support its program. If the average teacher salary was $30,000, then Lord Byron would receive $180,000 (6 × $30,000). This money was used to hire extra secretaries so that teachers had considerable secretarial support. Teacher assistants helped teachers in classrooms. Lab assistants set up experiments in chemistry; artists worked with students in class; professional musicians supported music classes; and audiovisual specialists made sure equipment was available and ready when required. While the work load was heavier for teachers, there was considerable support available.

Byron's departments were organized into cross-disciplinary units such as Social Sciences, the Arts, Mathematics, Science, and Technology, with a department chair in charge as opposed to a department head. The number of formal leaders was therefore reduced from as many as 22 in some schools to 10. The major role of the chairman was to support the classroom teachers. Each chairman handled discipline and attendance issues within the department so that teachers had immediate assistance if necessary. In the first 4 years, because of the chairs, the assistant principal at Byron spent very little time on discipline and could direct his efforts to issues such as community relations. More important, with so many new courses, the chairmen had to be effective curriculum writers. If teachers had materials to develop or curriculum to write, the chairmen would also assume some of their teaching responsibilities. All departmental administrative tasks were dealt with by the chairmen, who had a secretary to ensure that they were not consumed by these responsibilities. They also formed the principals' cabinet to work out school policies and procedures and make sure that teachers were informed and had input on school issues. Guided by Bond, the chairmen worked out policy and procedures, but the actual approval was a staff decision. Chairmen was the proper term in 1970—all the appointees were men because no women applied. In 1974, the first woman was appointed as a department chair. This and many subsequent appointments of women at the school and in the district came as the result of an informal women's network that began at Lord Byron in the early 1970s with the encouragement and support of Ward Bond.

Teachers designed integrated curriculum units and course packages and employed alternative teaching strategies such as simulations, group activities, independent study, and outdoor education. Programs were developed to meet the diversity of student needs. Traditional competitive and elitist rituals and ceremonies were generally downplayed or even eliminated. Graduation ceremonies, which in some schools rivaled university convocations, at Byron became informal gatherings of graduates, relatives, and friends. Pep rallies to urge on sports teams did not exist. Lord Byron did not participate in the regional elite mathematics contest. Parents' nights were much more informal than in other schools and teachers more accessible to parents. Professional activities were opened to interested community members and a parents' advisory council was initiated.

The building was designed to be as flexible as possible. It had open architecture, few doors, air conditioning for year-round use, and the system's first main-frame computer. Every teacher had work space in a room separate from classrooms. The library (called and considered a resource center) was the center and hub of the school. Rooms were organized to facilitate interdisciplinary work. Lockers were designed into a central hallway "crush area," which meant that students' use of their lockers was not disruptive to classes. To the outsider, the lack of walls was the most obvious physical example of change. While many "open-concept" elementary schools had been built in the province, there were no open-plan secondary schools in South. Open education had evolved at the elementary level in the early 1960s but few secondary teachers, including those hired at Lord Byron, had ever worked in an open environment. This was a formidable challenge that was not entirely overcome. When an addition was planned for 1975, many teachers asked for the inclusion of some strategically placed walls.

The staff was young. The average age was under 30. The staff included a number of people considered by other schools to be controversial. Some of these teachers had been considered too progressive, or too friendly with students, or too confrontational with administration in their previous environments. As a senior administrator stated, "Ward Bond was the father of Lord Byron and he nurtured it in the years he was there. He knew what it was about and he had the skill and I would even say in those early years, the craftiness to hire appropriate people."

Over one-third of the staff was female, which was a higher percentage than that at most secondary schools. Ironically, consistent with the patriarchal leadership values of the time, the original department chairs were all males. The role of a department chairman was unique in the province and from the principal's point of view, the key to making the concept of a "humane school" work.

My Personal Involvement

I was hired as the Chairman of Social Sciences. My time at Lord Byron became a turning point in my professional career. Ward Bond, who knew of my work from mutual friends in the South Board, approached me to join the Byron staff in early 1970. His description of what he had in mind for Lord Byron intrigued and excited me. I made a quick decision to leave my comfortable situation in a rather conventional school and accept Ward's invitation. While this was hardly a reasoned judgment, my intuition paid off. I joined the first Lord Byron staff at a time when the opportunity to innovate was limited only by a person's imagination.

The next 3 years were a blur of teaching, program writing, travel, and presentations on the "Byron concept." Few periods of my long career as an educator were as energizing, arduous, and eventful. I revered Ward Bond. I tried to pattern my own leadership after his, and to this day he is my image of the "invitational leader" (Fink, 1992a, Stoll & Fink, 1996). I was part of that "critical mass" of leaders and innovators in the school. I believed in the Byron concept and still do, and worked diligently to support it both intellectually and publicly. I have always prided myself on my work ethic but the demands of Byron challenged even my capacity to work long and often draining hours. The weight of writing new programs, supporting teachers, ordering materials, monitoring a substantial budget, and maintaining ties to central office, to the feeder schools, to the Ministry, to the community, were wearing. My colleagues shared my commitment to the school, and the principal and his assistant led by example. Fortunately most of us were fairly young and we considered the challenge worth the effort. My life at this stage was made up of work and my family, and in retrospect my family got little of my time. I resigned from associations, community groups, and recreational activities because I did not have the time or the energy to do it all. My social life tended to orbit around Byron activities and its staff. As I look back, my life lacked balance, but I did not see it at the time because I had finally arrived in a situation that was congruent with my values and beliefs about education and the treatment of people. I was totally, almost obsessively, involved.

I was like most Byron staff members: We were so engaged in our work and various projects that we paid little attention to the district as a whole. Other professionals criticized Byron without ever knowing what was going on. Bond tried to explain to his fellow principals but he eventually gave up because "they weren't bothering to listen." Bond's successor, Bruce Grey, used exactly the same words. Removed from those early years by 25 years, however, I can recognize my own naiveté and even arrogance in advocating for Byron. I failed to realize how threatening we must have been to our educational colleagues. We worked hard to gain community support and ostensibly succeeded by force of personality and argument. We used the press to get our story across, but our success in gaining profile did not help relationships with other schools and the teachers' union. In retrospect we did not realize how the times contributed to our freedom and how much the patronage of Sizemore meant to the climate of innovation in which we reveled.

After 3 years I received a promotion within the system. I was the first of the critical mass to leave. Bond and other key school leaders left for promotions within the next few years. After a year as assistant principal in a middle school (grades 6, 7, and 8), I was reassigned to Lord Byron as an assistant principal. Since Bond had departed in the interim, I was told by senior administration that I was needed at Byron to maintain the direction of the earlier initiatives.

OVERREACHING AND ENTROPY: THE HISTORY TO 1985

I returned, however, to a very different Byron in the 1974–1975 school year. The forces of change that had been dominant in the first few years of the school's history were about to confront the constraints of continuity.

Ontario to the Mid-1980s

No sooner had the recommendations of Hall-Dennis made their way to policy in H. S. 1 than forces within the province attempted to modify the document's perceived openness and lack of rigor. The secondary teachers' union gave lip service to the directions of the Hall-Dennis Report, but in its official response reaffirmed the need for compulsory subjects and advocated rigorous streaming and rigid prerequisites. In spite of the rhetoric of recognizing individual differences, the union advocated a streamlining of the school system as it had existed before

H. S. 1 and the Hall-Dennis Report. Post-secondary institutions, deprived of easy-to-administer admissions criteria provided by the provincial-wide examinations, also joined the chorus of complaint about the state of secondary education and particularly the more liberalizing trends.[3] Many in the public at large, in the press, and among the politicians joined in questioning practices that were quite different from their own experiences and therefore suspect (Stamp, 1982). As long as the economic times were good the challenges were restrained, but that too changed rapidly.

The provincial government responded to the criticisms. It rescinded its earlier encouragement to develop curriculum suitable for local needs and to use provincial guidelines to design a variety of courses. The Ministry tightened the curriculum, increased the number and range of mandatory credits, created an elaborate approval process for experimental courses, restricted textbooks to those approved by the Ministry, and, in general, communicated a conservative message. One of the most significant changes for Lord Byron, which offered its program at only one level, was that the Ministry mandated that compulsory courses be offered at three levels of difficulty. The Ontario Ministry also reaffirmed that a credit was 110 scheduled hours, which effectively undercut the Byron timetable and its school organization.

These changes coincided with the worldwide recession, which began in 1973 and impacted education in Ontario in the 1975–1976 school year. Money became tighter as grants from the province gradually began to diminish. In the early 1970s, the provincial government paid over 55% of South's educational costs, with the remainder provided by local property taxes. Each successive year the province's proportion was reduced, so that by the 1990s, the province paid less than 20%. The provincial share has continued to diminish year by year. This retrenchment in Ontario reflected a general economic malaise in Canada that contrasted quite remarkably with the "glory days" of the late 1960s.

At the same time that its share of educational funding was diminishing, the province mandated a number of new programs. Among these, and by far the most expensive, was the requirement for boards to significantly increase their special education programs and support. Concurrently, the province also agreed to provide full funding for separate Roman Catholic schools as well as expanding French programs to promote bilingualism. While the province added funds to support these initiatives, the resources fell far short of meeting the challenges, and as a result school boards increased property taxes, which in turn precipitated taxpayer unrest. School administrators and trustees (school board members) accused the Ministry of playing a financial "shell game." By mandating significant initiatives, providing seed money, and then reducing grants to other board programs and therefore school budgets, the Ministry created a high degree of cynicism among local politicians and educators toward the provincial government. By 1984, the government had virtually completed its retreat from Hall-Dennis. A "Rip Van Winkle" who had gone to sleep in the 1950s and slept through the 1960s and 1970s would see great similarities between the school structures of the 1980s and those of the 1950s.

The South Board to the Mid-1980s

Jim Sizemore took early retirement in 1975. His last few years as director had been challenging and had affected his health. He had been one of the "great men" in Ontario's educational history. Many directors appointed in the late 1960s were from the same mold—male, autocratic, forceful, persistent, and self-confident. For Sizemore, colleagues have suggested that the turning point was a very public and acrimonious campaign by an evangelical clergyman and his followers against sex education, contemporary literature, and the entire concept of state-supported compulsory public education. Sizemore badly mishandled the situation and called it "a tempest in a teapot," which only inflamed the controversy. Shortly after this episode began, he retired. Those close to him have suggested that he recognized that his style of leadership was inappropriate for the changing times and dealing with such emotionally charged issues. The "great man era" had come to an end in South as it did in Ontario generally. Sizemore's replacement, Edward Stevens, was a man of recognized integrity, scholarship, and personal sensitivity. He often described himself as a "broker" among competing interest groups. By developing policies on who could visit classrooms, and dealing with controversial materials in the classroom, the new director used his brokering skills to defuse the situations he had inherited.

Subsequent elections produced single-issue candidates for the school board who were less cooperative with each other and certainly with administration. A new type of school trustee began to emerge. Board members had traditionally seen themselves as members of a corporate body whose job was to establish policy, while the administration was hired to carry out policy. Few trustees directly involved themselves in schools, and when they did it was only for ceremonial functions. Many of the newly elected trustees were less trusting of administration and far more involved in the day-to-day operation of schools. Previous boards had been content to allow schools to evolve in different ways. The school boards of the late 1970s wanted policies that could be applied across the system. The special advantages enjoyed by Lord Byron in Sizemore's time, such as differentiated funds, were affected by this trend.

The severe budget difficulties of the mid-1970s, the renewed protectionism of the teachers' unions, and the board's swing to a more conservative stance combined to curtail or at least circumscribe the spirit of innovation that had characterized the Sizemore era. For example, the board and the union agreed to a standard configuration of department heads for the entire system. This effectively ended the Byron chairmanship structure. Similarly, a policy on examinations was approved by the board that forced Byron, contrary to its original philosophy, to base 40% of a student's grade on a final exam. The board seemed more concerned with control and predictability than with creativity and experimentation. Policies on teacher appraisal, student discipline, balancing staff strengths, and common curriculum opportunities followed quickly on each other through the late 1970s.

With the retirement of Stevens in 1981, the school board appointed a new, dynamic, and politically shrewd director—Phil Stone. He proceeded to reorganize the system. In short order he found ways to demote, terminate, or push out all the senior leaders in central office. In addition, he terminated two middle managers within months of his taking over. The board appreciated his businesslike approach. Stone's political acuity enabled him to build bridges to the school board, the teachers' unions, and the community. Most people who had known the system at its peak applauded these early efforts.

The 1980s were years of both expansion and consolidation in South. As populations shifted, schools were built in newly developed areas of South, and closed in established areas. Special education services were expanded dramatically through the 1980s. Renewals in curriculum, technology, and technical education infused the system with money and energy. Class sizes were lowered and salaries increased, and resources became more plentiful. Once again, the system was seen as one of Ontario's most dynamic.

Lord Byron: To the Mid-1980s

In 1975, as part of the board's original agreement to gain the support of the local district of the teachers' union for the Lord Byron experiment, the board had agreed to a thorough evaluation of the school after 5 years of operation. A committee, external to the school and the board and composed of well-respected educators and researchers, reported that "Byron is a fine school; what is equally important, it is constantly striving to be better. The Byron staff is one of which the Board and the community can be justly proud." While the report praised the school and made no recommendations for significant changes, it did indicate some potential issues that indeed became problems. Among these concerns were:

- inordinate pressure and staff workload,
- communications among staff and students as the school grows,
- responsibility and self-discipline of a few students who gave the school a bad image,
- a rift that might grow between original and new members of staff.

The publication and distribution of the report was probably Byron's finest hour.

Overreaching. The departure of Ward Bond was a major turning point in Byron's history. He was aware of the need for succession planning because he required chairmen to train their successors in the event of their departures. By 1974, four of the original chairmen had been promoted and moved on to other schools and had been satisfactorily replaced from within the school. Succession planning for principals, however, was a system responsibility, and it had no special plan to replace Bond. Ward was such a revered and admired figure that virtually any successor would find it almost impossible to replace him. His departure occurred at a time of a dramatic increase in student enrollment, teacher hiring, and a major structural addition to the school.

Succeeding the Charismatic Leader. The new principal, Bruce Grey, was 34 years of age in 1974 when he was assigned by the system to Lord Byron High School. He had been a successful assistant principal in a very large traditional school. Openly ambitious, he moved very quickly through the ranks. Most of his colleagues recognized Grey as very intelligent, a superb organizer, a fine administrator, and in his own way an innovator. He embraced his conception of the Byron philosophy enthusiastically. Grey's tenure as president of the local teachers' union had endowed him with considerable political skill. In fact, he had been the president when the Byron philosophy and organization had been approved by the union. Senior system leaders hoped that a former union president, as principal of Byron, would quiet a union that had become much more adversarial, especially over the issue of differentiated staffing funds (DSF). In union terms, DSF cost teachers' jobs.

The union's renewed aggressiveness reflected the change in leadership at the central office. Sizemore had dominated through sheer force of personality. His successor was a better listener and more conciliatory. Byron had been Sizemore's project. In the midst of many inherited problems, it was not as high a priority for his successor. As Grey has stated, "I think South was a major force in the rise of Byron and a significant force in its decline." He felt that the system failed to support the school in two ways: It had allowed the union to win the DSF issue, and it had appointed an assistant superintendent to supervise the school who had been quite critical of its philosophy and was a weak advocate for the school. Conversely, some system leaders saw Grey as brash and overly aggressive.

This negative opinion of Grey among some senior leaders of the system was shared by a few people on the Byron staff, as well as outside the school. There was a feeling among some staff members, especially those who mourned the loss of Bond, that Grey used the rhetoric of Byron but he did not really believe in its philosophy. They felt that liberty had become license. Tendencies evident in the first 4 years did become manifest in the "Grey era." The halls were often littered. Students would sit in front of the school smoking. Some rather unconventional staff were hired—as one person described them, "flower children left over from the 60s." As the size of the staff increased, communications tended to be through department meetings as opposed to staff meetings. Some placed the blame at Grey's door; others more charitably saw school size, the promotion of many of the key players, lack of regional support, and attacks by other professionals in the system as factors in the perception that Byron was losing its way.

The year 1974 saw the completion of a large addition to Byron to accommodate the growth in the east end of Middleton. By 1977, when Grey moved on to a senior leadership role in another school board, Byron was one of the largest schools in the system. Grey felt that a number of people on the staff had difficulty transferring their loyalties from the charismatic Bond to the "Byron concept." He said that for some people on staff, change was personified in the originating principal rather than becoming part of the structure and culture of the school. From his present perspective as a successful senior leader in another school district he said: "Change has to be built into the processes. Change identified with a person has the roots of its own destruction. There has to be loyalty to broader issues. Life cycles of many 'light-house' schools have been shortened because people could not shift loyalties from the individual to broader concepts."

Grey pushed the DSF concept to the point that the Byron chairmen had over $300,000 to use to support classroom teachers. The money was spent on teacher aides, secretaries, lab assistants, and outside experts. He was able to get the board's senior administration to agree to use the money for "things" that enabled Byron to be the best-resourced school in the region. The union objected to "teacher money" being used for "things." Grey's accomplishment, in retrospect, might have been a "Pyrrhic victory" because it quickened the union's attack on the entire concept. There was resentment as well from less venturesome principals. They found themselves trying to save money because of the board's budget difficulties by restricting paper use and other such approaches, while a neighboring school had an abundance of resources.

Perhaps Grey's greatest contribution was his handling of a potentially critical community. The Byron concept was so alien to most parents' experience that even in the Bond era community restiveness was a serious concern. Individuals in the community had always expressed concern about the perceived lack of rigor in the curriculum, student free time, informality of the teachers, and discipline. As Grey said, "the criticism never went away but we did keep it to acceptable levels." When he left in 1977, Byron was a large, well-resourced, and ostensibly successful school,[4] but the seeds of its decline were evident to people in the school. Many thought the school had been so caught up in issues like DSF, adult education, community outreach, and adding programs such as an outdoor education immersion that the essential Byron vision had become blurred. In essence, Byron suffered from "innovation overload"—too many new approaches added before previous changes had been consolidated.

Entropy. Concerns that the original Byron concept had been lost resulted in the assignment of Graham Clark, the former assistant principal to Bond, as principal to replace Grey. By 1977, Clark had gained experience as a principal in another large school in the system, and was well regarded by those staff members who opened Byron and were still there. It was felt that he might be able to capture something of the essential Byron approach. Clark's arrival coincided with a number of logistical and organizational changes over which the school had no control. He inherited a school of nearly 2,000 students and 100 teachers and 135 staff in total. The school's enrollment declined by 150 students each year of his 3-year tenure.[5] This meant that each year the most junior teachers were declared surplus to the school. Since Byron had known only growth, this was an important psychological turning point for staff. The drop in enrollment coincided with two mandated organizational changes that further undermined the initial concept of Byron.

In 1977, the Ministry of Education required Byron and other experimental schools to conform to the province's standard 27 credit (or course) diploma. Byron also was obliged to adopt the standard timetable that was used by all but three schools in South, which largely eliminated the savings in teachers that had led to differentiated staffing funds from 1970 to 1977. By 1980, DSF had disappeared totally in the system with the approval of senior system leaders. Enrollment in South had leveled off and in fact declined in some schools in the system. This decline meant surplus teachers from declining schools had to be placed in other schools. Byron had never hired its full complement of teachers and had reallocated those unspent funds. Now teachers' positions were needed and Clark was obliged to accede to senior administration's requirement to abandon one of Byron's essential innovations.

When these changes were combined with the board's agreement to change its policy on department heads in 1981, which was the basis of the chair structure at Byron, another key pillar of Byron's innovative edifice crumbled. This meant an increase in formal leaders, a reduction of their time for departmental functions, and a return to a structure more closely aligned with those of other schools.

Staff members give Clark credit for implementing changes, which were unpalatable to most people at Byron, while maintaining the integrity of the basic Byron philosophy toward students. During Grey and Clark's tenures there was considerable staff mobility. By 1978 only 23 of the 135 staff members had been at Byron in its first 3 years. Only five of the original 10 chairmen remained. The five who had left, all for promotions in the system, were considered by Bond to be the heart of his original group. In September 1979, the system promoted Clark.

Attempting to Recapture the Past. His replacement, George Owens, was one of the original chairmen. Owens had been the highly creative chair of English when the school opened. He had been one of the most powerful intellectual and creative forces within the original group and was well liked by students and staff. He had enjoyed a successful tenure as principal at a small school in the north of the region, and his return to Byron was generally met with approval by staff. In spite of Clark's and others' best efforts however, Owens found a school that had changed profoundly from the one he left in 1974 and was now little different from other South schools. South as well as the rest of the province experienced rapidly declining enrollment in the early 1980s. When this occurs, administrators have little choice but to eliminate courses, declare teachers surplus, and reduce or eliminate extracurricular activities, with the result that staff morale plummets.

Compounding the problem was an exodus of students to neighboring schools whose numbers were remaining relatively stable. Many of these students were high performers who left to get more specialized courses, or to participate in Roxborough's elitist program for the gifted. The flow of optional attendance was creating great imbalance in the schools of east Middleton. This further erosion of the student base through optional attendance made public relations and not educational issues the main school priority. Staff members felt betrayed by the board, by the senior administration, and by the school's community.

To aggravate matters further, because of the decline in enrollment, the board's policy reduced the number of assistant principals from two to one. As a result the school lost its most accomplished organizer. Owens was an intellectual and a visionary, but had to spend much of his time dealing with mundane administrative functions. The pressure of managing through such difficult times affected Owen's health, robbing him of his usual ebullience and energy. He saw his role in those years as "to maintain and contain." With so much needed in the school, he felt he had little left "to fight the ghosts." When the Ministry, remembering his truly visionary English programs at Byron of the early 1970s, offered him a secondment to review provincial policies in the teaching of English, he leaped at the opportunity.

A Different Direction. By 1984, I was able to convince my colleagues within the senior management team that Byron required a different type of principal. The new principal, Patrick Garner, had never taught at Byron. His major challenge was to restore public confidence and rebuild a rather disillusioned staff. My only personal involvement came at the beginning and toward the end of this phase of "overreaching and entropy." My one-year tenure as assistant principal coincided with the tremendous growth in student population and the beginnings of what I have described as a stage of "overreaching," in which innovation was pushed beyond the staff's ability to consolidate the changes. I returned as the school's superintendent 8 years later, at a time many staff members considered the lowest point in Lord Byron's short history. The "entropy" that had set in was immediately evident to me and to its new administrative team.

SURVIVAL AND CONTINUITY: TO THE MID-1990s

Ontario to the Mid-1990s

After 40 years in power, the Progressive Conservative party's control in Ontario ended in 1987, and the Liberal party came to power. In short order the new government announced its "Restructuring of Education" initiatives. Government-sponsored committees developed consultation papers on all aspects of elementary and secondary programs. The most significant policy initiative for secondary education was the destreaming (detracking) of grade 9. Schools worked energetically to act on this initiative only to have a new government elected in the early 1990s put most of the previous government's initiatives on hold, pending the results of the $3 million Ontario Royal Commission on Learning, which reported in December 1994. No sooner had the commission reported than the Progressive Conservative party returned to power and shelved the progressive and "teacher-friendly" report (Ontario Royal Commission on Learning, 1994).

In its present incarnation the Progressive Conservative party follows the philosophical stance of the "new right." It has initiated severe budget cuts to public service, welfare, child care, health care, and education, while pushing through a 30% tax cut for the more affluent. Teachers, nurses, public servants, and welfare recipients have been demonized and demoralized. It would appear that Ontario is intent on following the pattern established in Britain, Australia, and some American states and Canadian provinces. The severity of the cost-cutting is unparalleled in Ontario's history. School boards faced by reductions in provincial grants are eliminating a number of programs, initiating user fees for some services, and altering collective agreements to increase class sizes and reduce or eliminate teachers' planning time. As this is written, teacher strikes and other forms of political action have brought classroom innovation in Ontario to a grinding halt—proving once again that "policy cannot mandate what matters" (McLaughlin, 1990, p. 12). Funds for centralized curriculum and standardized testing, however, are available in abundance. From the perspective of an educator, if the early 1970s were the best of times, 1995–2000 are the worst of times for education in Ontario. For the South Board and its director, the provincial move to the political right merely follows the shift that had already taken place in South.

The South Board to the Mid-1990s

The system's fourth director, Bill Wilson, was appointed in 1988. A well-regarded superintendent within the system and a former Byron original staff member, he quickly established himself with staff and trustees as a respected leader. His organizational and political skills enabled him to consolidate the gains of the previous decade and to branch out in new strategic directions (Stoll & Fink, 1994). His background in staff development and his understanding of the change process had convinced him that improving staff performance through professional development held more promise for improvement than mandates or appraisal systems.

Wilson viewed the school as the basic unit of change. The "top-down model" of the previous 18 years of South's history was changed to a "top-down, bottom-up" model of change (Fullan, 1991). The system provided a broad set of directions through a strategic plan, as well as resources, and the schools developed School Growth Plans to meet their unique needs within these broad system parameters (Stoll & Fink, 1992, 1994). To achieve instructional improvement and staff development, Wilson persuaded the board to increase the support for teachers and schools by adding a number of instructional consultants to each of the area teams in the district (Stoll & Fink, 1992). From 1989 to 1992, in spite of reduced grants from the province, the board continued to support Wilson's strategic initiatives.

This growth and development under Wilson was short-lived. By 1992, South and the rest of the province were in the depths of a recession. Taxpayer protest groups were springing up all over the province. The Middleton Taxpayers' Coalition conducted a highly public campaign to reduce educational costs, which resulted in the election of six neoconservative trustees in the 1992 election. They succeeded in reducing board meetings to confusion and disorder and brought most of Wilson's progressive initiatives to improve schools to a full stop. Little was accomplished in a climate of acrimony, personal invective, and political "grandstanding." Discussions on issues often led to personal attacks by a few trustees on the director, board officials, or other trustees.

Despite the challenging political climate in South, the Byron influence continues to be evident throughout the region. As of 1996, of the 17 secondary principals, 13 had spent significant parts of their careers at Byron. One reason Byron has come to look very much like other schools is that the other schools have become much more student-centered and democratic in their operations as a result of the dispersal of the Byron "mafia." Initiatives that began with Lord Byron such as semestered timetables, immersion programs, multitext English, recreation-based physical education, interdisciplinary departments, individualized mathematics and science courses, personal student counseling, and informal teacher-student relationships appear in every school in South. In spite of the pessimism that pervades education in Ontario, these leaders continue to exude a quiet confidence that schools will be able to respond to whatever comes their way. Perhaps Lord Byron with its many trials and tribulations has proven a useful training ground for dealing with adversity.

Lord Byron to the Mid-1990s

When Patrick Garner, Owens's replacement as principal, and his new assistant principal Betty Kelly arrived at Lord Byron in 1984, they moved quickly to reestablish the school's vitality. They encouraged the district to place both the life-skills program for mentally challenged students and the "Satellite" program for seriously learning disabled students at Lord Byron. Many of the students in both programs had behavioral problems and some were physically handicapped.[6] The addition of special education programs, while laudable, did nothing to stem the outflow of the more academically talented students to Roxborough. As Garner explained his challenge, "as a community resident, I heard so much about the problems with Byron from my neighbors, that I wanted a shot at doing something about it." It was, he continued,

> a number of years of getting input from the community that made me decide that when I got there, these were some things I was going to work on. You can't work on everything so you have to work on a few things and this whole issue of gifted, making Byron as much of an academic school as Roxborough, and we had to get the message out to the community and we had to do certain things. . . . The other was the whole issue of the athletic program, and whether or not kids who went to Byron and were concerned about representing the school at a higher level would get lost. By that I mean Byron's philosophy . . . was that everybody made the team and got an equal chance to play and winning was not that important. There was a concern in the community that the kids

> end up losing the game all the time so I want my kid out of Byron.

Garner responded by establishing self-contained classes for gifted students and elite athletic teams similar to those of Roxborough. He balanced the athletic program by extending an intramural program open to all students. To further retain the high-achieving students, Garner convinced staff to support the addition of a French Immersion program. Throughout their tenure Garner and Kelly sought to balance the traditional egalitarianism of Byron with the very real community and social pressures for excellence and elitism.

Garner was a much more directive and decisive principal than his predecessors. Pragmatic and less innovative in his approach, he and Kelly, who replaced him as principal in 1987, clarified decision-making processes and lines of reporting in the school as well as streamlining procedural issues. Their approach to the community was to use every opportunity to say "Byron has changed." In practice, though, the substantive changes had occurred long before Garner and Kelly's appointments. They recognized that Byron's programs were still as good as if not better than those of most schools and worked energetically to alter public perceptions of the school. When Kelly was transferred to another challenging school in 1991, her successor, Dennis Lawrence, was able to report:

> The parents I speak to and the type of issues which come across my desk tell me that parents feel very good about this school. Occasionally . . . some of the old ghosts still make themselves known, not in any great way that really makes me terribly concerned, but it's still there, just a reminder that public relations needs to be attended to.

Lawrence, who had been a practice teacher at Byron in its early days, acknowledged that Byron was more similar to than different from most other schools. He stated, however, that "it is still a pretty unique school in terms of the programs it offers." It still seems to be more willing to respond to change than many schools in South. Perhaps it does not initiate change but responds to external innovations that fit its continuing student-centered philosophy.

At present, Byron's future is once again in doubt. With enrollment at the 700 mark, rumors of Byron's closure, especially at a time of financial cutbacks, are beginning to surface. As its present principal describes the condition of Byron:

> Right now we are in a phase of survival, and survival as an institution and an organization, and that we will continue to exist and be viable—believe it or not this is a major fear of our staff. Everyone is worried that we are closing down. I'm trying to remain positive and say we will survive but so much of it is dependent on being proactive about wanting to survive.

In many ways the scenario that Byron followed in the late 1970s and early 1980s is being replayed in the 1990s. It is being played out in a climate of retrenchment and some have used the word *fear.*

This brief history of Lord Byron has provided the historical context and a point of reference for the subsequent six analytical chapters, which look at the school from each of the six lenses or frames identified in Chapter 1: context, meaning, leadership, structure, culture, and the lives and work of teachers.

CHAPTER 3

Context

One of the myths of the school-improvement literature is that all schools are unique (Miles, 1998). Schools, of course, have many things in common. Unfortunately, school-change efforts have tended to operate on the opposite (and equally flawed) premise when it comes to new policies and practices—"one size fits all." As the preceding chapter argues, a starting point in understanding a school is to know its historical context. Similarly, a school's social geography, demographics, and political and cultural networks help to define its uniqueness.

THE CONTEXT LENS

This chapter develops the context "lens" introduced in Chapter 1 to view Lord Byron. In addition, it intends to assist readers to determine the relevance of this study to their own settings. Since the examination of context is potentially so extensive and complex, I have limited my discussion to those aspects of context that are most relevant to the Lord Byron case.

Internal Context

Students. "Educational change depends on what teachers do and think—it's as simple and complex as that" (Fullan, 1991, p. 117). The contextual factor that matters most to teachers is their students (McLaughlin, 1993). Teachers' responses to their students, however, are as diverse as teachers themselves. An individual teacher's sense of efficacy will vary depending on the classes he or she teaches, the socioeconomic background of the students (Teddlie & Stringfield, 1993), the subject(s) taught, the school's mission, and the teacher's individual knowledge, beliefs, and skills (Grossman & Stodolsky, 1994). Certain broad patterns of teacher response to the challenges students present have emerged in the research literature. McLaughlin and Talbert (1993) report that one type of adaptation occurs when teachers consider that the achievement and discipline problems students bring to the classroom are the result of external factors such as inadequate parenting or societal failures. These teachers, therefore, tend to respond by reinforcing traditional standards of discipline based on authority, transmission approaches to pedagogy, and concentration on a fact-based curriculum. Teachers who react this way are inclined to become cynical, frustrated, and burned out. The lowering of standards of achievement and discipline is a second response to student-created problems. "Regardless of teachers' rationale, both teachers and students in classrooms of this stripe find themselves bored and disengaged from teaching and learning" (McLaughlin & Talbert, 1993, p. 6). The third orientation is one in which teachers attempt to change practices and adopt more flexible student-centered strategies that involve teaching for understanding, activity learning, and such student-engaging strategies as cooperative learning. This adaptive approach is also fraught with difficulty. As McLaughlin and Talbert (1993) explain:

> Some teachers who attempted such changes in practice . . . were unable to sustain them and became frustrated and discouraged. This is because learning how to teach for student understanding goes against the grain of traditional classroom practice and so entails radical change and risks obstruction. Those teachers who made effective adaptations to today's students had one thing in common: each belonged to an effective professional community which encouraged and enabled them to transform their teaching. (p. 7)

There is also some evidence that students' responses to change often inhibit innovation (Rudduck, 1991; Rudduck, Day, & Wallace, 1997). Unfortunately this is an area we know very little about because as Fullan (1991) states, "no one ever asks them" (p. 182). What evidence is available suggests that students respond in one of four ways: indifference, confusion, temporary escape from boredom, and heightened interest in learning and school. Fullan declares that "effective change in schools involves just as much cognitive and behavioral change on the part of students as it does anyone else" (p. 188). In considering the context for change, he concludes that educators must "stop thinking of students just in terms of learning outcomes and start thinking of them as people who are also being asked to become involved in new activities" (p. 189). Corbett and Wilson (1995) go even further and recommend that "student role redefinition is a critical linchpin between adult reform behavior and student success, and the failure to acknowledge and accept this connection is a potentially fatal flaw in promoting our understanding of reform and in creating effective change initiatives" (p. 12).

Departments and Subjects. In some situations, a teacher's subject orientation, department, and/or professional network provide a "professional community." Conversely, in other circumstance these contexts promote patterns of professional adaptations that reinforce traditional and often "watered-down" curricula and teaching (Grossman & Stodolsky, 1994). Subject departments are also a critical context for secondary school teachers (Ball, 1981; Hargreaves et al., 1992; McLaughlin & Talbert, 1993). As Siskin (1994) indicates, departments have become "a crucial part of the context of teaching in high school, for it is the department which organizes teachers spatially, temporally, administratively, and symbolically" (p. 12). Membership in certain departments provides prestige, influence, and resources, whereas other departments and their teachers tend to be marginalized and less influential. Bennet (1985) argues that a teacher's subject and department affiliation can influence promotion opportunities. A teacher from a marginalized department such as visual arts, for example, has less chance for promotion than a teacher in a mathematics or science department.

Little (1993) identifies three factors that determine departmental strength and status: membership of full-time specialists, a substantive department chair position, and a coherent stance toward curricular policy (p. 157). In Britain, Canada, and the United States, academic departments such as mathematics and science enjoy greater status than nonacademic departments like the arts, physical education, and vocational training (Ball, 1987; Hargreaves et al., 1992; Siskin, 1994). Departments with enhanced status may, however, be different in schools with a special mission. Talbert (1993) found that in vocational schools, technical departments had higher status than academic departments. University and college requirements and outside assessments can also influence status (Stodolsky, 1993). Graduation requirements that emphasize certain subjects add to or diminish departmental prestige and influence. Assessment programs that tend to focus on a few subjects, such as mathematics, science, and English, reinforce these departments and marginalize nonassessed areas.

There is little agreement on the efficacy of departments as vehicles for school change McLaughlin and Talbert (1993) seem to promote collegial departments as a prerequisite for change in schools. Others have suggested that departments tend to work against schoolwide initiatives and promote balkanization (A. Hargreaves, 1994). Siskin's (1994) study describes how departments get involved in issues of power and politics in a school:

> The realm of academic departments creates boundary lines which constrain high school communications, and social worlds which can sustain

> subject colleagues within their small groups, but they are also micro-political arenas where critical "material endowments" of funding time and space are "defended" and "distributed." (p. 113)

Ball (1987) has described some departments as fiefdoms where teachers enjoy rewards for loyalty and experience punishment for treason. Departments are also differentially effective (Sammons, Mortimore, & Thomas, 1996) and require different improvement strategies (Harris, 1998). The department one belongs to has a significant bearing on a teacher's sense of purpose, practices, and ideas on organizational learning.

Studies of school subjects have indicated that they also provide a context that "can be characterized by conflict between subjects over status, resources and territory" (Goodson, 1983, p. 3). In addition, subjects "exert differential effects on teachers' ideas about academic knowledge and about classroom instruction" (Yaakobi & Sharan, 1985, p. 196) and can have a powerful effect on teachers' responses to change (Grossman & Stodolsky, 1993). English teachers, for example, tend to respond more positively to progressive methodologies such as individualization of instruction, whereas mathematics teachers are much more inclined to group by previous achievement (Ball, 1981). It appears quite clear, therefore, that teachers' subject orientation and the departments in which they teach have a significant effect on their classroom practices and willingness to entertain new ideas (Ball & Bowe, 1992; Goodson, 1983; Lacey, 1977). Indeed, it seems that secondary teachers' academic orientation is a major impediment to change in secondary schools (Goodson, 1983; Siskin, 1994). Attempts to promote more interdisciplinary programs often fail because of the hegemony of subjects and departments (Hargreaves et al., 1992). These divisions or academic "tribes" (Grossman & Stodolsky, 1993) are reinforced by such external contextual factors as university compartmentalization and provincial and national subject organizations.

The School as Context. There is a substantial body of recent school-effectiveness literature that shows the impact of the school on teachers' efficacy and students' achievement (Mortimore, Sammons, Stoll, Lewis, & Ecob, 1988; Rutter, Maughan, Mortimore, & Ousten, 1979; Teddlie & Stringfield, 1993). Mortimore (1991) defines an effective school as one in which "pupils progress further than might be expected from consideration of its intake" (p. 216). This line of research has identified a number of contextual factors that have enabled some schools, regardless of their socioeconomic context, to promote more effective teacher practices, which in turn enhance students' accomplishments.

- "High consensus schools" (Rosenholtz, 1989) in which the staff members share a vision of what they are trying to achieve, and identify and support goals to carry out their vision, are more effective for all students.
- Schools that socialize new teachers to a vision of school growth experience greater cohesiveness and less turnover than less effective schools (Teddlie & Stringfield, 1993).
- The degree of teaching collaboration appears to be an important determinant of more effective schools (Rosenholtz, 1989).
- The importance of the school's principal is reinforced in numerous studies (Mortimore et al., 1988; Smith & Andrews, 1989; Teddlie & Stringfield, 1993). Principals who support teacher improvement, promote a positive learning ethos, and expect high standards of performance from teachers and students are a crucial part of the internal context.

External Contexts

Just as classrooms exist within a context of subjects, departments, and schools, schools function within a much larger context that often dramatically influences their effective functioning.

District Context. The district in which the school resides is the first line of influence. As Louis and Miles (1990) advise "Always keep one eye on the district. Be prepared to negotiate steadily but discreetly for special status, especially in a rule oriented bureaucracy" (p. 188). Evidence suggests that more effective schools are located in districts where supportive interactions occur between schools and central office staff (Coleman & LaRocque, 1990; Fullan, 1991; Rosenholtz, 1989). Indeed, Rosenholtz (1989) found that districts with strongly bureaucratic, top-down structures were considerably less effective than districts that allowed teachers to experience more autonomy to learn and to improve their work within a context of overall regional direction and support. Similarly, schools unsupported by larger networks find school improvement exceedingly difficult (Barber, 1995; Fullan, 1991; Stoll & Myers, 1998). This theme of top-down/bottom-up change permeates the change literature (Lieberman & Grolnik, 1998; Louis & Miles, 1990; Stoll & Fink, 1992, 1994).

Conversely, it is unlikely that an ineffective school will continue to be ineffective within an effective school system. At their best, school systems can be powerful partners for schools (Brouillette, 1996; Stoll & Fink, 1992, 1994). Districts that promote positive change in schools and classrooms are characterized by the following attributes:

- Effective districts engender improvement in schools through the thoughtful and careful selection of instructional leaders as principals (Smith & Andrews, 1989) and the careful "matching of principals with schools" (Teddlie & Stringfield, 1993, p. 223).
- Successful districts tend to capitalize on naturally occurring change efforts by encouraging the school's leadership team and supporting change in context. Stoll and Fink (1996) have suggested that different types of schools require different leadership and school-improvement strategies. Successful districts tend to "nurture and create improvement processes that are indigenous to particular school contexts" (Teddlie & Stringfield, 1993, p. 223).
- Coleman and LaRocque (1990) concluded that effective districts have an active and evolving accountability ethos that combines interactive monitoring with a respect for school autonomy.
- Effective districts recruit and select teachers who are committed to district goals for students' learning and continuous improvement. In addition, these districts do not just transfer or try to hide less successful teachers. They focus on supportive practices, and if help is unsuccessful, they facilitate the teacher's dismissal (Smith & Andrews, 1989).

As Fullan (1991) states, schools cannot redesign themselves. "The role of the district is crucial. Individual schools can become highly innovative for short periods of time without the district, but they cannot *stay* innovative without the district action to establish the conditions for continuous and long term improvement" (p. 209).

Community Context. Mirel (1994) provides a detailed examination of how macro-politics disrupted a school district, its communities, and its schools. The arguments that erupted over a federally initiated "break-the-mold" reform effort in the Bensonville district[1] in the United States destroyed the project and the potential of significant school improvement. Local rivalries and the inability of the district to anticipate and handle the macro-political environment were contributing factors. Mirel suggests that significant change will not occur unless reformers address the material and political dimensions of reform "well before embarking on a campaign of change." He indicates that reformers

> must face the power-brokering reality of the reform process, clearly recognizing which issues strike deeply at vested interests . . . they must be as well versed in strategic negotiation and alliance building as they are in devising breakthrough educational programs. In the process, they must also become competent in judging when to compromise, redesign or stand fast. Reformers will have to recognize that the process of change involves not just building constituencies but also maintaining them, not just gaining power but exercising it wisely. (p. 516)

Mirel (1994) also suggests that "less is more." This advice is directly contradictory to McLaughlin (1990), who concludes in the Rand study that large change efforts have a greater chance of success. Mirel suggests that large projects that undertake to make dramatic change threaten a community's concept of a "real school" (Metz, 1991). The conception of a "good school" as defined by professional expertise in Bensonville was quite out of line with the public's perception of what a "real school" looked like. The public saw many of the advocates of new ideas, with their associated exclusionary jargon, as out of step with what the public believed was common sense (Brouillette, 1996; Fletcher et al., 1985; Gold & Miles, 1981; Grant, 1988). As in the case of Bensonville, many projects that were touted to be "innovative," "break-the-mold," or "state-of-the-art" promised too much and delivered too little. Mirel (1994) suggests that smaller scale, low-key, rather understated reform efforts have a greater chance of receiving community support. Since education has always been highly politicized perhaps this is good advice. He suggests that the way to avoid the pitfalls of macro-political conflict is

> to recognize from the start that efforts at educational change inevitably deal with such powerful issues as control of highly prized institutions, levels of taxation, and job security. Reform also confronts deeply held values and exposes some of the most fundamental passions surrounding parents' hopes and fears about their children. (p. 518)

In recent years, the role of the community has become an increasingly important topic in the change literature (Edwards & Jones Young, 1992; Epstein, 1995; Fullan, 1991; Morgan & Morgan, 1992). Governments have concluded that decentralizing some decisions directly to schools and councils of parents will lead to better decisions. This can create more problems than it solves. In some situations, parents with little expertise in educational issues are making decisions that more properly should be made by people with some understanding of the educative process. Participatory democracy, on occasion, can also conflict with representative democracy, as the following case reveals.

The State Context. Brouillette's (1996) case study of the Cottonwood school district[2] provides a useful example of how a district that by all measures could be considered a successful school district was undermined by its context within a state. In spite of the district's best efforts to promote growth in its schools, it found itself caught between the larger political influences of the state and the more localized political issues of the various school communities. In its attempt to promote more decentralized decision-making, the paradoxical forces of representative democracy, as played out in the state legislature and the district's board room, and participatory democracy as reflected in parent councils challenged the district's ability to support its schools. More particularly, in a district that had promoted greater openness with parents and greater involvement in decision-making, community members attacked it for issues that often did not apply to the district but were part of the larger educational context. When the state engineered severe budget cuts and "schools of choice," community members took out their wrath on the nearest source of frustration, the district. The authors of the changes, the state legislators, were too remote to access. The district and the schools also took the brunt of national and international criticism of schools engendered by the state and national press. The community attacked the district for a lack of communication and fiscal irresponsibility when in fact it communicated more openly than most districts and, by any standard, was quite fiscally responsible. It would seem that the more schools and particularly districts communicate with their communities, the more they are subjected to criticism. Brouillette (1996) concludes that Sarason's (1990) advice, that school improvement will not occur unless power relationships within schools are addressed, is insufficient. She argues, based on the challenges faced by the Cottonwood district, that "the effectiveness of restructuring (or reform) efforts will be limited unless power relationships in the social context within which public schools are embedded are also transformed" (p. 208).

In recent years, governments in various countries have adopted neoconservative reforms in the name of national economic competitiveness. Local autonomy over the things that matter in education such as curriculum and assessing student progress have been trampled by central governments' rush to national curricula, more student assessment, and the cult of efficiency. Educators have gradually awakened to the omnipresent role of the state in determining the context in which teachers work and schools function. Criticism of this invasive role of government into the functioning of schools has been widespread and largely ineffective (Ball, 1993; Barlow & Robertson, 1994; Bracey, 1991, 1992; Mortimore & Whitty, 1997; Whitty, 1998). While the change literature has attended to micro-politics (Ball, 1987; Blase, 1988) within schools, districts and schools are buffeted by macro-politics. Certainly the history of new schools speaks to the inability of educators to deal with political vicissitudes (Fletcher et al., 1985; Gold & Miles, 1981; Moon, 1983; Riley, 1998; Smith et al., 1987).

Teachers' Union Context. Another contextual area on which there is relatively little research is the role of unions in the life of schools. Teachers' unions are a significant and somewhat elusive component of the contextual landscape for most schools and school boards. As Mirel (1994) reports, the Bensonville unions reversed their original support of the reform project in order to preserve teacher contractual rights and as a result came to stand for the status quo. Some observers argue that unions place too much emphasis on economic and political priorities to the detriment of school programs (Kerchner & Koppich, 1993; Louis, 1990). Others contend that collective bargaining creates the perception of teachers as laborers rather than professional workers (Johnson, 1984; McDonnell & Pascal, 1988; Mitchell & Kerchner, 1983). This line of argument blames unions for formalizing lines between administrators and teachers, and the standardization of teaching tasks.

At the local level, there is ambivalence about union roles. Bascia (1994) looked at case studies of individual schools and found that the better "the match between union strategies and professional community, the more likely the union will secure teacher commitment as well as enhance the practical and intellectual value of the professional community for its members" (p. 8). Conversely, she reports that

> in situations where district-level concerns are out of synch with the conditions and issues of a particular school faculty, there may be differences between teachers' values and occupational needs and issues of relevance to union leaders. These differences are probably more likely in larger districts. (p. 67)

In Ontario, where union membership is mandatory, this ambivalence within the secondary teachers' union has been a feature of its history over the past 25 years (Martel, 1995).

The following discussion of Lord Byron High School focuses on how the intricate interplay of these external contextual factors—the province, the district, the community, and the union—affected its life cycle. Subsequent chapters on leadership, culture, and teachers' work and lives attend to issues involving the internal contexts of the school.

LORD BYRON AND ITS CONTEXT

Byron's creation in 1970 was a response to pressures that school and system leaders felt intuitively, but could not identify or articulate with precision. Their collective experiences, insights, and sensibilities led them to design a school that in many ways was ahead of its time. What resulted, however, was a change process with an ill-defined, or at least partially developed, theoretical base. As George Owens reflected:

> We were like Thomas Kuhn's (1962) paradigm pioneers. We didn't have the statistically validated basis for what we were doing, some of us acted based on experience. My feeling after 25 years is the precepts we enunciated clearly enough in 1970–1974 have been validated in the following 20 odd years.

Lord Byron was a product of its times. As a former teacher recalled:

> We were largely very young, largely single, not everybody, but many were beginning their careers and they were people who not only brought youth and idealism but also a particular philosophy because they had come through the universities of the 60's. The times were significant for the things we did. Byron could not have happened in the 80's and couldn't have happened in the early 60's either.

Years of Creativity and Experimentation

Byron was the result of that "particular philosophy" which came to characterize the 1960s—an age that exalted the individual as opposed to the corporate, identified with the disenfranchised rather than the majority culture, and prized intuition and creativity over rationality and conformity. The challenge at Byron was to translate these ill-defined ideals into a workable school. The timing could not have been better. The political and social contexts of Ontario and South were ripe for experimentation.

The District's Influence. It is difficult to trace the exact origins of the Byron concept, but certainly "the genuine interest" of the director of education was vital. The district's role in the establishment of Byron was crucial. The director of the South Board established the Innovations Committee, which provided the initial impetus for the school. Perhaps unwittingly, however, by authorizing a fairly elite group of South's staff to envision a school of the future, he created what Fullan and Eastabrook (1977) have described as "a group of people working on a common problem independently of the larger community, tending to grow in a direction incomprehensible to their co-workers and associates who had not experienced the learning process undergone by the committee members" (p. 224). Most of South's other employees, and virtually all of the potential parents and students of Byron, had no idea what was being contemplated (Fullan et al., 1972).

Certainly the appointment of Ward Bond as the first principal was an important system decision. As one observer commented, "I don't know if the system realized how radical Bond really was." By giving Bond a year to plan, the opportunity to hire most of his staff, and the agreement to use a different staffing process, the system enabled him to design what for the times was a radical alternative. It required a politically confident chief executive officer to convince or, as some have suggested, coerce the board and reluctant senior administrators to support the Byron concept. Sizemore was also able to influence the teachers' union to permit differentiated staffing and an alternative organization at Byron.

The district teachers' union was very much on everyone's mind when Byron was established. A senior official of the board at the time recalls:

> I'm not sure the staff was aware of this but Byron was under siege from a number of sources including the local union and particularly its leaders. . . . They held great suspicion and opposition to the notion of the reallocation of resources, the abandonment of the traditional department heads.

This opposition occurred within a climate in which the provincial union had taken a public stance in opposition to the broadly progressive Hall-Dennis Report and had opposed H. S. 1 (the curriculum plan for secondary schools). In spite of its professional rhetoric, the union and particularly its South division tended to be more concerned with creating jobs for teachers than with supporting experimental approaches to school and classroom organization (see page 14). As the school's superintendent at the time of its opening said, "[the union] was never open-minded on the chairmanship organization." The union's compliance with the Byron experiment was bought at the price of a full review of Byron after 5 years.

Despite his silence on the topic, Sizemore appeared to see Byron as a way to push the newly created South system and particularly its secondary schools into more progressive educational directions. He always took great interest in the number of visitors to Byron and the number and type of presentations made by Bond and his staff to other schools and provincial organizations. He hoped that as a result of Byron "the entire level of the system would be raised." Since Sizemore was also a dominant provincial figure, he was certainly in a position to extend Byron's influence to the province.

Sizemore's forceful style and his recent promotion to director of the newly created South Board had created enemies. Byron was seen by many as part of the Sizemore agenda, and as such it experienced some of the ill-feelings derived from what dissident elements in the region considered a "takeover." They believed that Sizemore had created a school that threatened their values and beliefs, to say nothing of their organizational structures. A young teacher in one of the schools in a section of the region that felt it had been annexed by Middleton, and later a principal at Byron, recalled that the people at Byron were seen as

> the flower children of the 60s. That was the perception. They had this beautiful school that the Board had pumped all kinds of money into, selected the very best of the best to go there, and they were free floaters, free thinkers. They were literally likened to the flower children and some of that never went away.

Many South staff members shared the view that Byron enjoyed unique benefits from the newly created school district—a new building, unrestricted staff recruitment, and more resources than other schools. The reality was quite different. Byron was not alone as a "new" building. Significant growth within South County in the 1960s resulted in the building of five new secondary schools from 1965 to 1970. Bond had agreed to accept his share of teachers displaced by the building of Byron and some of them were not the "best of the best." In fact, Bond's successor had to terminate the contract of one of the "force transfer" people. Certainly the early staff members were not flower children. While the staff was young, its average age was approximately 28, a significant percentage were over 30 years of age and 90% had some previous experience in conventional schools. In addition, Byron received the same amount of money as any other school. Sizemore insisted that if Byron was to be credible it "must be within the budget listed for all other schools; it must be fair." What Bond did do, however, was to use staff differently and reallocate resources. Only a few other schools accepted Sizemore's offer to differentiate staff.

A persistent theme of Byron respondents was the antagonism they experienced or felt from other colleagues in the region. A young teacher in 1970, who was transferred to Byron after her first year of teaching, described this tension:

> Because Byron was different and proud of being different, because it felt it was doing things for kids, the worst comments came from other schools. When I would ask them, they had never been to the school, had really never talked to anybody in the school. Rumor and the sense that these people at Byron were doing something different, all they wanted to hear were the negatives. They never heard the positives.

Bond found this rather "mindless" opposition confounding. When asked to identify the critics in the system he replied:

> The whole gamut, the principals in other secondary schools, teachers in other secondary schools—elementary schools tended very much to understand and support. There were "snipers" in the community, some Board members. If I might make an attribution, the reason that most of it went on was that by virtue of what we were doing and changing without coming out and saying it, we were saying you're doing it wrong and that was offensive. Simply, people didn't like the fact that we wanted to change all these things so they took "shots at us." That was enormous pressure.

This reaction was understandable, because in the early 1970s Byron was a threat to the entire "grammar of schooling" (Tyack & Tobin, 1994) that gave meaning to the careers of system colleagues.

From the very beginning, what staff members at Byron perceived as unwarranted opposition created a siege mentality. A teacher at Byron for all but its first year commented that he was "really tired" of arguing the merits of the Byron approach. The criticism had two effects: First it created a determination to make the Byron concept work. As Bond stated, "This made me more determined. This is going to work." He was not alone. Second, it resulted in Byron's purposely isolating itself from the rest of the system and closing in on itself. A veteran teacher commented, "Nobody outside the school supported it so we had to support each other." There is some evidence to suggest that this collective introversion was not unique to Byron (Hargreaves et al., 1992; Moon, 1983).

The Community Context. One and a half miles from Byron stood another secondary school, Roxborough, a well-respected and rather typical school of its time. Continuity and change sat uneasily side by side for everyone to see and compare. The staff at Roxborough made no secret of their contempt for Byron and its innovativeness. Its principal never referred to Byron by name, but only as "that school down the road." Ironically, Roxborough had been the Byron of the early 1960s. In its own way it had been less traditional than other schools of the time. Its principal had recruited fine teachers and many had been promoted in the system. As a former Roxborough teacher explained, even Roxborough had been resented because of its own newness and there was talk of the "Roxborough mafia" in the early 1960s. Criticism was not unique to Byron in the region. What made the situation tense was the physical proximity of the two schools and Roxborough's reputation as the "academic" school. Like many schools in the 1960s and 1970s, Roxborough tended to sort and select its students. Conversely, Byron's philosophy rejected this approach, and the school opened its doors to students who had not succeeded in other schools. Since most of these students were not high academic achievers they contributed to Byron's reputation as a school for the nonacademic. As one teacher recalled, "Because Byron was such an open school, when things went wrong they usually ended up in the newspaper." Many "pushouts" from Roxborough and other Middleton schools ended up at Byron.

Sizemore had allowed two schools to develop side by side with significantly different approaches to secondary education. He established Byron as a "pilot venture" or a "demonstration school" to shake up the system. Whatever his motivation, his plan resulted in intense competition between a well-regarded traditional school and the avant-garde school. "It has always been a Byron-Roxborough comparison, not Byron and any other school."

In the early years, from 1970 to 1975, Byron people tended to ignore Roxborough. For the most part, the Byron staff was more worried about daily survival than a contest with other schools. The insularity of Byron was often interpreted as arrogance. What was particularly damaging was the manner in which colleagues within the system undermined Byron with its parent community. Byron became stigmatized as the nontraditional, nonacademic school—a legacy that still haunts it 25 years later.

The Byron community first found out about the Byron plan through a series of meetings Bond conducted in the community. A fundamental principle of the school was not only to reach out to the community but also to include the community in the school. Byron had the first active parents' advisory committee in South, and adult participation as students in regular classes. In comparison with other schools, Byron was much more open, inviting, and parent-friendly. In 1975, the External Evaluation Committee stated: "In its relations with the community . . . Lord Byron is a model worthy of study by other schools." In contrast to this glowing testimonial, however, many members of the public remained skeptical. Criticism was muted because of Bond's political skills and the smoothness with which the school operated in the first few years. In spite of the best efforts of Bond and his colleagues, however, the community never totally "bought" the concept.

Another teacher provided a succinct and insightful summary.

> I think one of the problems Byron had is that very good things were happening but the public didn't necessarily understand the changes and changes which are not understood are perceived negatively. It takes a long time to change an existing perception once it's in the public's mind.

Tyack and Tobin (1994) provide two reasons to explain the difficulty of changing the "grammar of schooling." Both are appropriate to Lord Byron. Most reforms tend to be "intramural." This was certainly true of the Byron experience. It evolved from Sizemore to the Innovations Committee to Bond and to the staff with virtually no involvement of people outside this limited network of educational professionals. The second problem they identify is the burnout of reformers. This became an increasing problem for Byron. Two of the major causes for this burnout were the failure to gain community support and the presence of Roxborough. People were working themselves to exhaustion on behalf of their students while the parents, the teachers' colleagues, and the larger community sat back and criticized. George Owens's frustration was typical:

> I had ideas in 1970 that I thought as I worked through them were validated at the school but I wasn't sure. There was an immense amount of criticism. We were innovative but didn't have the sup-

port of people in the field and didn't have the body of data we have now that validated what we were doing.

In many ways the response of Lord Byron's external context in its early years made the internal context even more meaningful than it might otherwise have been. I well recall how we turned to each other for mutual support and reassurance that we were indeed on the right track. This introversion in the face of criticism became more pronounced as the school moved into the second stage of its life cycle.

Overreaching and Entropy

When the first students arrived at Byron in September 1970, the school had no history, no traditions, no mythologies, no reputation, and no culture—in effect, no "identity." By the time Bruce Grey became principal in 1974, he inherited a short but very rich school history, some traditions, and not a few myths and legends. He was appointed to a school that in the educational community was either revered or reviled. Few remained indifferent. It had an identity based on its perceived progressive philosophy, its open building, and the public images of its key leaders. There were rumblings of discord in the community but they had not surfaced in a coherent form. The parents who participated in the Parents' Council were enthusiastically supportive. Within the school, a dynamic, energetic, and closely collaborative school culture had developed.

By the early 1980s, however, the school had closed in on itself, lost its initial energy, and reverted to structures and cultures similar to those in most of the other schools in the South Board. Owens explained what he saw from his perspective as a chairman from 1970 to 1974, and Byron's principal from 1979 to 1984:

> The people who were capable of doing anything went on elsewhere and the people who depended symbiotically on the change agents and dropped back in the pack and was imposed on them from administration from above and not just from administration but from the community. Those first four years, we really resisted community attempts to impose conventional patterns on us and we were able to do it by force of personality, force of argument and by the demonstration of competence in the classroom.

When interviewed later, he said with a huge sigh, "When I went back in '80, it was just like any other high school." Some very small but consequential things had changed—the formal commencement, principals' pictures on the walls. Pep rallies for sports teams had been introduced. "I think of the physical education program based on noncompetitive lifetime activities in the '70s and the goddamn hockey team of the '80s. It was the toughest hockey team in the South Board. A year after I left, the principals of Roxborough and Byron had to cancel the hockey playoffs because of violence." That, he said "was completely antithetical to the mood of the early years."

Staff learning was an integral part of Byron's culture in the first few years, but as time went by, that learning became isolated from the rest of the region. As Fullan (1993) states, "The learning organization must be dynamic inside but perforce must be highly plugged into its context" (p. 83). Changing circumstances in Byron's environment impacted significantly on the evolution of Lord Byron. The most significant external shift occurred at the board's central office.

District Context. In 1975, the retirement of Jim Sizemore had greater repercussions for Lord Byron than perhaps any other secondary school in South. It was not that the new director was unsupportive of Byron, or uninterested in it, but rather that he perceived he had to be equally supportive of all South's schools. He inherited a legacy of significant political difficulties, which occupied his time and attention. Sizemore's style had created some adversarial relationships. In addition, Sizemore's successor had become director at a time when the political climate had changed both in South and in the province. The educational pendulum, which in Ontario had never swung very far to the right or the left, was perceived by the governing party to have moved too far to the left in terms of student choices and teacher and school decision-making; consequently, steps were taken to redress the historical policy balance.

Byron was also losing its uniqueness. Other schools were selectively adopting Byron's innovations. Semestering had become very popular because it had advantages to both students and teachers. More to the point, however, if employed within the regular 27-credit diploma requirement, semestering reduced teachers' workloads. Even the teachers' union, which was skeptical of most things that had the Byron stamp on them, approved because teachers liked semestering.

Less to the union's liking was Sizemore's final policy initiative. With some minor differences, he gained board approval for the imposition of the Byron chairmanship model on the rest of the system's secondary schools. It meant that all department heads were removed and new jobs were posted and opened to all qualified candidates. The local union legitimately opposed the move because it would cost some of its members their jobs. The conflict led to the provincial union's "pink-listing" South. This meant that all union members in and outside of South were forbidden to apply for any of the new jobs. The result was a compromise that reduced the number of heads in all schools in South, increased responsibility allowances, and gave each head more time for leadership activities. More important for the more adventurous principals, it gave them an opportunity to bring in some more energetic people.

In the milieu created by the progressivism of the Hall-Dennis Report in the early 1970s, schools throughout Ontario and particularly in South had begun to adopt different organizational structures. In addition to semestering, many schools, particularly in South, began to experiment with some of Byron's structures. A new school opened in Middleton in 1975, for example, that in building design, program organization, and philosophy resembled Byron. In fact, eight Byron teachers transferred to the new school and five of the eight went as department heads. In the meantime, two former assistant principals of Byron had become principals in other schools and were gradually moving them toward their concept of the Byron image. Even Roxborough adopted longer teaching periods.

However, those at Byron who had enjoyed the "golden years" felt abandoned. As one teacher recalled: "I felt like nobody outside the school at the Board level trusted what was going on in the school or supported it." This feeling of betrayal pervaded people's recollections of the late 1970s and early 1980s. These emotions were exacerbated by demographic changes beyond the school's or even the board's control. The highs and lows of student enrollment contributed significantly to the "attrition of change" at Lord Byron.

Changing Demographics. Byron began with fewer than 900 students. By 1975 it had doubled to 1,821 students and reached its zenith in the 1976–1977 school year with 2,006 students. Ten to 20 teachers were added each year. The careful selection that characterized the recruiting of the initial staff was lost by the sheer urgency of adding staff. More teachers were "force transferred" from other schools that were declining in enrollment. Bruce Grey, who was principal in the years of rapid growth, stated:

> I'm not sure people really appreciated the impact of size on Byron, not so much in terms of philosophy but in terms of the ways

> you had to do things in a school of 2,000 as opposed to a school of 900. You tend to have to systematize procedures which tends to depersonalize things.

Departments became large. Meaningful staff meetings were out of the question. Communications within the school became an issue of major concern. In the words of an experienced teacher:

> The large hirings at the time meant that people didn't really know what the philosophy of the school was. People hadn't bought into the philosophy. Do something for the sake of doing it without looking at all the consequences of it. I think that is where we are still fighting the image of Byron.

A review of school documents in those years reveals this dilemma. In 1975–1976 one of four school goals was "strengthened communications linkages"; in 1976–1977 the first school goal was "improved communications among students, staff and the community outside the school"; by 1977–1978 the staff was looking for ways "to further the involvement of staff in school decision-making." Each year new procedures or school policies were initiated to ensure liaison among staff and to maintain connections with students and their parents. Where flexibility and common sense once reigned, rules and regulations crept in. Perhaps the most challenging aspect of size was the anonymity it created for many students and some teachers. With anonymity came concerns over student discipline, attendance, smoking, work completion, and vandalism. Plans to tighten requirements for students to change courses, finish incomplete courses, and attend to the basics speak to the emerging problems created by size. At the same time, increased enrollment meant more teachers and more DSF, which enabled Byron to "throw money at problems," much to the chagrin of other schools and their principals. For example, size meant more students skipped classes; therefore an attendance secretary was hired to keep track of students and inform their parents. Cohesive staff action to attend to issues became an increasing problem. Specialization replaced cooperation as the way to solve schoolwide problems (Grant, 1988).

After the 1977 school year, enrollment began to decline, slowly at first and then dramatically. By 1980 when Owens became principal there were 1,661 students. When he left in 1984, Byron had bottomed at 975 students. Owens lamented the circumstances he faced between 1980 and 1984:

> It was a big school of around 1,700 students in 1980 and went down to somewhere in the 900s by 1984. When you go from approximately 120 staff to somewhere around 60 in four years it is very difficult to maintain any thrust, to maintain any ideology, to maintain any enthusiasm. I dealt with a lot of unhappiness because people didn't want to leave the school.

The system's negotiated surplus procedures, which generally meant the least experienced and younger staff members were transferred, significantly altered the staff composition. Not only were the staff members who remained from the early 1970s getting older, but any opportunity to create age and gender balance was out of the principal's hands and depended on centralized procedures that were carefully scrutinized by the regional teachers' union. Reduced enrollment meant the contraction of programs and the further loss of students to Roxborough, which did not experience the same kind of enrollment decline until the late 1980s. It was my responsibility as superintendent for both Byron and Roxborough to approve all requests for optional attendance. These applications to move to Roxborough from Byron tended to be from the parents of higher-performing students who wanted to transfer to Roxborough to take advantage of Roxborough's French Immersion program and its self-contained program for gifted. The impact on Byron's staff morale was significant.

The Community Conundrum. The most perplexing contextual problem Byron faced was its reputation in the community. As one teacher recalled: "We spent all of our energy in the last two or three years I was there, '78, '80, '81, working on public relations. That was our main focus. How were we going to change the perception of the community? What did we do? I really don't know."

Evaluations of the school by the staff and various principals list a myriad of notable activities such as a community council, special evenings, and newsletters to mention a few, but the perception of Byron as a school for "special" or the "artsy" school or the "permissive" school or the "Hall-Dennis" school never went away. As one teacher said, the reputation "frustrated the hell out of us, because it wasn't true." As a secretary whose own children went to the school said, "I don't know why the community perceives, Byron, you know, 'Oh! Byron, you are going to Byron type of thing,' and yet academically we rate higher than many of the schools." Regardless of the cause, the image issue caused the staff to become very defensive and insular, and to expend incredible emotional and physical energy with little result.

One of the most respected people at Byron, who was often mentioned by others as one of Byron's more "heroic" teachers, was very blunt about Byron's image. Blair Alden, who joined the staff in 1975 and left in 1987, said:

> The school in my time, never explained well and did some "dumb" things. For all the good things people do in the school, the community would remember the one "dumb" thing. Teachers were allowed to do "dumb things," like the teacher who told the class we are going to experience silence which they did for most of the period. From my own personal point of view, I gave up. If our own professionals won't send their kids to the school we will never convince the community. In the beginning Byron did shape its own destiny but over time it was shaped by outside forces one of which was "reality."

A teacher who came to Byron in the late 1970s stated:

> When I got there it had changed . . . the community had disowned the philosophy because of some of the hiring—they took it too far—you don't have to go to class, there were no consequences—some courses were experiential and out of the mind-set of most people, like chanting mantras—50 or 60 kids not showing up on a given day.

This theme of individuals pushing the boundaries to the point of public reaction reoccurs in many interviews. Miles and Huberman (1984) describe a set of schools in their study that tried too much in too short of time and experienced problems resulting from policies that were a "poor fit with organizational norms and procedures" (p. 147). They call this phenomenon "overreaching." This would seem to be an appropriate description of Byron during this phase of its evolution.

Other respondents who addressed the "image" problem focused outside the school. "The community was afraid to change." "Social and cultural changes in the 1980s worked against Byron." "All outside forces tried to make Byron like every other school—entropy." The evidence, however, suggests two overriding factors. In the words of Blair Alden:

> I can't believe you can be too different. If you are too far ahead or behind you have to judge how fast or slowly to move—to chal-

> lenge without alienating. You have to explain yourself and that is hard to do. The hardest thing is to explain yourself in language they can understand. I would not use words like "new" and "change."

Byron pushed too far too fast. Initial structures and processes had not been consolidated before new initiatives were undertaken. A community that understood that "real schools" looked like Roxborough had to be nurtured very carefully. Byron's problems were not unique (Fletcher et al., 1985; Gold & Miles, 1981; Riley, 1998; Smith et al., 1987). The message for innovative schools such as Byron would seem to be "make haste slowly" and without a great deal of fanfare. A second factor, perhaps less amenable to influence, was that Byron was a product of the 1960s and increasingly out of harmony with the values and aspirations of both students and parents and the larger community in the late 1970s and early 1980s.

Like most innovative schools, Byron tended to operate on an intellectual paradigm of change, and its community on another paradigm that was based on continuity. This collision resulted in miscommunication and misrepresentation. Many parents in the community had their sons and daughters "vote with their feet" by opting for Roxborough, while in the school, staff members like Blair Alden responded by "giving up"; others departed for other schools, while many who stayed became more entrenched in the correctness of their version of the Byron philosophy and refused to adjust to changing times and circumstances.

Survival and Continuity

By the mid-1980s, the Byron staff had for the most part accepted the fact that Byron was not much different from other schools in Ontario and South. Respondents who reflected on the late 1970s and early 1980s expressed disappointment and in some cases anger with both the province and the region over the manner in which their policies had eliminated the uniqueness of Byron. The transition from the "lighthouse" school to a "real" or conventional school like Roxborough evolved slowly and incrementally. Most people interviewed could not recall how or when Byron became part of the mainstream of education in Ontario. Some respondents spoke nostalgically of the past, but recognized that the world had changed and Byron with it. Most teachers accepted and in fact supported attempts to tighten the curriculum and restrict freedom. As the school's principal from 1991 to 1995, Dennis Lawrence stated, "I think Byron has come in line with the South system and certainly provincially." He elaborated by describing educational policy as a swinging pendulum and presently the school has "just swung along with a more conservative swing of the pendulum." In his perception, Byron had become more traditional and the system and the rest of the schools more liberal and innovative. A teacher who joined the Byron staff in 1982 summarized the Byron of the past decade:

> There has always been a collection of teachers who have been here from the beginning who have been very supportive of Byron's original philosophy, and of course their numbers are dwindling as the years go by, but they have always brought back that philosophy that students come first, that the compassionate teacher is the effective teacher. They are still here and they are a minority, but they are a vocal minority. I think they are very good for the school.

Contextual influences had supported experimentation in the early 1970s, and eroded Byron's uniqueness in the decade from 1975 to 1985. Even though Byron by the mid-1980s was a "very traditional type of school," its public image remained at least 10 years in the past. In the mid and late 1980s, the school made a concerted effort to convince its community that it was a conventional academic school like Roxborough.

Dealing with the Community Context. As the Byron and Roxborough situations reveal, public perceptions of a school play an extremely important role in the internal school dynamics. A high percentage of Roxborough graduates complete university, and its teams are generally successful. The influential parents would naturally feel their students are getting a good education, especially because it is not much different from their own. Less academic and less elite athletes have found Roxborough a challenging place (Hargreaves et al., 1992). There is a great deal of contemporary advice in the educational literature on creating an image (Davies & Ellison, 1997), but for Byron leaders and the staff, the challenge of altering a negative image was largely uncharted territory. Many of the innovative schools of the late 1960s and early 1970s contended with "image" problems (Doremus, 1981a, 1981b, 1981c, 1982; Fletcher et al., 1985).

In 1984, Byron's public perception was perhaps at its nadir. The educational program offered at Byron was very similar to that of its competitor "down the road." Some departments were stronger, some not as good, but on the whole, as the supervisor for both schools in 1984, it seemed to me that the products of each were broadly comparable. What was not comparable was the public's perceptions of the two schools. Byron's new principal and vice principal, Garner and Kelly, presented a very conservative and confident image. Garner in particular had dealt with sensitive political issues in his previous assignment, and possessed the type of background and skills to help him deal with Byron's problems. He described how he saw his role when he moved to Byron:

> I arrived at the school when I think it was in drastic need of new direction and I was sort of the stabilizing force for three years. I certainly wasn't a change agent. I never saw myself as a change agent that all of a sudden turned it around and put it in the opposite direction, . . . I came when probably it was on a downslide . . . something needed to happen to sort of stabilize it before it took its next leap.

Changes to the initial Byron organization initiated by provincial and board policies had been generally accepted by staff. Enrollment had bottomed at 975 students in 1984 and remained fairly stable for the next 6 years. Garner and Kelly did not have to face the frenetic addition and then disheartening reduction of staff of the previous decade. Indeed, they did have some limited opportunity to restructure their heads group and infuse the staff with some younger people. By 1985, only four of the original chairmen remained and they too would either retire or move to other schools within the next 5 years. Since many of the key people in senior administration were products of Byron, they were aware of the school's history and prepared to provide support to the school. At the same time, successive principals of Roxborough worked cooperatively with Owens and later Garner and Kelly to reduce the debilitating features of the rivalry between the two schools and helped to organize joint staff-development activities, which contributed to better understanding between the two staffs. External circumstances were favorable in the late 1980s to attempt a Byron renaissance.

By the late 1990s, however, government budget cuts and declining enrollment once again threatened Lord Byron's existence. While it is beyond the purview of the present study, if one were to look at the present and speculate on the future, a wager on Lord Byron's survival into the new millennium would be unwise to say the least. Both Lord Byron and Roxborough have experienced a significant decline in enrollment. In addition, the South Board, because of reduced provincial support for education, has eliminated some of the unique special education programs that helped to keep Byron viable. At present Lord Byron has fewer than seven hundred students and Roxborough only about 1,000 students. One school could accommodate both enrollments. If politicians have to decide between the school with the rather conventional history and the perceived innovative school, the decision will be a foregone conclusion—good-bye Lord Byron.

There is, as the preceding discussion suggests, an inevitability to the "attrition" of change at Lord Byron and, I would submit, at most innovative schools. It would appear that the more innovative a school is, the less sustainable are its changes. There is no question that the changing external context influenced the internal context of Lord Byron and contributed substantially to the erosion of its pioneering spirit. Provincial policies that became increasingly restrictive, district policies designed to promote uniformity among schools, a community that lost confidence in the purposes and practices of the school, wildly fluctuating school enrollments, and a more militant teachers' union were external contextual factors that interacted over time to undermine the viability of Lord Byron as an innovative school. The interplay of the two sets of contexts—the external and the internal—provides the substance of the next few chapters as we see how this interplay affected the meanings people brought to the school, the school's leadership, Byron's structures and culture, and finally the lives and work of the teachers.

CHAPTER 4

Meaning

What made Lord Byron unique in its early days was its principal's and teachers' intent to challenge the essential meaning of education in the South Board and the province of Ontario. Meaning or purpose in education is an obvious but often ignored or avoided topic in the change literature. Critics of the school-improvement literature point to its relative neutrality on issues of purpose (Fink & Stoll, 1998). Only recently have researchers and educational commentators addressed the fundamental question of why we do what we do (Boyd, 1998; Fullan, 1993; Robertson, 1996; Stoll and Fink, 1996; Wells, Carnochan, Slayton, & Allen, 1998). In a world enamored of the three contemporary gods—the market, competition, and efficiency—the ethical question "why" often gets lost. Efficiency overrides effectiveness. Moreover, if change is not grounded in some shared sense of educational meaning, then improvement efforts become unfocused and change often occurs just for the sake of change. All changes are not created equal—some changes introduced by policymakers require strong support and others are worth fighting against with all one's might, or at least subverting (Hargreaves & Fullan, 1998). Unless schools and educators address the fundamental "why" question they have no moral compass on which to base decisions of support or opposition.

Bennis and Nanus (1985) state: "All organizations depend on the existence of shared meanings and interpretations of reality, which facilitate action . . . an essential factor in leadership is the capacity to influence and organize meaning for the members of the organization" (p. 39). Fullan (1991) makes a similar point in the context of educational change: "The presence or absence of mechanisms to address the on-going problems of meaning—at the beginning and as people try out ideas—is crucial for success, because it is at the individual level that change does or does not occur" (p. 45).

THE MEANING LENS

The question that arises, however, is whose meaning should prevail? Brouillette (1996) has summarized the four most common ways of viewing the purposes of education as humanist, social efficiency, developmentalist, and social meliorist. To the *humanist* the purpose of education is to prepare students for citizenship so that they understand the values and traditions embodied in their societies' institutions. To this end, students must be sufficiently literate to communicate with their fellow citizens and have the knowledge necessary to comprehend current issues and cast their votes appropriately. In practice this has tended to be interpreted as an emphasis on the teaching of the liberal arts with a focus on the "basics"—grammar, spelling, and an understanding of Western, Eurocentric values and traditions.

To those who advocate *social efficiency,* the purpose of schools is to prepare students for jobs and for contributing to the economic well-being of society as a whole. The concept of students as "human capital" evolves from this point of view (Sweetland, 1997). As Brouillette (1996) suggests, business-oriented politicians tend to focus on the non–college bound students and inquire into their employability. While this view places an emphasis on the basics and sees education as a very linear "input-output" process, it does stress the need for vocational education.

The *developmentalist* position holds that education should help individual students to develop their personal potential "so that they are prepared to be creative, self-motivated lifelong learners who are effective problem-solvers, able to communicate and collaborate with others, and to meet the varied challenges they will encounter in their adult lives" (Brouillette, 1996 p. 224). While humanists and developmentalists have similar aspirations for students, they diverge on where to put the emphasis in curricula. The humanist is much more concerned with forms and precision than is the developmentalist. The developmentalist would entertain invented writing and focus more on the content and ideas of a student's work than on the syntax and spelling. To focus too early on what they might see as cosmetics, they would argue, inhibits a student's creativity and imagination.

The purpose of education to the *social meliorist* is to bring about a more just society "through using the schools to help those children whose background puts them at risk, to get the resources they need to succeed, and through teaching all students about diverse cultures and ethnic heritages, thus helping them to grow into open-minded, tolerant adults" (Brouillette, 1996, p. 224). Those who advocate this view would see the humanist approach to be narrow, traditional, elitist, overly Eurocentic, and perpetuating the tyranny of the majority. In a similar vein they would view the social-efficiency perspective as exploitive and "unthinking replication of social injustice." The developmentalist view with its focus on individual growth and development, from a social-meliorist point of view, tends to ignore the social context and social ills that prevent students from taking advantage of opportunities. The developmentalist emphasis on cooperation can easily mean co-optation by forces that should be confronted. These positions help to explain the challenge of developing shared meaning in a high school where all four purpose positions often coexist somewhat uneasily. When one adds the conflicting and sometimes inchoate views of a school's community, the notion of shared purpose becomes even more daunting.

The importance of "shared meaning" is, however, well documented in the literature (Fullan, 1993; Joyce & Showers, 1988; Louis & Miles, 1990; Rosenholtz, 1989; Sammons et al., 1995). Many of the situations of struggling innovative schools (Fletcher et al., 1985; Gold & Miles, 1981; Riley, 1998), in which schools and communities conflict over school issues, result from different perceptions of the purposes of education. In general, new schools tend to emphasize developmentalist and social-meliorist goals. Conflict emerges when dominant community groups perceive that more traditional humanistic and social-efficiency goals are subordinated or ignored (Fletcher et al., 1985; Fullan et al., 1972; Gold & Miles, 1981; Smith et al., 1987; Watts, 1977). Similarly, change within schools suffers when strongly held but divergent purposes conflict (Ball, 1981; Grant, 1988; Woods, 1979). It is clear, however, that meaning cannot be imposed from outside. Hargreaves and his colleagues (1992) in their study of secondary schools' responses to the destreaming of the first year of high school found that the more academic and more affluent schools were most resistant to what they perceived was a social-meliorist set of purposes, which they considered more appropriate to culturally diverse communities.

In any change effort, teachers and schools should know where they are going, and broadly speaking, they should agree on where they are headed. The most positive approaches to change were where teachers faced overwhelming challenges in urban schools and were energized by the resolve to work on them together (Lightfoot, 1983; Louis & Miles, 1990; National Commission on Education, 1996). Many teachers enter teaching because they care about children in particular, or contributing to social improvement in general. Often these purposes become submerged as teachers succumb to the daily classroom pressures and routines (Fullan, 1993). Teachers' purposes can also differ, leading to confusion and inconsistency for children and creating difficult or superficial staff relationships. It is important that teachers engage in dialogue about them, and that their purposes are somewhat convergent. Dialogue about and coalescence of purposes among teachers is a significant step toward the development of shared meanings.

For change agents, the change literature suggests that answers are required to the following questions among many others:

- Does the change have a clear moral purpose (Sergiovanni, 1992b)?
- Is the purpose an imposed one or does it come from within (Fullan, 1993)?
- Are purposes surrounding the change fragmented or do they cohere into broadly common vision (Barth, 1990)?
- Is the change demonstrably connected to purposes of teaching, learning, and caring in classrooms in ways that matter for teachers (Newmann & Wehlage, 1995)?
- How do teachers connect with "other people's children" with backgrounds and cultures that are different from the teacher's own (Delpit, 1988)?
- Does the initiative provide a balance among competing policy directions of quality, equity, and efficiency (Stoll & Fink, 1996)?

LORD BYRON AND ITS MEANING

The preceding discussion provides insight into the second lens through which to examine Lord Byron: the changes and shifts of meaning or educational purpose over 25 years as the school responded to various internal and external contextual factors provide insight into the "attrition of change."

Years of Creativity and Experimentation

In the early years, Ward Bond hired people who bought into his vision of an innovative school. This image has had a powerful influence.

Defining Purposes. In spite of opposition, criticism, and disappointment, what has persisted over these past 25 years is a collective sense of meaning of what Lord Byron was about. Every person interviewed for this project articulated two concepts: Byron was intended to shape the school to the student, not the reverse; and Byron was about innovating, experimenting, and challenging the prevailing paradigm in Ontario. Regardless of time period, longevity at Byron, or the role the person performed at Byron, these messages were fundamentally the same. A school secretary said: "Byron puts students first—mutual respect, co-operation and the intermingling of different types of kids. There has always been that."

A technical education teacher who taught from 1972 to 1976 at Byron and whose two sons attended the school said Byron created a "positive environment, in which kids could reach their potential." Another teacher indicated that Byron "provided a breadth and depth of opportunities without barriers to students" and "much better teacher-student relationships than I have seen in any other school." George Owens, who was an original chair and later Byron's principal, said that Byron was about "different strokes for different folks—individualization—treating kids with intricate sensibilities. I used the term 'structured multiplicity' where you take a group of kids in grade 9 and you develop a program to develop the talents of each student to his or her best."

A teacher who has remained at Byron for the past 25 years explained that the school's philosophy was

> that you had to be able to answer the question is this good for the students in the affirmative in order to justify actions. There were sort of peripheral things like fewer rules, and that you teach more by modeling than you do by precept, and that the aim of all discipline was self discipline . . . the idea was to offer kids a choice, and when they make a choice they make mistakes. You have to be prepared to live with these mistakes. If you can't then you modify your program to limit the number of choices.

Various respondents described Byron as "a second-chance school," a school that believed in the "goodness of kids," one that "emphasized co-operation not competition" and "learning not just teaching."

At a second level, Lord Byron was intended to challenge the prevailing paradigm of secondary schooling in Ontario. As Bond explained:

> What made it unique in the eyes of others in the community and education generally was that it was the first semestered school in the province. That was the most obvious mechanical thing and then the philosophy that was designed to surround that. The philosophy included how staff and students should be treated; the en-

> vironment in which they should work. We were all there to enable all students to learn, to remove obstacles, to remove their problems and to prove to them that they could learn. We did not convey the idea that discipline comes first which I think a lot of us felt was the attitude in many other schools. In addition the school was open in design and open in attitude as well. Our intention with regard to the community was to welcome the community at any time and to invite them to participate at any time in what was going on in the school. This was unique at the time.

In response to my question, "What do you feel has made Byron unique among schools in South and the Province?" virtually every respondent, regardless of teaching era, noted the student-first philosophy. When asked to articulate factors that challenged the prevailing educational paradigm, most mentioned semestering, open-concept building design, the chairmanship leadership structure, the variety of course offerings, the innovative programs such as individualized mathematics and science, the paucity of rules, and the unsupervised cafeteria, to mention only a few innovations. Each change on its own was not unique. In combination they challenged the essential "grammar" of secondary schools in Ontario.

Developing a Shared Sense of Meaning. What became clear as my interviews proceeded was the influence of Ward Bond in shaping the "meaning" of Lord Byron. As one teacher recalled, "Ward Bond would say, when you find them doing something wrong, pick them up, dust them off and start them out again, don't throw them out." Still another teacher recalled that Bond "had a student oriented view of education that was unique at the time." Bond described his vision in this way:

> It was largely wrapped around our aspirations for students. We wanted them to be self learners. We wanted them to realize what potential they had, and we approached it from the view that we weren't imparting all the answers to the students and they were responsible for sitting down and learning. It was that belief in students, and that belief in the approach to help students to learn, that encompass the philosophy or at least our attitude as to how things should be. This was perceived at the time as a more lenient attitude as we were trying to engage the students in their learning. We also had distinct ideas as to how people should be.

While Bond articulated the original vision, it was shaped by the people he recruited as they tried to bring it to life in the school. As Senge (1990) suggests, organizational visions grow as a by-product of individual visions and ongoing conversations among them (p. 212).

The congruency between vision and action is illustrated by perhaps the most controversial concept at Byron in its first 8 years, the provision of free time for all students. The belief held by Bond and most staff in the early years was that if students were to be responsible they must be given responsibility to make decisions, and particularly decisions over their use of time. Bond's explanation of that policy reflected his faith in students' ability to use good sense provided the environment was nonthreatening and supportive.

> We provided access to the learning resource center, study spaces around the school, the remedial reading room and teachers. We all know it did not succeed with all students. There were abuses which in other schools would have led to regimentation of all the students. We did have a belief that students needed some unstructured time during the course of the day, and I don't believe as a total staff we believed their use was improper. We didn't mind students in the hallway. The design of the school facilitated that. It was structured to provide socializing space.

As Bond suggests, staff acted on the premise that most students could use time productively and adapted facilities and developed strategies to assist students to use their time effectively. What Bond did particularly well was to manage meaning (Bennis & Nanus, 1985; Fullan, 1991). The sense of meaning initiated by Bond but internalized and acted on by Byron's staff encouraged integration, cooperation, responsiveness to individual needs and alternative ways of knowing such as intuition, all of which may be considered more stereotypically feminine qualities. Student use of free time, to continue with this example, was an innovation for which there was little precedent in Ontario at the time. Pure rationality would suggest that such a policy was asking for trouble. Bond felt that it was worth the risk as a way to give students the opportunity to learn responsibility by having important decisions to make.

The values espoused by the Lord Byron staff were clearly at odds with the self-asserted patriarchal values that dominated Ontario and South's educational systems. Most schools and school systems encouraged and rewarded power, competition, control, domination, and linear analytic rational thought. The South system was a very male-dominated, patriarchal system. All the senior leaders were male; all but two of the curriculum coordinators were male. The prevailing metaphors were those of male-dominated team sports like football. A favorite saying to encourage hard work was, "If you're not ruptured, you're not pulling your load." Ironically, it was Bond, a former intercollegiate athlete and physical education instructor, who had the confidence and inner resolve to "go against the grain." As a system leader stated, "Ward was the father of Lord Byron, he nurtured it in the years he was there. He had the skill and the craftiness to hire the right people." Equally ironic was the fact that all of his first department chairs were men. When asked about his choices, he said no qualified women applied, which spoke eloquently to the state of women's leadership in South at that time.

The values espoused at Byron were of course influenced by the 1960s. Nascent feminism, multiculturalism, and environmentalism had gained currency. Phrases like "self-actualization" and "human potential" were part of the educational climate. The Hall-Dennis Report, for a short time, made such ideas the topics of conferences and seminars, and of course criticism and ridicule in the popular press.

A few schools around Ontario acted on the concepts of more open education. Thornlea (Fullan et al., 1972) in Toronto predated Byron by 3 years, and Bayridge (Fullan & Eastabrook, 1977) in Hastings County and Governor Simcoe in Lincoln County followed a few years after the establishment of Byron. In retrospect we can see manifestations of a humanist response to the rigidity and inflexibility of the "factory-model of schooling" (Morgan, 1997), but at the time most people still believed in the profoundly modernist conception of progress—if we can just know more about the world, and in this case education, progress will result.

The frustration expressed by many of the Byron respondents, many years removed from events, was that they were certain they were moving in the right direction but could not prove it. Much of what went on at Byron was the product of people's experience, intuition, and trial and error, rather than "solid empirical research." Mistakes were made that in other, less visible settings would have been ignored, or at least used as internal learning experiences. Byron tended to be so visible, public, and open that its missteps were magnified and publicized. As one long-serving teacher recalled, "Being so open, the failures that kids had, and they probably would have failed in other schools, were quickly blamed on Byron." "They are experimenting with my child and that is why my child has failed"—and we were quick to be blamed for things that were not necessarily our fault. Other elements of the educational community, such as superintendents, other principals, teachers, and even the press criticized Byron for its lack of "hard data" to support its innovations, which resulted in Byron's being almost obsessive about evaluating its efforts.

To use Brouillette's (1996) categories described previously, Byron might be categorized as fitting into the developmental category because of its stated goals of advancing the academic and social growth of each student. The critics tended to speak from a humanist perspective. They believed that the purpose of schools was the preservation of the dominant culture, with a focus on the basics. Their criticism of Byron was consistent with Brouillette's description of the humanists view of the developmentalist approach to education—lack of discipline, inappropriate student choice-making, a lack of respect in teacher-student relationships, concern for the arts and other non "hard-core" subjects, a lack of competitiveness among students, and a perceived deficiency in standards.

What Bond had succeeded in doing was recruiting people who supported his progressive developmentalist view of education. Acting on this image for education required a profound shift in thinking in the school and its community. While Bond and his colleagues succeeded within the school, they faced a wider educational community and a social hegemony that were firmly rooted in maintaining continuity with what most people perceived to be "real schools."

Overreaching and Entropy

In the first 5 years of the school, the staff had internalized and acted on a very definite shared sense of meaning. By 1980, the Byron staff did not experience the same certainty of direction and confidence in their activities. As Blair Alden explained:

> Byron now is like a regular school. . . . Byron's philosophy was to do anything that is good for the student. I don't think that philosophy has changed, but what people perceive is good for the student has changed. I think in the beginning, if it sounded like a good idea let's try it, and eventually reality forces any new changes to fit into contemporary reality.

Shifting Meaning. Others make similar points when they talk about Byron's shift in meaning over time. One teacher said the breadth of course offerings, which had been developed to meet the multiple needs of students, "has closed down" and the notion of caring and cooperation is "more talk than reality." Another teacher, who has spent the past 24 years at Byron, declared that "Byron was a student centered school—student needs dictated curriculum and organization. The philosophy has changed direction drastically—it is much more academic, much more image conscious, much more driven by standards, much more." Another teacher, who has moved from Byron, stated that "it became more like an assembly line." Another described a "shifting from a student focus to a more political focus."

The climate of change and innovation that had been so much of the ethos of Byron in its early days had slowed appreciably. Buffeted by criticism and the enervating effects of declining enrollment, teachers took refuge in their teaching and their subjects. Its principal from 1984–1987, Patrick Garner, compared the original meaning to what he found in 1984:

> I'm putting it into my own words, but in the early days if you think of an idea, try it—so the whole idea of being a risk taker and being an innovator—whoever thought of an idea, if it seemed reasonable, there was encouragement to try it. It's not as open as it was, certainly in the kind of innovation, as it used to be—that has certainly changed.

A teacher reflected that

> this school was focused on what was best for the kids, that was the question that was always asked. It is not asked in staff meetings to the same degree as it was. In discussions of change there is less discussion and more acknowledgment and announcement, but that is the way things are in the face of declining enrollment and resources. The best we can do is say how can we make this work for our kids. Not how can we survive as teachers, but how can we make it work for the kids.

A teacher who has been at Byron for 24 years captures the shift in "meaning":

> Definitely there has been a philosophy change. The philosophy of Byron in the 1970s is not the philosophy of Byron now, I think the philosophy now is much more of a universal thing—a district thing—more of where are we going as a district. There doesn't seem to be the same focus as a school. I think the philosophy has drastically changed and I think its largely due to change of personnel.

Survival and Continuity

By the time Garner and Kelly arrived at Byron in 1984, the original meaning still existed in the hearts and minds of many of the school's teachers, but seemed to have little bearing on day-to-day activities. In retrospect, Kelly described the decade from the mid-1980s to the mid-1990s:

> I have to say in the early years, in the "golden years," certainly Byron was master of its own destiny. When that innovative leadership was recognized for their strength and appointed to other positions, Byron then became a follower not a leader in the late 70s and early 80s. We were able to capture back some of that leadership when we accepted responsibility for things like the Satellite, French Immersion, and Life Skills [see pages 32–33]. We started to look at our strengths and recognize what we do well.

Garner and Kelly inherited a staff that somewhere along the way had lost or at least misplaced the sense of meaning that energized its early years. A teacher who joined Byron in 1982 described the school staff during her tenure:

> Byron has pretty well progressed from being that kind [progressive] of school in the beginning to becoming or trying to become a fairly traditional school today. It has become quite a traditional school. Maybe a little more student focus and that might reflect the original philosophy. Although I don't know if the philosophy is that different from other schools. I think the philosophy of all the schools in South is to take our students and make them productive. I don't see that we are any different than any other school. I think there is a genuine caring for students here but I think most schools are the same.

A teacher who also joined the staff in the mid-1980s stated:

> I think that the people who have been here longer are sometimes more apt to change than people who have been here a shorter time, and maybe just because of the nature of the people. People talk about the beginnings of Byron—teachers who have been here a long time. They say that some of the things in the Transition Years [destreaming or detracking grade 9] are like 20 years ago so

> they see that as a good thing whereas some of the people would like to take things more slowly when we have things written down and have content and courses and direction.

Reshaping a Sense of Meaning. By accepting programs that few schools in the system would or could deal with, Garner and Kelly adopted a risky strategy, but in the long run one that helped Byron to recapture something of the spirit of its early days and support its continuation. As one teacher explained,

> We have a very mixed clientele here, and we have more special education kids than in most schools, and at least as many problem kids as in any other school—maybe more, but we tend to work with them better because there were some strategies set up from the very beginning [see pages 17–19]. The school had a very well trained staff and an active special education department. We have a place where our kids can be dealt with on a one-to-one basis and looked after.

A long-time school secretary responded to the question of what makes Byron unique.

> I think it is the diversity of program that we have at this school. We have Life Skills, day care, the Satellite program, we also have the ACLD [Association for Children with Learning Disabilities]—which is the learning disabilities resource. When our life skills first came into the school, some people wondered how are the students going to react. I have never seen a life skills student made fun of or retaliated against in any way. They are usually intermingling in the foyer at lunch and I think it is just great. Even the little tykes in day-care—they have their lunch in the cafeteria—they have little tables in the back of the cafeteria.

A female teacher who left the school in the early 1970s described the contemporary Byron:

> I think the philosophy of the school is well grounded and I think that has something to do with the staff that you bring in, the kinds of professional development, the kinds of experiences. I still feel that when I walk into Byron, and I was in Byron last week, and I still felt it. I feel it in the way the Satellite is set up,

> the Life Skills unit has been set up there and all those things. I know that they take their toll but nevertheless I still feel that the basic philosophy, that kids come first is the overriding philosophy.

A teacher who moved to Roxborough in the late 1980s told the story, with pride in his voice, of an autistic boy who wandered into his drafting class and was welcomed by the regular students. Each day the boy returned and actually learned to do a little drafting with the help of the students in the class. Another teacher described how welcoming the school had been to her own son and how he and his friends found the school atmosphere "very warm and not as formal."

By the late 1980s, Byron's response to innovation demonstrated the school's altered sense of meaning. The Ministry of Ontario provided money for pilot programs related to untracking the first year of secondary school. The concept of heterogeneous classes was a Byron innovation in the early 1970s and part of its tradition. One would have thought, considering the school's history, that it would have enthusiastically embraced the government's direction. While other schools embarked on quite adventurous programs, Byron submitted a rather modest proposal to provide extra counseling for incoming students, a tutorial system for underachieving readers in grade 9, and some interdisciplinary grade 9 units. I was the board's official responsible for the six regional projects, and it was clear to the committee I chaired that the Byron plan was the least ambitious of the five that were funded. It should be added, however, that while Byron did apply, 11 other schools did not. The first two aspects of Byron's project that were initiated and pursued by individual departments were quite successfully implemented. The third project, which necessitated interdepartmental cooperation, never got very far. From a cultural point of view, balkanization had replaced collegiality. Innovativeness that had once helped to define Byron now resided largely with certain departments, particularly special education and guidance, both of which were ancillary to the regular program of studies in the school.

What had evolved by the mid-1980s were at least three parallel narratives that gave Lord Byron meaning. The first suggested that Byron was like most other schools, perhaps a little more student-oriented but even here there were other schools at least as caring as Byron. The second narrative implied that Byron, because of its acceptance of a diverse student population, was quite different from most schools.[1] There is a certain amount of truth to each claim. The student-centeredness of the early days continued to exist in pockets, if not pervasively. It was well accepted among the special education professionals in South that Byron was more responsive to the needs of less-advantaged students than were more traditional schools. At the same time, there were other schools in the system that were as open, if not more open, to attempting to meet a diversity of students' needs. A new school built in the late 1970s in the northern part of the region, for example, included not only the regular range of students, but also mentally handicapped students and students from the adjacent school for the hearing impaired. A third narrative, which in some ways made Byron's staff somewhat schizophrenic, was "We are an academic school and as demanding and rigorous as 'the school-down-the-road.'" To summarize, using Brouillette's (1996) categorization of meaning, Byron's initial developmentalist and social-meliorist aspirations, which had united staff in the first few years of the school's life, had yielded, at least in part, to the humanist and social-efficiency arguments in the immediate community and the general educational context. To accommodate these purposes, the school created self-contained gifted programs, elitist school teams, and French Immersion programs, and promoted participation in academic competitions, among other initiatives. Byron philosophy had evolved over 15 years from a shared sense of meaning to a more fragmented and less coherent idea of what it was about.

Good Schools and Real Schools. In recent months, my colleagues and I have developed a process for analyzing change called the Change Frames (Fink, 1998; Hargreaves, Shaw, & Fink, 1997). To illustrate the challenge of developing and sustaining a shared sense of meaning for a school, we employ an interesting workshop activity. We first explain Brouillette's (1996) four perspectives on purpose, and then indicate that each of the four corners represents each of the four perspectives. We ask participants to congregate in the area that represents the perspective closest to their own meaning position. Almost invariably the majority of educators move to the corners that represent the developmentalist and social-meliorist perspectives. After a discussion of why they have chosen their respective positions, we ask them to speculate where they believe various other stakeholders like parents, politicians, and the press might assemble if they were present. Almost without fail, participants believe that virtually every other segment of the community operates from the humanist and social-efficiency paradigms. Not only does the activity illustrate the diversity of educational purposes, it also demonstrates why educational change is so difficult. In a sense it reflects a theme of this study that professionals have an image of a "good" school that is often at odds with the larger community's perception of a "real" school. The external context overwhelms the internal context. It is no wonder that in the ongoing interplay of change and continuity, continuity tends to win out more often than not.

CHAPTER 5

Leadership

The importance of the leader in the determination of meaning in an organization is one of the few concepts in school effectiveness and school improvement literature about which there is fairly consistent agreement (Bennis & Nanus, 1985; Smith & Andrews, 1989; Stoll & Fink, 1996). In recent times, this literature has referred to managers as people who do things efficiently and to leaders who do things effectively (Bennis & Nanus, 1985). Others have described transactional leaders as those who use conventional rather than political means to get the job done, and transformational leaders as those who unite their associates through a shared vision to achieve organizational goals (Burns, 1978). Certainly the effective-schools literature is in general agreement on the importance of the principal's role as an instructional leader (Louis & Miles, 1990; Mortimore et al., 1988; Rosenholtz, 1989; Smith & Andrews, 1989). Leadership as defined by much of this literature places inordinate pressure on a few leaders in a crisis. The concept of visionary leaders propounded by the management literature (Bennis & Nanus, 1985), however, requires these few to have extraordinary foresight (Stacey, 1995). The evidence of this study suggests that Ward Bond, Byron's first principal, was indeed a visionary in the context of his time as school leader. His ability to conceptualize and articulate a sense of meaning for his colleagues profoundly affected the school, the school district, and the leaders who succeeded him. The leadership frame or lens provides important insights into the life cycle of Lord Byron.

THE LEADERSHIP LENS

More recently, scholars have moved beyond identifying the components of leadership that seem to produce results to more global or holistic approaches that encompass both the rational and the nonrational aspects of leadership. Some have applied Burns's (1978) concept of transformational leadership to education. This style of leadership includes the pursuit of common goals, empowerment, maintenance of a collaborative culture, teacher development, and problem-solving (Leithwood, 1992). These qualities are reflected in teacher-led professional development committees and staff-led school planning teams. The clear implication in much of this literature is that attending to management or operating in transactional ways—exchanging services for rewards—is clearly inferior to being a transformational leader, who is people-oriented and focuses on transforming the beliefs and attitudes of followers.

Stacey (1995) provides a different image of leadership by describing the need for leaders to manage in times of diversity, complexity, and unpredictability. In effect, he suggests that traditional views of leadership, which are based on a rational, predictable, linear world, are relatively useless in a society that is becoming increasingly "chaotic." In his *Managing Chaos* he argues for the development of learning organizations that are sufficiently prepared and flexible to respond to an unknown and unknowable future.

Others suggest alternative approaches to leadership that are more specific to education. Sergiovanni (1992a) advocates an approach that encourages teachers to unify around moral purposes. Block (1993) suggests that the future requires stewardship, not leadership: "Stewardship is defined . . . as the willingness to be accountable for the well-being of the larger organization by operating in service rather than control, of those around us . . . it is accountability without control or compliance" (p. xx). Deal and Peterson (1994) criticize the artificial debate between management and leadership and suggest that schools require leadership that blends the technical skills of an engineer and the creative imagination of the artist. They declare that

> high performing organizations have both order and meaning, structure and values. They achieve quality at reasonable costs. They accomplish goals while attending to core values and beliefs. They encourage both fundamentals and fun. They embrace the dialectic between expression of values and accomplishment of goals. They encourage both leadership and management, symbolic behavior and technical activity. (p. 9)

While these images are useful, they do not capture the complexity and challenge of school leadership. Most school leaders play many roles in the course of the day; they are at once administrators, politicians, parents, counselors, publicists, and transactional leaders—and on occasion, transformational and moral leaders. Recently, my colleague Louise Stoll and I have suggested still another approach that reflects both the rational and nonrational, the predictable and unpredictable aspects of leadership in schools, and recognizes the multiple roles school leaders are required to fulfill (Stoll & Fink, 1996). It is a view that also captures both personal and professional aspects of school leadership. We have called this approach "invitational leadership." Invitations are messages that communicate to others that they are able, responsible, and worthwhile (Purkey & Novak, 1984). Leadership therefore "is about communicating invitational messages to individuals and groups with whom leaders interact in order to build and act on a shared and evolving vision of enhanced educational experiences for students" (Stoll & Fink, 1996, p. 109). We argue that leadership of schools should be dynamic, holistic, flexible, and humane. This vision is quite at odds with leadership in many schools, particularly secondary schools.

The leadership structure of most secondary schools would appear to be inimical to the development of schoolwide learning communities (Hargreaves et al., 1992). Decision-making lodged in a management group, or a small cadre of department heads, tends to inhibit efforts at school-based decision-making (Wohlstetter, 1995). Most secondary schools and school systems are not only "balkanized" by the departmental structure; they also are hierarchical and bureaucratic. It is very clear that present legislation and organizational structures create schools in which the struggle for "turf" is paramount. As Sarason (1990) has stated:

> Teachers, principals, supervisors, curriculum specialists, superintendents, members of boards of education, . . . with rare exception, those who belong to these groups think and perceive in terms of parts and not a complicated system, *their* parts, *their* tasks, *their* problems, *their* power or lack of it. (p. 24, emphasis in original)

Broadening decision-making to involve teachers can contribute to a reduction of these internal rivalries (Walter and Duncan Gordon Charitable Foundation, 1995; Wohlstetter, 1995). The danger, as Fullan (1997) points out, is that teachers who become involved in change initiatives or participate in teacher decision-making committees can become distanced from their colleagues. Teacher participation in decision-making is not a panacea. Conley (1991) suggests there are three decisional states related to teacher participation: deprivation, saturation, and equilibrium. How does a school find equilibrium? How does a school design a system that responds to the bureaucratic demands of the larger context while meeting teacher needs for participation? Fullan (1997) states "The key issues . . . are twofold: broadening the leadership roles of more and more teachers; while reshaping the culture of the school that produces in-built collaboration involving all (or the majority of) teachers" (p. 9). This solution suggests a complicating paradox. Structures such as departments, subject specialization, and inflexible timetables in secondary schools obstruct more collaborative cultures. In addition, teacher cultures of privatism, individualism, and academic specialization also tend to preserve divisive structures. These paradoxes influenced the nature of Byron's formal and informal leadership structures over time. In addition, a revolving door of formal leaders at both the school and district level had a profound influence on Byron's ability to sustain its innovative ethos.

LORD BYRON AND LEADERSHIP

In many ways Ward Bond was an amalgam of the leadership types described previously. Perhaps the best description of his leadership was as a "leader of leaders" (Barth, 1990). He firmly believed that he should lead less, and disperse power, control, and resources to enable staff, students, and parents to lead more. In secondary schools, micropolitical tension usually exists among the senior leadership team, the department heads or chairs, and the staff as a whole (Ball, 1987; Blase, 1988). Managing these three elements in such a way as to ensure that everyone's needs are met is a challenging balancing act for a principal.

Years of Creativity and Experimentation

Bond believed strongly that formal leadership should reside in the department chairs. When asked the source of leadership at Byron in the early days he responded:

> There is no doubt in my mind it was the chair. Leadership was one of the elements considered when the chairman was chosen, and I believe it was an expectation that they understood, it was to be their leadership and their school, and in their areas they had control of programming and instruction.

He went on to add:

> I don't think that major decisions should go back to the staff. There should be complete involvement where that can be possible, but unless you can couple the accountability with the

> decision-making, I don't see total decisions resting with the staff . . . the accountable person is the one who has to end up saying I made the decision. . . . In talking about leadership and the leadership provided, I think it is expecting too much of teachers to do more than have input into decisions when the decision lies outside their realm of practice—but in the classroom, management, instruction, program, curriculum design, sure. . . . One of the significant factors was that chairmen had time to provide leadership to the people with whom they worked . . . it demonstrated to me if you have an expectation for leadership you have to provide time to do the job.

Each chair Bond hired was expected to demonstrate leadership, particularly instructional leadership in his area (Smith & Andrews, 1989). The chairs acted as an effective cabinet as Bond had intended. As one teacher, now a principal recalled, "I think one thing that was significant was how Byron was organized. I came through as a department head in another jurisdiction. The way the chairs functioned at Byron as a council gave immediately an accessible leadership target to people because those people did meaningful things."

At the same time, staff, especially those who had experience in other schools, felt involved and committed to the process of staff participation in decision-making. One teacher who is well known for her intolerance of pretense reported that

> everybody knew what was important and again part of the leadership qualities of Ward Bond was that he didn't lay on "nit-picking" things—staff meetings were not called the first Monday of every month whether you needed them or not. They were called when you needed them. You didn't have trouble getting staff members there, they knew it was important. . . . Now you think oh God! another staff meeting. It never occurred [to us] to say oh God! a staff meeting . . . there was something that was going to come out of it.

She added:

> I am not a hero worshiper but when I look back, he had a quiet leadership style rather than a really aggressive one, but I think his encouragement made people want to follow. In fact, he tended to make leaders rather than followers. He would ask pertinent questions and lead you down the path to start something new . . . he

> assumed you would do a top notch job and you did. You tended to live up to expectations.

Bond succeeded in his tenure in creating a balance among potentially competing micro-political components of the school. In its comment on leadership in the 1975 evaluation of Lord Byron, the external committee observed:

> As well as observing those in formal positions (principal, assistant principals, chairmen) exercise enlightened leadership, we noted that teachers are able to contribute significantly to the decision-making process, not only within the departmental structure. The administration has consciously provided opportunities for recognition of leadership among staff, other than those formally designated as chairmen. This approach has not only guaranteed high quality leadership within the school, but has served as a training ground for an exceptional number of persons who have moved on to positions of leadership within the system.

The report concluded its discussion of leadership by commending the school "for its effective leadership development program" (p. 20). Bond was indeed a "leader of leaders."

Bond of course was not only a visionary leader. He had the interpersonal skills to build a shared sense of meaning. People used words and phrases like "charismatic," "revered," and "the perfect person" to describe Bond. He could be "crafty" and "tough" if necessary, or "quiet and caring." He could be both a transactional leader as his wringing concessions from central office attests, and a transformational leader as his many disciples confirm. I asked each of my interview respondents to name the heroes in the school. Virtually every person named Bond, even people who had never met him. He would fit the description of the invitational leader who invited others both personally and professionally (Stoll & Fink, 1996).

Ironically, perhaps the members of staff most influenced by Bond and his leadership style were the women. One evening I recorded the comments of a female group of seven former Byron staff members who have all moved on to leadership roles in South or in other systems. In the room was a director of education, two principals, three department heads, and a consultant. They were part of a larger women's network that had emerged from Lord Byron in the early 1970s. They still try to meet at least six times a year. The group has not only been instrumental in helping women to achieve formal leadership roles; it has impacted significantly on the culture of South. One woman remembered seeing the chairs work as a council to solve problems in a collaborative way and saying to herself "I can do that." "It was more collaborative and there was discussion. It wasn't a decision made by a principal, which everybody carried out. My guess is that women are good at that kind of leadership and prefer it." Another participant stated:

> Ward had a philosophy but he was open to anybody's input. I remember it was significant that he was going to let women wear pant suits. I just remember it being an issue for working women. You just had a sense if you took something to him, an idea, it was going to be heard. I think that in 3 years we were willing to say as women "we must go further." I almost felt that was the ethos that was there—readiness to accept and an invitation to proceed.

Few women in the 1970s sought leadership roles, partly because of the prevailing patriarchal value system of most schools and school districts. As the women explained, they felt comfortable, affirmed, and empowered to aspire to formal leadership roles as a result of Bond's leadership and the value system that gave meaning to the Byron experience. When I pointed out that it took 4 years to appoint the first female chair and that the original complement recruited by Bond was entirely male, one of the women's group commented:

> Yes, but look at those males. If you go back and look at the leadership within that school over the years . . . they have an acceptance of females and an acceptance that they treated you as equals and you never had the feeling that you were anything less, in fact you were encouraged to be more—I think that is a really important and significant difference from other schools. I was head of the largest department [in another school] before I came to Byron and I worked hard to be the best because they expected you not to be the best. At Byron you were expected to be the best and you were the best.

Paradoxically, it was a "critical incident" (Ball & Goodson, 1985) related to the departure of Bond from Byron after 3½ years as principal that galvanized the women to organize a network to attend to women's issues. When Bond was promoted, the male staff members organized a two-day "men only" stag party at farms a number of staff members owned in northern Ontario. The women were incensed that an event for Bond was planned strictly by the men. As one woman recalled: "We felt respected and our individuality was important to us and he was important to us as well." A woman who is presently a principal in South recently recalled:

> The main issue was that it was exclusive to men. It was *the* major social activity planned by the group to honor Ward, and no women were part of it because there were *no* women on the leadership team. It was the catalyst that got us talking together about not being part of decision-making. It was a very symbolic representation of the fact that we, as women, were not considered part of the decision-making because we were not in formal leadership positions, and that we were the only ones who were going to do anything about that. We certainly felt valued as staff members, but were not encouraged by our male leaders to take on formal leadership, and that was where things were happening—so we decided to set up our own leadership, encouragement, training and support group, because we felt the other groups were not open to us. So it was a case of experiencing a need, talking about it and doing something about it.

They organized an alternative event to which they invited all staff members and their partners. The success of this event and the enjoyment of working together to achieve a goal led to subsequent meetings.

They helped each other professionally and personally. They were there for each other at the "birthing of babies" and the seeking of advancement. Since there were no women in the chairs group, for instance, they asked why not, and encouraged their colleagues to apply, which over the next few years many did with success. Of the present nine department heads (chairs), six are women. Sexist jokes and gender-based language were discouraged at Byron by men and women alike. The movement spread throughout the district. In the early 1980s, members of the group helped to found an organization in South called "Men and Women in South," which dealt with gender-based issues in the region. One of its successes was a board policy on inclusive language and a review of curriculum to ensure gender equity. Bond and the ethos of Lord Byron had supported and empowered women to create a network that engendered the kind of self-confidence required to pursue leadership opportunities. This is quite different from the scenarios described by Shakeshaft in the United States (1993) and Edwards in the United Kingdom (1994).

Bond's impact on both male and female leaders in South was profound. The staff of Byron in its first five years produced two directors, three superintendents, ten principals, four vice principals, and a number of consultants and department chairs. In fact the rest of the South system often referred to the "Byron mafia." Virtually all of the mafia have tended to lead in Bond's image. I can trace much of my own leadership style and subsequent writing on the topic (Fink, 1992a, 1992b; Stoll & Fink, 1996) to my 3 years with Ward Bond. A woman who has been principal in two secondary schools reflected, "I think the thing that Ward taught me was to be a leader, to keep positive, listen to people's ideas and offer ideas."

To a number of respondents, Bond's premature departure was *the* major factor in the attrition of change at Byron. A former system leader observed that "Byron changed the month and day that Ward left." A former chairman with Bond used almost the same words when he stated: "The shift came down to the month, if not the day that Ward left." One teacher felt "somewhat betrayed" because 3 years "was not enough with his kind of leadership when you are trying to make change." Still another teacher reflected that Bond had such a powerful persona that he "was an almost impossible act to follow."

Bond admittedly enjoyed unique circumstances. He not only had a year to plan the structures of the school, he was able to recruit staff members to his vision. He opened a school of 900 students and when he left it was still only 1,200 students. This compares to the more than 2,000 students who would attend the school by 1976. He enjoyed the support of the central office and was able to bask in the spotlight of provincial and national interest. At the same time, it would be difficult to diminish his stature among the staff and much of the parent and student community. While his style was not in the "heroic" tradition (Senge, 1990, p. 340), the significance of the Byron experience in the lives of so many people who became influential in the South system led to a mythology around Ward Bond that indeed made succeeding him difficult. Principals who came to Byron 20 years after Bond's departure felt they were being measured against Bond's mythic persona. As one respondent who had taught at Byron long after Bond had left reported:

> He still walked the halls when I got there. I never saw the man for years, but the way people talked about him and the references to what he had done that helped people be the way they were, they were legion. People were always turning to me in great shock and saying "Oh, you don't know him, your style is like you know him."

Bond created a strong leadership group. The chairs saw themselves as mini-principals and with Bond, made most of the major policy decisions. Over Bond's tenure the chairmen grew so collegial, collaborative, and confident of the "Byron approach" that the potential for "groupthink" existed (Janis, 1972). Groupthink occurs in highly collegial groups in which participants will often accept decisions with which they disagree or to which they mutely dissent in order to be perceived as team players. Typically, Bond was aware of this possibility and shared copies of Janis's book with the chair group and discussed its implications with them. This tendency lay dormant under Bond. As external criticism increased over time, groupthink was to contribute to Byron's isolation in the system. Since the school was relatively small, Bond was able to involve staff in providing input to decisions and to communicate directly with the entire staff. He was able to spend time both informally and formally with staff members. He always said, "I do people things during the day and paper things at night." He often said that "he would know when he had succeeded when he worked himself out of a job." Bond had skillfully shaped the micropolitical balance in productive ways. In the process he created a group of chairs who saw themselves as wholly involved in running the school and similarly a staff that felt totally involved and consulted. Four of the original group became principals in the system and interestingly, their replacements also became principals. With this nucleus of strong leaders, the heads groups functioned in the ways that Bond had envisaged in the first 10 years of the school.

The paradox of leadership for new schools is that new, innovative schools appear to require exceptional leadership. All respondents agreed that Bond was an exceptional leader and very difficult, if not impossible, to replace. Conversely, as Hargreaves and his colleagues (1996) have suggested, exceptional leaders can often create problems for their successors, which can negatively affect the school in the long run. The power of the Bond persona and the delicate decision-making balance that he left would prove to be difficult challenges for future principals.

Overreaching and Entropy

Bruce Grey replaced Ward Bond as principal in 1974. Grey observed that "people who are ruthlessly obsessed by goals sometimes pay the price." From his present perspective as director of education in a rural school district, he recognized that his ambition to be a principal before he was 30 years of age had created some ill will. He was seen as aggressively ambitious and to some, he seemed more intent on personal advancement and profile than attending to the best interests of the school. More serious for his leadership, however, was that Grey never engendered the trust and respect enjoyed by Bond. Grey acknowledged the challenge of following Bond but asserted:

> I didn't have any trouble following Ward. I think other people had a lot of trouble with the transition—there is no question about that. One of the reasons change dies is that it gets personified with one person rather than becoming part of the culture and structure of the organization.

The Legacy of the Charismatic Leader. Grey felt that he was a "transition person." What he tried to do was move people from loyalty to a person to loyalty to a concept, because he perceived that the school had lost its initiative with Bond's departure. At the same time, he was to lead Byron through its period of greatest growth, which placed him in a "catch 22." Strains were showing in Byron's structures. He could pursue consolidation and retrenchment. To do so, however, he risked alienating a staff that was really not sure of him and mourned for its previous principal. "I think," he said, "changes had come so quickly at Byron that I think for a lot of people, they had become very conservative in protecting what had gone on." At the same time, as a very young and ambitious principal, he recalled, "I was at a stage in my career in which I was not interested in the status quo." He therefore decided that the best course for the school and for himself to establish his leadership credentials in the school and region was to reenergize the school by pushing the change processes even further. Day and Bakioglu's (1996) research suggests that "making too many changes in the first year without getting to know the school culture, staff, and community was identified by the experienced headteachers as an error" (p. 210). From the first day he arrived in the school, Grey moved very quickly to continue the change agenda. He expanded DSF; poured time, energy, and money into a community-school concept; introduced immersion programs; and supported innovations throughout the school. Some have suggested that many innovations were not well thought out and in the words of Blair Alden "some people did dumb, dumb things." It would appear that Grey's efforts to create an identity separate from Bond contributed to a backlash at the board office and with the union. His immediate superior in the system described him as "young and bright but there was a smartiness about his manner." As Grey himself admitted, he made a conscious decision to concentrate on the parent community. He was "not particularly interested" in the larger educational community. "They just weren't listening too well." He chose to ignore them. Unfortunately, the perceived deterioration of order, discipline, and academic rigor in the school tended to work against his best efforts to develop community support.

A number of interview respondents questioned Grey's appropriateness for Byron in 1974. Some even suggested that the "attrition of change" began with his principalship. The question remains: Could *anyone* have replaced Bond? From the board's perspective, there were no incumbent secondary principals or vice-principals suitable, or for that matter, interested. It would appear that little thought had been given by senior administration to succession planning for the principalship of Lord Byron. An appropriate successor had not been identified when Bond was promoted. The logical successor, the vice-principal, Graham Clark, was by his own admission not ready. Grey was thrust into a situation in which the seeds of problems from decisions made in the first 4 years germinated during his tenure. His successors experienced the results.

Grey left the school district after 3 eventful years at Byron. He was succeeded by Graham Clark, who led quietly and by all accounts efficiently, very much in the way his mentor, Bond, would have handled things. He was the principal when government and board policies undermined or eliminated many of the key components of Byron's innovative structures. South Board's evaluative documents for the period, and my interview respondents' lack of comment on these contextual pressures, suggest that Clark was able to lead this retrenchment with a minimum of upset. Those who commented at all felt that his appointment was 3 years too late. Respondents saw that after Grey "as political wariness crept in, principals took fewer risks. There was less 'future think' because other social forces had taken over." Successive principals inherited the policy changes of both the province and the board and had to administer a school experiencing unprecedented demographic changes.

After 3 years, Clark was promoted within the system to be replaced by George Owens. Within the course of 6 years, Byron had had four different principals and innumerable vice-(assistant) principals. It was board policy to rotate vice-principals every 2 years, which meant that between promotions to principalship and normal rotations, the vice-principals' role at Byron provided even less continuity than the principal's.

Preserving Programs Versus Teachers' Jobs. Owens's difficulties have been described previously, in Chapters 2 and 3. He was overwhelmed by the "catastrophic" decline in enrollment and the need to reduce the staff complement from 120 to 60. In addition to the trauma of reducing the staff by 15 and 20 teachers each year that he was principal, he also had to deal with a group of strong union people who constantly monitored his administration of the surplus procedures. While Owens worked to keep the staff that could offer a breadth and depth of programs, the union worked to preserve the jobs of the most senior people based on the collective agreement. It was a "no-win" situation for either side. Byron faced unprecedented reductions in students and therefore staff. These cutbacks had to be achieved within a systemwide policy that had been negotiated by the board and the regional union. These procedures were designed to place teachers regionally, but took little account of the impact of enrollment decline on individual schools. Within individual schools these policies forced principals and staff to try to balance the maintenance of important programs for students and the preservation of teachers' jobs. Decisions of this nature often created adversarial relationships among staff members. A procedure designed to cover all possible situations in the region proved particularly inappropriate for a unique school such as Byron.

Owens, occupied by enrollment decline and teacher attrition, tended to have little time for the festering community problem. When asked about the ongoing problem of lack of community confidence, he conceded it was beyond his influence. As he stated, "I'm the last person to answer that question. I never felt the community council worked effectively. Personally I never had time to talk to parents in that mode, I only had time to talk to them about their kids."

Owens's in-school difficulties compounded by health problems meant that one of Bond's innovative structures, the Chairs' Council, had to step up and take a leading role in the operation of the school. In the words of a former department head (board policy replaced the word *chair* with *head*), "Heads were the real leaders of the school."

The Decision-making Conundrum. "Principals came and went, but the heads were the continuity. Different principals didn't hurt because the heads and key teachers were so strong they carried the school." Blair Alden's observation on the key role of the head was corroborated by others, but many respondents still felt deeply that the lack of continuity at the principal level was damaging to the school. The problem for the school, however, was that with some exceptions, the type of head (formerly chairs) had changed. Owens commented that when he arrived in 1980,

> the staff had changed, the originals had got older, "the critical mass" of innovators had moved on, and the Chairmen's Council in my view needed direction. When you lose that critical mass

> and you have a bunch of people who felt abandoned and then you have people who want a commencement, a yearbook, and then you end up with a very normal high school. The heads were competent, but to my mind they were pedestrian people. They didn't have the larger vision of where to go and what to do. They did want detailed instructions and resented the fact that I didn't give them a detailed guide of what to do.

One of his successors described the leadership situation in this way:

> The source of leadership was not in the administrative offices, in my opinion, but rather rested in the hands of a few heads and a subculture of strong teachers. Not to put down the administrators that were there, one person left to go to another county, and the principal was having health problems and couldn't do the job by himself, there was too much to do. So a few very strong heads . . . seized the opportunity and rightly so, and were given the opportunity and they literally ran the school. The seat of power was with the Heads' Council.

She continued to describe a rather telling story:

> A good example of that: in June, Patrick and I were appointed to go to Byron. We were invited to a heads' barbecue. The department heads had gathered together and to sort of support themselves and to maintain the control they had been given. They gave Patrick and me, the new principal and vice principal coming in, all of the policies they had passed in the two weeks after our appointment—the name of the game, here are the rules, and here are the expectations, and here are the policies, and this is how we do things. I will never forget that, I almost fell over. . . . Certainly they were protecting their turf. For all the right reasons, they worked very hard at doing that, but it was really two or three people doing it in absentia from the office. There was another subculture, that was within the staff and some very strong staff members . . . who were tied very closely to the Union. They had a strong hold on staff in the sense of direction, what was acceptable, what wasn't acceptable. Not always did the subculture agree with the hierarchy of the Heads' group. There was some friction at the time, that subculture certainly didn't agree with the administrators so the Heads were literally caught in the middle. I think, they did the best they could and for those three years did a super

> job of trying to hold it together. Not that we were saviors but we did identify those issues and went forward with them.

As Patrick Garner analyzed the situation he inherited:

> The first major issue we had to deal with was who was going to make the decisions and whether it was going to be the department heads, the staff or principal and vice principal—who was going to have some say in, and who was going to make what decision. It probably took six months until . . . there was some agreement as to how the decisions were going to be made.

In Bond's time he had been able to balance the leadership roles of the administration, the chairs (or heads), and the staff. The dramatic increase in enrollment with its concomitant increase in staff meant that the principal had to rely for advice on the Chairs' Council and on a staff advisory committee rather than the whole staff. Over time, the rapid changes in the school required the Heads' Council (same as Chairs' Council) to assume unusual power in the school. With rapidly declining enrollment and surplus staff, however, the staff became represented by a vocal few. Rather than the administration, heads, and staff working in harmony through difficult times for the improvement of the school, they tended to conflict, in part because of regional procedures, which further contributed to the attrition of change. As structures were altered or totally changed and conflict over decision-making replaced the harmony of the early years, the culture of the school gradually changed from a collaborative culture to a balkanized and, in some respects, an individualistic one (Hargreaves, 1994).

In the early days, the formal school leaders shared power *with* the department chairs and the staff of the school. Over time, stakeholders with power *over* the school changed organizational structures in such a way as to undermine the more positive politics of the Bond era. The politics of decline were adversarial and debilitating.

Survival and Continuity

Garner was appointed to Byron for quite different reasons than his predecessors. Bond, Grey, Clark, and Owens were all seen as innovators, and to use Burns's (1978) term, transformational leaders. Clark and Owens had been original members of the Lord Byron staff assigned to Byron to recapture some of "the Byron spirit." Senior administration of the board, however, appointed Garner because he was a proven manager and administrator and politically astute. His style and experience would more closely fit those of a transactional leader (Burns, 1978; Leithwood, 1992, 1993). At Byron he was obliged to negotiate a new meaning for Lord Byron in the face of compelling contextual pressures. He also had to work with a divided and in some respects hostile community, as well as with his educational colleagues to establish the school's credibility. At the same time, he and his assistant principal implemented the "Satellite" and "Life Skills" programs, which helped Byron's survival.

The leadership literature often implies that managerial, transactional leadership models are unproductive, and that transformational leadership is the only way (Bennis & Nanus, 1985; Burns, 1978; Leithwood, 1992). As my colleague and I have suggested elsewhere, however, it is really the situation that tends to dictate the style and the methodology (Stoll & Fink, 1996). Leaders who build trust, exude optimism, respect others, and operate with integrity can respond to shifting contexts effectively (Covey, 1989). While Garner tended to lead in more conventional ways, it could be argued that the circumstances required this style of leadership. It could also be suggested that his handling of affairs reflected "principled" leadership. He made his intentions very clear to staff and acted consistently to reestablish Byron's viability as a school. His handling of the competing micro-political elements at Byron when he arrived reflects his approach.

An important part of Byron's legacy from the early 1970s had been the balance of leadership among administration (senior management), the Chairs' (Heads') Council, and the staff. Ward Bond had fostered leadership at all levels, and was described by a number of respondents as the leaders of leaders. By 1984, the vicissitudes of the previous 14 years had destroyed this leadership balance and replaced coherence with confusion. Garner's first action, therefore, was to sort out decision-making issues. He made it very clear, as Bond had many years before, that since the principal was accountable, he would be the ultimate decision-maker. As he explained,

> From my point of view, I have to have a greater amount of say if you like. I'm willing to give the heads' group a certain amount of authority, but certainly not all of it. It is a reflection of my style of principal. The other aspect of that is a function of the strength of your heads. In some cases throughout the history of Byron there were some extremely strong heads' groups and therefore the principal was probably inclined to give them greater say, whereas, there were looking back over the years some heads' groups not

> nearly so strong and looked to the principal to be more directive, as well as staff. At times staff say the same thing "tell us what you want." Staff wanted a leader who was going to make a fair number of significant decisions, although they didn't want to be told everything—they just wanted some input. Well, at the heads level there was still strong feeling, because it was made up of quite a few old Byron people. They wanted to have control, and they wanted to direct things because they saw the ways things should go, simply because they wanted some of the old philosophy to continue, because we were new and they weren't sure in what direction we were going to go. So, from the heads' group there was certainly a strong feeling that they should continue in their position of leadership. However, at the staff level I found there wasn't necessarily that overwhelming feeling that they wanted to be involved in all the decisions. In many cases, they got tired of having everything brought back to them . . . oftentimes they would say "why don't you just go ahead and make the decisions, we don't want involvement in that it's something you should be doing anyway," whereas there were other, more crucial issues that they wanted to have some input . . . certainly when I arrived on the scene there was willingness to let administration make decisions on less crucial issues.

As Betty Kelly recalled:

> Our hardest task was to get the Heads' Council to understand that their role was one of decision-making certainly, but also one of facilitation and one of engagement. They needed to gather the opinions and views of all the staff and it became shared decision-making. I can remember sitting down and developing a decision-making model and taking it to heads and saying okay, there are some decisions administration is going to make and some decisions that Heads' Council is going to make and some decisions that need to go to staff. Can we look at the kinds of decisions that would fall into these categories and can we agree that we will start to do some of these things and engage all people?

By the end of Garner and Kelly's first year, much of the bickering over who makes what decision had disappeared. In a sense, the two administrators with the heads and the staff had arrived at a consensus that was very similar to arrangements in most other schools. If anything, Byron's leaders were somewhat more directive because they perceived a need for fairly quick action to redress some imbalances that had evolved over time.

When their successor, Dennis Lawrence, was asked if decision-making at Byron was different from that at other schools in his experience, he replied, "I don't think so. I think when we get down to the crunch, the hierarchy still exists. People look to those hierarchies and that determines some decision-making as well, but the feeling still is that somehow it needs to be collaborative and people do try to do that to some extent." He went on to explain, however, that the issue "is very much alive" and how he had to set up a committee to review the patterns of decision-making in the school. It would appear that by the time Garner and Kelly appeared on the scene many staff were quite content to let the formal leadership make decisions. A decade of rapid growth and decline, crises and stress, had left many staff members content to work with their students and let others deal with the school-wide issues. Moreover, the evidence from at least three of the principals suggests that the quality of leadership at the heads level had deteriorated over time and necessitated greater direction from the senior management team. As a teacher who has worked with all eight Byron principals observed,

> I think there was a period of a lot more consultation and collegiality than we have time for right now. I think when you have a system under pressure like the 1990s you have an administrative group who deal with each other rather than the staff. When we had more flexibility people were prepared to put time into the process, now it is just not possible to consult. Staff says we really can't influence anything so tell us what to do and let us get on with it.

In the early days of Byron, leadership was purposely spread among many informal and formal leaders. Decision-making was a shared activity among senior managers, department heads, and the total staff. Ward Bond had the ability and perhaps the fortuitous context to maintain a delicate decision-making balance. Bond saw himself as the "leader of leaders" and acted on that conviction. His replacement, Grey, perhaps because of his inexperience or the changing school circumstances, moved the leadership dynamic in a somewhat more directive and less collegial direction. Clark and Owens attempted to resurrect the more democratic ethos of the early Byron experience, but found that the situation around them had changed. The rapid decline in enrollment, a more directive provincial presence, and the ongoing "image issue" forced Owens to make some very unpopular decisions, which alienated some heads and staff members. At the same time, many staff felt he should be even more directive and less collaborative—just make the hard decisions and get on with it. Owens was torn. He wanted to provide leadership and promote involvement, but found himself caught up in contextually created managerial issues. At the same time, the staff had become more argumentative because of the effects of declining enrollment. This is the situation Garner and Kelly found in 1984.

They assumed a more directive, transactional stance and moved quickly to clarify the balance among themselves, the heads, and the staff. Bond's delicate balance was purposely shifted to ensure more direction by senior managers. This tendency has continued to the present. Leadership would appear to be more centralized around the senior leaders and less with the staff as a whole. While it would be easy to suggest that this was a power grab by principals, a number of my respondents suggested that many of their colleagues just wanted to stay in their departments and classrooms, and leave schoolwide issues to the principal and department heads. With so much decision-making taken over by the province and by the board, there was a feeling that "we really can't influence anything so tell us what to do and let us get on with it." This move from more democratic to more directive approaches to leadership has parallels in other new and innovative situations (Fletcher et al., 1985; Gold & Miles, 1981).

The Byron experience suggests some very clear patterns. The transformational leadership of the early days, over time, and often of necessity, became transactional in nature. Shared leadership became hierarchical. Power "with" became power "over" (Blase, 1998). While the characters and styles of the various school leaders no doubt influenced these trends, it seems clear that contextual factors, both external and internal, forced these shifts. It would be premature to suggest that such patterns are inevitable in innovative schools, but the examples available in the international literature of new and innovative schools would lend credibility to such a hypothesis (Fletcher et al., 1985; Gold & Miles, 1981; Smith et al., 1987).

One of the most obvious ways in which contextual factors forced changes at Lord Byron is the changing nature of its structures. Structures introduced in the school experienced mutations over time as external pressures forced Byron to alter its practices. Chapter 6 develops this story.

CHAPTER 6

Structure

As previously stated, structure is about the use of time and space, and the definition and arrangement of roles and responsibilities in an organization such as a school. Soja (1989) writes:

> Just as space, time and matter delineate and encompass the essential qualities of the physical world, spatiality, temporality and social being can be seen as the abstract dimensions which together comprise all facets of human existence. . . . Each of these abstract existential dimensions come[s] to life as a social construct which shapes empirical reality and is simultaneously shaped by it. (p. 25)

In a sense, these structures create organizational coherence and order in much the same way as grammar makes language intelligible. Tyack and Tobin (1994) have used this metaphor to describe the relationship of change and continuity in American educational history. They conclude that changes have come and gone, yet the essential "grammar of schooling" remains unaltered. As they state, "habit is a labor saving device" (p. 476). Cuban (1988) explains this pattern by discriminating between first- and second-order changes. First-order changes try to make "what already exists more efficient and effective, without disturbing the basic organizational features, without substantially altering the way adults and children perform their roles" (p. 342). "Second order changes seek to alter the fundamental ways in which organizations are put together" (p. 342). For the most part, Cuban contends that change in schools over time has been of the first-order variety, and efforts at second-order change have been uncoordinated and generally short-lived. This, in part, explains the persistence of the prevailing length of the school day, the length of the school year, and generally the temporal cycle of schools, which has remained relatively unchanged over long periods of time.

THE STRUCTURE LENS

What most outsiders to Lord Byron recognized as revolutionary were changes in the traditional structures of schooling. Bond's challenges to conventional uses of time and space and his redefinition of roles and responsibilities were the most obvious and the most controversial deviations from the accepted grammar of schooling. This chapter, therefore, looks at the school through this structure lens.

Time

Much of the rhetoric of school reform has been about effective use of time. As the U.S. National Education Commission on Time and Learning (1994) has stated:

> Learning (in our schools) is a prisoner of time. For the past 150 years . . . states have held time constant and let learning vary. . . . Our people and the people involved in them . . . are captives of clock and calendar. The boundaries of student growth are defined by schedules, bells, buses and vacations instead of standards for students and learning. (p. 7)

Critics have compared Western educational systems invidiously to those of Eastern societies, where students spend more time in school (Stevenson, 1992). Moreover, Western schools are criticized for inappropriate use of the time that is available. Commentators have argued that the allocated time for student learning does not translate into students' time-on-task. In turn, time-on-task does not necessarily mean academic learning time, that is, the time in which students are actually learning (Berliner, 1990). These arguments have been used to lengthen the school day and the school year, mandate curriculum, and impose a multiplicity of tests to ensure compliance. The irony is that the law of unintended consequences sets in, and teachers spend more time on noninstructional issues related to government mandates (Barber, 1995). These and other efforts to foster change through alterations of time have ironically had limited impact on classrooms (Elmore, 1995) because teachers do not have the time to respond (Adelman & Pringle, 1995). It is quite clear, for example, that teachers need time for staff development (Fullan, 1991; A. Hargreaves, 1994; Hargreaves et al., 1996; Stoll and Fink, 1996), yet paradoxically, time is usually not available. Watts and Castle (1993) conclude from a major change project in which they were involved that a clear finding "is that faculty development is necessary to student empowerment. And faculty development takes time; time to collaborate, communicate, ponder, and reflect with others is essential" (p. 307). Time alone, however, does not necessarily promote greater degrees of staff collaboration although it is a prerequisite for it to occur (Hargreaves, 1994).

Space

Space is as important as time in supporting or inhibiting change. As Giddens (1984) has suggested, "human beings do 'make their own geography' as much as they 'make their own history.' That is to say, spatial configurations of social life are just as much a matter of basic importance to social theory as are the dimensions of temporality" (p. 363).

The traditional egg-carton design of school buildings has promoted cultures of isolation and independence (A. Hargreaves, 1994). Similarly, marginalized subject areas have often been built on "the margins" of schools. Technical areas in Ontario are a good example. When the federal government transferred millions of dollars to the provinces for technical education in the 1960s, Ontario entered a few years of furious building construction. Almost invariably, these new structures were added to existing schools and were generally located far from the heart of the school. This distance is not only physical; in many schools, it is social as well. A similar pattern exists with guidance counselors (pastoral care workers), who often have their own separate offices in the general proximity of the administrative offices. This tends to accentuate the division between classroom and nonclassroom teachers (Grant, 1988), while opening up the possibility of guidance (counseling) becoming an extension of administration (King, Warren, & Peart, 1988).

Open space, comprehensive schools, vocational schools, staff-development schools, work experience, and co-operative education[1] are examples of alterations in space designed to promote different behaviors on the parts of teachers and students. Space allocations, for example, can often have "unintended" results from those anticipated. Department offices provide places for teachers to work, relate, and socialize. They can also reinforce "balkanized" cultures. Staff rooms designed to bring people together can also prove divisive, as various micro-political or social groupings stake out their territory. A colleague in his workshops asks participants to draw a map of the staff room and describe who sits where as a way to introduce the micro-political aspects of a school. The activity seldom, if ever, fails to make its point.

Roles and Responsibilities

Change also includes alterations in the roles and responsibilities of students, teachers, and parents. Virtually every innovative school described in the available literature endeavored through changes in time and space relationships to alter the ethos of the school and make the school more student-centered (Fletcher et al., 1985; Fullan et al., 1972; Gold & Miles, 1981; Smith et al., 1987; Watts, 1977). The move to comprehensive schools in the United Kingdom, in which the tripartite system of selective grammar schools, secondary modern, and in some cases vocational schools, were to be merged, was an attempt to break down stereotypes and promote greater equity for students. But old habits died hard. As both Woods' (1979) and Ball's (1981) studies demonstrate, changing structures through mandate does not necessarily change the roles and responsibilities in schools. In Ontario, efforts to change relationships among students and between students and teachers through destreaming (detracking) have experienced great difficulties (Hargreaves et al., 1992). Teachers, through within-class grouping, have found ways to shape the new structure into something similar to the old "grammar." School planning teams designed to empower broader segments of the school staff often face opposition from entrenched groups of department heads. Parent councils intended to provide more opportunities to influence the school have on occasion been thwarted by a school staff or its principal, or divided the parent community into those who are "in" and those who are "out" (Mortimore et al., 1988). These few examples provide evidence that changes in time, space, and roles and responsibilities are fundamental to school change, but without attention to culture, change agents who attend only to structure are, in Fullan's (1991) words, "doomed to tinkering." The remainder of this chapter outlines the changing nature of Byron's structures. The next chapter (Chapter 7) establishes the connections between structure and culture.

LORD BYRON AND STRUCTURE

To achieve his vision of a school that was sufficiently flexible to meet the diverse needs of students, Ward Bond created an organizational structure that was intended to alter conventional uses of time and space. He intended to create a very different "grammar of schooling" (Tyack & Tobin, 1994).

Years of Creativity and Experimentation

Bond recognized that to change the "grammar" he had to view Byron as more than a bundle of innovations. He had to begin with a vision of what education was about, design structures facilitating that vision, hire staff members who could bring the vision to life, and finally work with the architects to design a facility that would encourage the work and the learning of staff and students. At the same time there were certain "grammatical conventions" such as credits, credit hours, subjects, and department structures, among others, that were determined by forces outside the school—the Ministry of Education, the board, and the union contract—that had to be accommodated. While he had much more freedom to organize his school and to hire staff than do contemporary principals, he did not have "carte blanche" and had to be clever to work around externally imposed impediments.

He began with the concept of time (Donohoe, 1993; A. Hargreaves, 1994; Harvey, 1989)—time for teachers to teach, time for leaders to lead, and time for students to learn, experience, make choices, and socialize. His answer was to semester the school, design a 32-credit diploma, and schedule a one-hour teaching period. Students had an individualized timetable that required that they take eight subjects per year, and four per semester. As one teacher recalled:

> I am looking back 20 years, and I still think those kids were the best educated kids, simply because they had such a broad base and they were able to overlap. It was not unusual for a kid to do a project where he or she took the information from the music course, maybe in Renaissance music, brought it into English class and combined the music, with Renaissance literature and history to complete a given project.

Since each student's minimum requirement was four classes out of a six-period day, students could choose to use the nonlunch period to accelerate their program by taking an additional course, pick up a failed course from a previous semester, or as a free period. The structure provided flexibility and also the opportunity to make choices.

Teachers had the same timetable, which gave them four classes to prepare for at any one time compared with six in every other school in South. At the same time, they had one-hour classes, not the traditional 40 minutes. It was thought that longer periods would oblige teachers to use a greater variety of teaching strategies to utilize the additional time effectively. It also gave teachers the time to provide more individualized attention for students in nonstreamed classes. Department chairs taught two classes per day and had three periods available for leadership activities.

In establishing the initial organization of the school, Bond, with the advice of the Innovations Committee, not only thought about altering time patterns for teachers and students but also looked at the use of space (Harvey, 1989; Rosenau, 1992). He worked with the school's architect, system consultants, and those chairmen and staff members that he was able to hire before the school opened to design a physical facility to accommodate flexible teaching strategies, teacher collaboration, interdisciplinary learning, individualized student timetables, and student free time. Every teacher had a desk in a workroom for private preparation. Each interdisciplinary department like the Social Sciences Department had a workroom in which meetings could be held or teachers could collaborate on joint projects. As one teacher recalled:

> One of the wonderful things about this school was that they had wonderful department workrooms where you could store material. It used to be in other schools that you "held court" in your classroom, where you also kept all your stuff. We didn't do that. We moved from classroom to classroom. In the English area, the books for the courses were stored in one room so you may have three classes you taught in so you needed a workroom. That was a philosophical thing that was supported by the architecture.

A large, comfortable staff room was also designed to encourage informal staff socialization and discussions. This was the one place where coffee was available. An English teacher recalling the debates in the staff room exclaimed, "Those were wonderful, I learned so much." The resource center was accessible from all parts of the school. As one teacher remarked, "The resource center was a hub, that was a real resource center." Perhaps the most controversial feature was the openness of the school. Open concept had been tried and perceived to have succeeded in elementary schools by the professionals but parents were still suspicious. Open space in a secondary school was largely untried in Ontario. Some saw it as a real asset:

> The open concept was so important because the walls were so flimsy and there were few doors, people wandered in and out. You

> couldn't be ignorant of what people were doing because it impinged upon your space all the time. Nor could you run a class that wasn't working or where kids misbehaved. There was responsibility to one another.

Others were not so sure. One teacher who left Byron for Roxborough felt the open concept worked against innovation because it was difficult to use strategies that might be noisy. Another teacher felt that open concept "did not work well." She remembered

> teaching at Byron with six classes in the open area and it got to be a bit of a competition of noise and you are trying to override the noise in other areas. . . . If you wanted kids to discuss in groups and they got into an argument, that became very disruptive for another class to have an argument going on.

To alterations to time and space, Bond added the third piece, which was the use of resources, both human and material. It was Bond who introduced differentiated staffing, augmented guidance (counseling) resources to help students make choices, reduced the number of formal leaders, hired a community relations coordinator, and structured interdisciplinary departments. Rather than utilizing teachers in formal supervision of students in hallways and the cafeteria, he encouraged incidental supervision in which staff spent time talking to students in the foyer or cafeteria. Teachers ate their lunch in the main cafeteria, which eliminated the need for "laid-on" supervision.

The thousands of visitors found when they visited in the early years a relaxed, informal ethos, in which teachers and students mingled quite naturally and usually productively. The external committee for the 1975 evaluation of Lord Byron commented that the school had made "significant progress towards achieving the overall goal of creating a humane environment for students" (p. 11). A system superintendent recalled that in his first visit to the school he walked into the cafeteria and asked who was supervising. When he was told no one, he was amazed. He said it was the most orderly secondary school cafeteria he had ever seen. To many in the educational and parent communities, this was not, however, the grammar of a "real school." As long as Byron's use of time, space, and staff worked in concert, the system worked well for students and teachers, but each of these innovations pushed too far or removed from its original context had the potential to produce problems, as many of them eventually did and as many of the critics were only too ready to point out.

Overreaching and Entropy

Part of the discouragement for long-serving staff members was to see structures, which they believed in and which had benefitted students, gradually eroded by forces over which they had no control. Alden's words that "reality forces any new changes to fit into contemporary reality" were particularly true of the 1977–1984 period in Byron's history. Bond had created structures that were holistic, integrated, and based on a very clear notion of how schools should operate. Tinkering with one structure inevitably unbalanced every other tangible and intangible structure in the school. Two major structural factors contributed to this retreat to "reality": enrollment instability and macropolitical decisions.

Enrollment Instability. The rapid increase in enrollment and the infusion of DSF money when combined with ambitious and somewhat inexperienced leadership created an overheated environment in which new initiatives were piled on top of old. The most enterprising proposal was to create a number of semester-long immersion programs in various studies. This plan to create in-depth courses located in the community consumed a great deal of time and energy, but produced only one lasting program. The commitment to a "community school" concept in the mid-1970s in the hope that the community would become more supportive also deflected staff from its main task within the school. These imaginative and innovative uses of time and space, however, required a reallocation of financial and human resources away from the instructional program to create opportunities for adults.

The community effort during Bruce Grey's tenure did keep the community's underlying discomfort with the school quiet for a few years, but many teachers perceived that it was at a cost to the school and its staff. Similarly, Grey's success in gaining the approval of the South administration to use DSF funds for "things" antagonized an already adversarial teachers' union and quickened its attacks on many of Byron's structures, particularly DSF. As a teacher who began his career at Byron in 1972 recalled:

> As a new teacher I wasn't too aware of what the Union was doing. I remember the DSF fund gave us a lab assistant. Some people would say everybody else in the region is teaching three classes, we're teaching four, and the money is going from our salaries to pay for these other aspects and reducing the number of teachers in this school. Most of us accepted what we were teaching.

Byron teachers were caught in a difficult situation between loyalty to a structure they believed had helped the school and to their union, which could argue that by teaching more classes Byron teachers were costing other teachers jobs. This argument was particularly powerful in the late 1970s because the enrollment in the South Board had declined and there was the very real potential that teachers would become surplus to the region and ultimately dismissed.

Equally damaging was the increased effort required to make systems designed for 900 students work for 2,000. Free time for every student was a key part of Bond's original thinking. He recognized that some students would have difficulty using time wisely and put supports in place to assist these students. If 10% of the school population fell into this category, this meant dealing with 90 students in 1970, which was manageable, but it also meant dealing with over 200 in 1976, which was not. The existence of a significant number of students with time on their hands and no supervision led to vandalism, litter, and generally a very poor public image. One of George Owens's first acts as principal was to tear down a tin shed in the smoking area because of drug use. Almost overnight, hundreds of "Fuck George" buttons appeared throughout the school. He found this a dramatic change from the students he left in 1974. As he said, "I inherited a lack of control, there were lots of things I was over my head with."

Attendance and work completion were relatively easy to monitor with 900 students, but very difficult with over 2,000 students on individualized timetables. Not only did the student enrollment more than double, so too did the staff complement. Coordination of ongoing procedures and practices became increasingly complex. New teachers, recently hired to Byron with little sense of its essential student-centered meaning, tended to overlook problems and interpret students' skipping class and failure to complete work as part of Byron's philosophy. To be humane in the Byron approach was not only to care for all students, but to care enough to hold high expectations. Inadequate induction of new staff tended to result in an emphasis on the caring and less focus on expectations. In addition, school size meant that some departments had as many teachers as some elementary schools. There were, for example, at least 15 full- and part-time teachers in the English Department during Byron's peak enrollment period.

Staff members who were new to the school began to question structures that were different from those of other schools. As Alden recalled, they began to say: "Why am I teaching my history class in an open area next to a geography class? Since the original idea had been to timetable compatible courses together in order to promote interdisciplinary studies, the answer would be to teach social integration when it really didn't." Old answers did not suffice for new issues resulting from Byron's changing context. "Why do we teach four 60-minute periods when teachers in other schools teach three 70-minute periods?" Many practices had been just accepted as "part of the Byron way" and unquestioned. As Alden recalled, "people just assumed this was a good thing and in the beginning there was an attempt to make the open concept work. Time took care of all these things."

Divisions between the "old guard," who believed fervently in the original structures and beliefs, and questioning "newcomers" began to surface as a result of school size. The limitations of the building became apparent with the increased enrollment. As a teacher who arrived at Byron in the early 1980s recalled:

> I think the open concept has changed, the walls have been going up, the doors have been slamming shut, physically the plant is not an open concept any more. Our ventilation system is balking at the fact that there are walls where there shouldn't be. I don't think there is a lot of integration. I think that is something that everybody has on paper but is not actually happening.

Enrollment decline was even more destructive to the structures of the Byron program. Fewer teachers and students meant the loss of many courses that at the peak in the 1970s had been very useful to many students. When a school loses staff, it also loses people who coach teams, run choirs and clubs, and generally contribute beyond the classroom. It loses secretarial, guidance, and administrative support as well. Flexibility of staffing and program delivery were further eroded, which made the competition with Roxborough even more difficult, because programs that would attract students could be offered only in the larger school and had to be eliminated in a declining school such as Byron. Departments in Byron tended to become more insular and protective. Falling enrollment resulted in interdepartmental competition for the remaining students in order to preserve low-enrollment courses and keep the jobs of younger teachers in a department. This pattern was consistent with Siskin's (1994) study of the reaction of secondary school departments to restructuring initiatives. She states that her study was about

> how under conditions of stress from the external educational community even a group of teachers dedicated to a restructuring design, convinced of the need to overcome departmental fragmentation and divisiveness, com-

> mitted in extraordinary ways to the needs of students, and willing to take extraordinary means to address those needs, retreat into the traditional departmental divisions which they originally defined as part of the problem. (p. 11)

Loss of students also creates excess building space. Since system administrators abhor a vacuum, they tend to want to either fill the space with regional programs or close the surplus areas. In Byron's case, two regional programs were established at Byron. Both were for special education students, which added to Byron's image as the "school for special students." Few if any schools in South's history have experienced such highs and lows in enrollment in such a short time. Compounding Byron's attempts to adapt to these extreme swings in enrollment was the shift back to a more traditional philosophical stance by both the provincial government and the South Board. Byron's internal problems were further complicated by changing policy directions at the provincial and board levels.

Macro-political Decisions. Between 1975 and 1985, decisions by the Ministry of Education and the South Board totally altered the structure of Byron. The ministry's insistence on a 27-credit diploma not only affected the flexibility and "renaissance" nature of the students' programs, but in combination with the South Secondary Teachers' Union's opposition, effectively ended DSF resources, which in turn terminated the use of para-professionals in academic areas. Byron's 32-credit diploma had required each teacher to teach slightly more students per year than in other South schools, which meant that fewer teachers were required at Byron. The board had given the money for "teachers not hired" to the school to use as DSF funds. The decision to end DSF impacted on Byron's use of time for department chairs to provide support to teachers. Ironically, it was the creative and progressive former department chair Owens who as principal in the 1980s was obliged to enforce the ministry's guidelines for streaming students. At the same time, declining enrollment across the system meant that South needed placements for surplus teachers in other schools. Since Byron had differentiated some of its staff allocation, the South Board during contract negotiations agreed with the union's insistence on the elimination of DSF funds.

Moreover, pressure from trustees to have uniform systemwide policies forced Byron to conduct formal exams and to eliminate the chairmanship system and replace it with the system's leadership model, which increased the numbers of positions of responsibility. By the early 1980s, the forces of continuity had virtually eliminated all of the experimental structures that Ward Bond had designed in better times.

Survival and Continuity

The only structure from the original Byron concept that remained in 1995 was the semestered timetable. In most other respects Byron's structures are the same as or very similar to those of other schools in South and the province. In virtually every other facet of schooling, the Ontario Ministry and the South Board have progressively reduced school discretion by raising expectations while mandating organizational structures, curriculum, and assessment procedures. The days of creation and experimentation for Byron are, for the moment at least, history.

In 1984, Garner and Kelly used what little room they had to maneuver to try and reenergize the school. They therefore altered or added structures to effect change on two distinctly different levels. On one level, to exorcise the "ghosts" of Byron's past, they initiated structures that would appeal to the parents of the more able students who might opt to attend Roxborough. A redesigned program for gifted students, the introduction of French Immersion, and elite athletic teams moved Byron closer to the more traditional Roxborough (see page 16). At a second level, to ensure that the excess space in the school was filled, they added the Life Skills program, and the Satellite unit (see page 32). The difficulty of integrating challenged students into regular classes helped to renew Byron's historic commitment to students, regardless of ability or background. This balancing of the twin pulls of perceived quality and equity reinvigorated Byron and stopped the "entropy" of the late 1970s and early 1980s.

Changing Perceptions. Middleton, as one staff member described it, is an "unbelievably middle-class community. A school like Byron would be loved in Toronto." Since most identified gifted students in South came from middle- and upper-middle-class homes, Garner congregated these students in specifically identified classes so that their parents were assured that the students' learning needs were being met. Previously, their program was enriched through a pull-out program in which they were congregated for certain themes and activities. Interestingly, this program had received a provincial award for its innovativeness, but parents of brighter students still did not consider it to be the equal of Roxborough's more elitist segregated program (Kohn, 1998). What Garner did was more cosmetic and organizational than educationally different, but it did create a perception that met the parents' expectations and enabled Byron to retain many of the brighter students.

Similarly, Byron's reputation for allowing anyone who wanted to participate to play on school teams created an impression among influential elements of the community that Byron was not interested in winning in sports events and reinforced the image of a noncompetitive, "artsy" school. Garner supported his new physical education head's desire to establish competitive teams, while at the same time redirecting resources to improve intramural sports. Byron soon became a power in South's hockey league and competed quite successfully at the provincial level. At the same time, Garner and Kelly encouraged the dramatic arts program to expand. Led by a well-known teacher, and supported by administration, the Lord Byron Players brought Byron considerable positive public notice. Another strategy Kelly promoted was to involve Byron in the Canadian Academic Decathlon. Byron had traditionally avoided elitist academic competitions and its image had suffered because of this apparent avoidance of competition, although Byron had participated quite successfully for many years in board and provincial mathematics competitions. Teams of students of different ability levels competed in the academic decathlon. Byron won the Canadian championship 2 years in a row and remains very competitive every year. A veteran staff member who lived in the community praised the public relations efforts of Kelly and Garner:

> Betty did a lot of being in community, and rah rah Byron. She brought Byron from that, I don't know, if the word is crisis in the early 80s. There was a real down that everything was at fault. Patrick was the beginning of the turn-around and Betty carried on with it and really gave Byron much more high profile to the point that there were people saying very positive things about this school.

He provided the following example, "One thing about Betty, things had to be done with style. She insisted that you do things really well. We have neighbors whose son came to Byron for his last year, they couldn't believe our commencement ceremonies. There has been a shift."

School procedures were tightened. Students were required to take a full program. Dropping a course was made more difficult. Discipline and attendance were closely monitored. With these visible changes in place, both administrators met with community groups and communicated one message: "Byron has changed." As Garner admitted, we just kept repeating the message "Byron has changed" and in time we began to hear back the same message, "Byron has changed." As Garner admitted, the Byron program, organization, and in some ways philosophy had changed long before he arrived, but his and Kelly's task was to get the message out to the community, which they did with considerable success.

The board's optional attendance policy is a useful barometer of their success. Before students can change schools, parents must follow a procedure that requires the involvement of a school board official. In the early 1980s, as the board official responsible for Byron and Roxborough, I would receive 50 to 75 requests from parents to move their students from Byron to Roxborough. By 1988, the flow had reversed. Roxborough students who opted to finish their school careers early wanted to move to the semestered system at Byron. It became an issue at Roxborough because many of these students were among Roxborough's most academically proficient. The principal at Roxborough even initiated an attempt to organize Roxborough into two five-month semesters to stem the tide of students moving to Byron to graduate early. A community backlash prevented this attempt. A major argument used was that semestering would make Roxborough like Byron.

Reviving the Byron Past. At the second level, the inclusion of a diversity of programs and students became a source of restored pride for the school over the next 10 years. As Dennis Lawrence commented:

> Let me say this, although our school looks similar to other schools, it is still a pretty unique school in terms of the variety and spectrum of programs that we offer at the school. Let me list them. We do have a day care program here for the little kids. Although the "Y" (a community group) runs its own program they are integrated not only in terms of the facility being here but in some of the activities we have. We have the Satellite program which is a regional program and that provides an interesting mix for the school. We do have a program for learning disabled students. We do have the Oak Creek program (an outdoor education immersion program) which is now regional but administered out of this school. These five programs certainly make this an interesting school to be in and to administer.

While the inclusion of less-advantaged students in the Byron mix did little to enhance its reputation in middle-class Middleton, it did provide Byron with a uniqueness in the South school community, and it did reconnect the school to its egalitarian past.

Term Appointments for Heads. Lawrence also highlighted another Byron difference, the staff's collective desire to retain some difference in its headship structure.

> When I came here and did my entry plan, one of the things the staff got into that they felt very strongly about was this notion of term appointments, and it goes back well to the whole notion of being a democratic staff and what that means basically is that every three years every position of responsibility is open and anyone can apply, the incumbents as well as people from across the system and I was told that the staff felt very strongly about this.

When board policy established regional guidelines for department heads, which allowed staffs to have some say in their schools' structure, the Byron staff decided to make their headship a 3-year term appointment. The move for term appointments was led by a teacher who was a past president of the union and a member of the math department. In the words of the former union president, headship positions "should not be held sacred." He stated that the notion that "once a person was appointed a department head he or she was a head for life made little sense at the time." He indicated that some department heads at Byron wanted a graceful way to step down. Others were considered by other staff members to be inept and the principal needed to make a decision, and—more important—he saw it as a way to provide opportunities for potential leaders. The mathematics department, for example, had a number of aspiring leaders. The members agreed among themselves to try to have a rotating headship similar to university departments. A survey of staff on the issue revealed that a significant percentage of staff was supportive of the idea. The two teachers who led the initiative were able to convince the principal of Byron at the time, Garner, and the former union president was able to persuade his colleagues to support this departure because the staff had voted for it. Perhaps the underlying reason for this support for the concept was the feeling that Byron had strayed too far from its democratic roots.

Lawrence described the importance to Byron's collective attitude:

> We felt very strongly, whatever you do don't tamper with that [term appointments] because we the staff feel strongly about that. I accepted that and I like the notion and strongly support it. What's interesting of course as we put it to practice is that when these six positions came open we made one change. One incumbent did not get his position back. Now it's weird, we really sup-

> port the notion. Indeed when the decision was made there were some ripples. In spite of that, the people conceded that the best person got the job and this was a person from outside the school as well. The friendships and the ties to the individual who was the incumbent made some people unhappy or maybe sympathetic or even sad but somehow the philosophy held up.

Principals such as Lawrence supported the idea of term appointments because it gave them the opportunity to hire to their concept of the school. This is something Bond had in the early days. From the staff's point of view, control over headship appointments was one of the few ways in which they can feel truly empowered. The idea of term appointments has been adopted at a few schools in the South Board, but not in the comprehensive form operating at Byron.

Throughout, this chapter has tied structure and culture closely together. It was suggested that changes in structure affect culture, and conversely changes in culture influence structures. The development of a humane but rigorous learning culture for students and teachers motivated the original plan that Bond and his colleagues tried to put into place. To promote this kind of culture, the originators of Byron restructured the use of time, altered spaces, and rearranged the roles and responsibilities of staff members. For the most part, with a few previously mentioned exceptions, structures unique to Lord Byron disappeared over time, which resulted in changes to the cultural patterns that made them effective. Chapter 7 continues this discussion of the interaction between structure and culture by focusing on the changing nature of Byron's organizational culture over its history.

CHAPTER 7

Culture

As stressed in the previous chapter, Lord Byron's structural innovations were designed to encourage a more humane and inclusive culture for students, staff, and parents of the school. Since structure and culture became inextricably intertwined, and concurrent (Fullan, 1993), this chapter attends to the other side of the equation—culture. Contemporary change strategies such as school effectiveness tend to look at the parts of schools rather than the interconnections (Fink & Stoll, 1998; Hargreaves, 1994; Stoll & Fink, 1996). Similarly, school-improvement processes tend to focus on rather linear rational planning models, which are useful in a predictable world but less valuable when the future is unknowable (Stacey, 1995). Neither school effectiveness nor school improvement alone has proven satisfactory in effecting change (Fink & Stoll, 1998). The reason, as Little (1982) explains, is that

> the school as a workplace has proven extraordinarily powerful. Without denying differences in individual skills, interests, commitment, curiosity or persistence, the prevailing patterns of interactions and interpretations in each building demonstrably create certain possibilities and certain limits. (p. 338)

THE CULTURE LENS

Fullan (1993) goes so far as to suggest that what is needed in contemporary change efforts is not restructuring but reculturing: "Changing formal structure is not the same as changing norms, habits, skills and beliefs" (p. 49). Wheatley (1994) refers to "fields" in the natural world as unseen forces whose presence is known only through their effects. Magnetism and gravity are two examples. Culture is an example of a "field" in the social world. Change agents tend to concentrate on tangible structures to the exclusion of those forces that are unseen, but represent the interconnections and interrelationships in the organization that make the organization whole. The reason of course is that culture is not only hard to define, but difficult to identify and difficult to change. As mentioned previously, the simplest definition is that of Deal and Kennedy (1983), who describe culture "as the way we do things around here" (p. 4). Culture is a "way of life" (D. H. Hargreaves, 1995). It defines reality for those who work in a social organization; it also provides support and identity and "forms a framework for occupational learning" (A. Hargreaves, 1994, p. 165).

David Hargreaves (1995) offers one way to analyze a total school culture. His model is based on two dimensions, the instrumental domain, which includes social control and an orientation to the task, and the expressive domain, which includes social cohesion through the maintenance of positive relationships. Four types of school cultures sit in different and extreme places on the two dimensions:

- traditional—low social cohesion, high social control—custodial, formal, unapproachable;
- welfarist—low social control, high social cohesion—relaxed, caring, cozy;
- hothouse—high social control, high social cohesion—claustrophobic, pressured, controlled;
- anomic—low social cohesion, low social control—insecure, alienated, isolated, "at risk."

He proposes a fifth culture, that of an effective school:

- effective—optimal social cohesion, optimal social control—fairly high expectations, support for achieving standards.

As he explains, schools tend to fit into one category or another, but schools display characteristics of more than one type. In fact, large schools may display several different cultural types.

Andy Hargreaves (1994) offers five fairly distinctive types of teacher subcultures. The first suggests another way to look at school culture—from the perspective of the teachers working in a school. He considers the most pervasive subculture that of teacher individualism. Reinforced by self-contained classrooms, teachers operate in isolation, not only from one another but also from ideas and outside influences—not only is blame avoided, so is support. This individualism is distinguished from individuality—the power to exercise independent discretionary judgment—and solitude—"a withdrawal to delve into one's personal resources, to reflect retreat and regroup" (p. 180).

The second type is collaborative. Collaborative working cultures tend to be spontaneous because they emerge from the teachers themselves as a social group. They are also voluntary since collaboration is initiated by teachers in response to perceived needs. Since teachers work together on projects to which they are committed, collaboration is development oriented, and characterized by informality and unpredictability. The outcomes of collaboration that is teacher-directed and flexible in the use of time and space are uncertain and therefore unpredictable (A. Hargreaves, 1994, pp. 192–193).

A third type of culture A. Hargreaves (1994) calls "contrived collegiality." It differs from a collaborative culture in that it is initiated and regulated by management. It is therefore usually compulsory. Staff members are compelled to work jointly as opposed to doing so of their own free will, and to work together to implement the mandates of others. Management, therefore, determines meeting times and places to ensure a high degree of predictability of outcomes from the teachers' efforts.

A. Hargreaves (1994) explains that the fourth type, a "balkanized" culture, has low permeability because subgroups within the school are isolated from one another. At the same time the structure and membership of each subgroup have high permanence over time. People therefore become attached to the subculture such as a secondary school department, often to the detriment of the school as a whole. Teacher subcultures are not only a source of loyalty but also "repositories of self interest." Subcultures compete for power within the larger environment, which results in some being more influential than others (pp. 213–215).

A. Hargreaves's (1994) fifth cultural type borrows Toffler's (1990) metaphor of the "moving mosaic." In this subculture, teachers group and regroup based on problem-solving requirements. The emphasis is on flexibility and teachers' continuous learning. This culture is characterized by collaboration, opportunism, adaptable partnerships, and alliances.

Whereas both David Hargreaves (1995) and Andy Hargreaves (1994) concentrate on the "forms" of culture, Deal and Kennedy (1982) provide a useful way to analyze the "content" of an organization's culture. Deal and Kennedy suggest that a culture is composed of the shared values that are espoused and acted on. Some schools advocate child-centered learning, others emphasize preparation for the world of work, and still others stress the traditional humanist values of the academic school. To understand the culture it is useful to identify the heroes, among staff *and* students. How could one study the famous Summerhill school without knowing about A. S. Neil (1960, 1966)? School rituals and ceremonies tell an observer a great deal about who and what is valued in the school. In some schools for example, where football defines small communities, the athletes are honored at pep rallies and given time off school for practice, while academics and the arts do not enjoy this kind of support. The stories people tell provide "concrete examples of values and heroes who triumphed by following the culturally prescribed ways" (Deal, 1987, p. 6). Each school has its informal priest/esses, gossips, spies, and storytellers "whose primary role is to reinforce and protect the existing way" (p. 6) and provide clues to the cultural networks that communicate the cultural norms to newcomers to the school. This structure was used in my interview schedule to delve into the culture of Lord Byron. The following analysis of culture in the school, however, attempts to integrate both the content and the form of culture.

CULTURE AND LORD BYRON

New schools such as Byron have a unique opportunity to create structures and also to create a school culture where none had previously existed. The challenge for Bond was to design structures that would contribute to his vision of a student-oriented school and a culture in which teachers work together to provide each student with the best possible learning experiences. There are, however, no guarantees—changing structures does not necessarily create predictable cultures. Culture is so subtle that two schools with exactly the same structures can have quite different cultures (Schein, 1985).

Years of Creativity and Experimentation

Bond, however, had one other advantage that principals of established schools do not: He could hire most of his staff. By communicating his sense of meaning for the school, designing a physical and organizational structure based on this vision, and then recruiting appropriately, he was able to encourage a culture that was collaborative while recognizing and encouraging individual differences. Elsewhere, I have (with Louise Stoll) detailed the cultural norms of a collaborative school. The following discussion uses these norms in relationship to Lord Byron in its early years (Stoll & Fink, 1996).

Shared Meaning. Rosenholtz (1989) contends that "the key difference between moving schools and stuck schools lies deep within the organizational goals: whether or not they exist, how they are defined and manifested, the extent to which they are mutually shared" (p. 13). The consistency and repetitiveness with which Lord Byron respondents, quite removed in time and space from Byron, articulated its original goals and directions were quite astonishing. Before I began this work I had always thought that Byron might have prospered more over the years if the original staff had developed a mission statement and a set of written goals. Such an activity would have been redundant. If Byron lost momentum over time, it was not because of a lack of clarity of goals. As one very experienced teacher who left Byron shortly after Bond departed because she felt the school's tone had changed recalled:

> Byron kids came in and the staff were saying we are all here for one purpose, we are all here for a common goal. Kids were also empowered. At the end of a course they were encouraged to evaluate and talk about things and they got to the point where they could offer very constructive criticism. Sometimes they just needed to know why they were doing certain things. I found that really good so that they had a sense of a common goal. It is not abdicating power it's just working together rather than separately. We were told that we were going to get rough kids when the school opened. They came from rough areas and these were not ideal kids to be starting a new school with and yet they were wonderful and very encouraging and very helpful.

She went on to explain that students in her present school are not as well educated because government requirements have narrowed the programs for students. She added that her present students

> don't have the same attitude. Partly at Byron the staff attitude was infectious because the staff was hired to a purpose and had a goal and a mission. Whereas now the staff here does not have any particular purpose or goal and so they have different priorities in life. We can't get the staff to agree on anything including enforcing school rules. We didn't have that problem at Byron.

A present-day principal in the Byron Women's Group believed the difference between Byron and most schools then and now was that "in the beginning of Byron, we knew where we were heading, we knew what the bottom line was, and we knew our scope within there." This "bottom line" focused directly on students' academic and social growth and development.

Responsibility for Success. A major tenet of the effective-schools literature is that all students can learn and achieve (Edmonds, 1979). Schools that make a difference for students have positive expectations for all students (Mortimore et al., 1988). This optimism is vital to any reform process if it is to have a chance to succeed. As Joyce and Murphy (1990) state:

> School improvement efforts depend on the belief that curriculum, instruction, and social climate affect student learning. If the culture of a school is permeated with a belief that the causes of student learning lie largely outside the school, in the genes and social background of the students, school improvement efforts appear hopeless and even ridiculous. (p. 248)

Much of my interview with George Owens dwelt on the challenges he faced as principal of the school in the turbulent early 1980s. When we began to talk about the early 1970s when as chairman he had pioneered innovative approaches to the teaching of English to students regardless of their ability levels, his face lit up, and his old optimism resurfaced as he asserted: "I still think if we had been there 20 years later we could have sustained that establishment." He went on to elaborate how much the collective efforts of staff members in his own department and from across the school had meant to him both professionally and personally. "I guess that period really sustained me, interested me. I learned so much from my friends, I learned how to manage people."

Collegiality. When the original staff arrived at Byron 2 weeks before the school opened, there was no curriculum, few resources, no procedures or policies. As Bond described the situation:

> Set aside all the things that would normally go with equipping a school—the ordering etc.—set that aside, and just take into account the factors involved in writing program to fit the philosophy of continuous progress: writing program to fit into a semester, the one hour period, the need to change instruction that had to take place, add to all that over 7,000 visitors, then you see the challenge for teachers.

Bond had articulated a broad set of operating principles, designed the comprehensive structure, recruited the staff; now the rest was up to the staff. As a member of the women's group described the situation:

> We were into something together that was really powerful and created its own dynamics and we brought our own excitement to it. It was a young staff and when things got rolling a lot of stuff spun off. It was a school that operated on ideas that were significantly ahead of their time. A high level of collegiality was expected by people who were there. They simply assumed they worked in teams and partnerships. I haven't seen that degree of interdependence and influence until very recently at a school. An off-shoot of that is that the staff felt very strongly that they owned the school as much as the kids or the administration did. And I think that accounts to some extent for the increase in women's interest in leadership.

Another teacher who left Byron in 1980 to work at another innovative school said, "It just broke my heart to leave. We really tended to give our lives to the school. I used to dislike holidays because I had to leave. I was not originally into the togetherness thing but I developed a liking for it." A member of the women's group described collaborating at student promotion meetings: "I remember those huge teams of people who would meet and we would look at every single report card. We discussed the kind of follow up we would do for each student."

Collegiality just happened, almost spontaneously. It was not planned as a separate project or initiative. Although the school building facilitated collaborative action to some extent, in many ways it occurred out of necessity. The size of the task, the urgency to get the operation running, the considerable public scrutiny of other professionals, many of whom hoped the school would fail miserably, compelled the staff to collaborate, if for no other reason than to survive. As Owens had stated, "We were like most 'paradigm pioneers,' we felt we were on the right track but couldn't prove it empirically." As a staff, it dedicated itself to continuous improvement and rigorous evaluation of all aspects of the school's operations.

Continuous Improvement. This commitment to improvement was one of Byron's great strengths in relation to other schools but also a source of frustration and exhaustion. The preamble to the terms of reference for the 5-year evaluation of Lord Byron stated:

> Lord Byron has already been the subject of more evaluation by more people than any other school in the region. The thousands of visitors who have visited the school have expressed their opinion. The annual evaluation report of the assistant superinten-

> dents and the Superintendent of Instruction and other members of the Executive Committee have been completed each year. The school has been the subject of study by faculty members at O.I.S.E. [Ontario Institute for Studies in Education] and McArthur College. But perhaps the most thorough evaluations have been those conducted annually by the school itself in surveys of parents, students and staff. Certainly, these internal studies have been among the most rigorous done on the school and they have some added validity because they are based on the school's objectives.

In 1975, the External Evaluation Committee reported on Byron's commitment to continuous evaluation for improvement:

> The large amount of documentation produced by the Byron staff over the years attests to this commitment. At the same time this commitment caused our group serious concern. In essence we wonder if Lord Byron is "evaluating itself to death." Evaluation consciousness is praiseworthy; too much may be counter productive.

The wisdom of this prediction was to become evident over time. The staff members who came to Byron in the first few years had an almost messianic sense that they were venturing into unknown territory and that a progressive, optimistic, student-oriented direction for education in South depended on Byron's success. At the same time, as a teacher who was there in the early 1970s declared, "We were always on display, trying to do things in a way that hadn't been done before." Others, like Owens, confessed to ambiguity about this boldness: "I had nowhere to look to sustain the innovations especially process writing. Sometimes I would wake up at two o'clock in the morning and say I have created a monster and didn't know how to sustain it."

A combination of the meaning of their work and the fear of failure derived from the uniqueness of their efforts, as well as Byron's high profile, contributed to "hothouse" tendencies (D. H. Hargreaves, 1995). The continual internal scrutiny at its best led to improvements, but pushed too far led to fatigue and a "siege mentality." As Bond was to reflect years later, in addition to the workload what really hurt was "the sniping at what we were doing, and sniping in the sense that the critics would not accept the invitation to come and see what was going on. They simply wanted to find fault and pick at what we were doing from a base of no knowledge, so that created stress." It also created a pressure to demonstrate by the best empirical, rational methods available (what George Bernard Shaw called "brute sanity," quoted in Fullan, 1991, p. 96) that Byron was indeed a better way. The effort for the most part was futile, because the critique was largely emotional and nonrational. Byron people did not understand that at the time, but the effort helped to shape a culture of continuous, almost frenetic, search for improvement and justification.

Learning Is for Everyone. In the 1975 evaluation report, the External Evaluation Committee reported on 5 years of professional development:

> Each year a theme has been determined, and all programs dealt with the particular theme. It is worthy of note that professional development programs have almost totally replaced "staff meetings." The program for the first two years dealt with the building of curriculum. . . . In the ensuing years, topics have included:
>
> 1. Teacher Effectiveness Training,
> 2. Reality Therapy,
> 3. The School and Society,
> 4. The Community School,
> 5. Stress and How to Handle It.
>
> After four years of involvement of experts from outside the school, there is developing an increased utilization of the expertise within our own staff (e.g., workshop by G. O. on the Therapeutic Community), and teachers are now traveling to other centers in search of stimulation and innovative practices. In conclusion, professional development has always been an important aspect of the Byron program. (p. 70)

This focus on professional development was unique in the region, if for no other reason than D.S.F. (differentiated staffing funds) enabled Byron to finance it. The choice of topics reflects the changing nature of issues confronted by Byron, and the culture of intellectual inquiry that developed in the early years. As Owens reflected, "The one thing about Byron above all other schools was simply intellectual acuity. People were thinking at a level I haven't met in other schools."

Byron's approach to professional development was unique in the system at the time. While most teachers in other schools were usually involved in subject-based professional development, the teachers at Byron attended to schoolwide issues. Most learning opportunities in the region might better be described as in-service in that teachers were treated like quasi-professionals who must be exposed to the "right" way to do things. The Byron approach tended to be more professional because it came from the needs identified by the staff, not the principal or central office. From the beginning, the professional development committee was a major school committee. This group, which was broadly representative of the staff as a whole, was provided with funds to develop a professional program that teachers identified as useful and necessary. Each June staff members were surveyed to determine issues for the program in the next school year.

Risk Taking. Each new year at Byron meant "constant change, constant experimentation." It also implied learning from mistakes. Bond created an ethos in which teachers learned from mistakes "because mistakes were open and acknowledged." "At Byron we decided if we made mistakes we were allowed to learn from those mistakes." One teacher provided an example from the early 1970s:

> I remember doing an English course in grade 11 where I did it on a contract basis. I made up dozens of units and put a point value on them for the amount of work involved in research. I noticed that I hadn't taken into consideration the fact that by the end of the course they didn't know each other and the whole social element was missed so I decided that was not a good system. Social interaction is important and they weren't getting it because they would go off in their own little niche and do their thing and I was not happy with that. Things like that would come up and you could see that educationally they were sound but there was an element missing.

Experimentation implies making mistakes. In a highly visible and antagonistic environment mistakes become magnified, publicized, and criticized (Fletcher et al., 1985; Hargreaves et al., 1992). When this happens the experimenters pull back to the "tried and true," and learning ceases. Experimentation leads to higher levels of learning only if it is sustained by the environment and supported by the administration. Bond created this ethos.

The teacher quoted above described Bond's style:

> I appreciated him more after the fact than at the time but in retrospect when I look back probably one of the things that made him a good leader was that he could talk about what you had done

> and say—he would remember and come back a couple of weeks later and say "how did such and such work out" and I would say, it was either "great" or it "bombed." If it bombed, he would say "did all of it bomb or did only part of it bomb? Do you have to change it all?" It became a questioning routine so that it got you thinking again as to the evaluation of it and then you would start over again and make the changes you needed.

Bond had made the need to support staff experimentation very clear in 1970 when he stated, "The most significant contribution to the success of our experimental position at Lord Byron will be made by the staff. It is obvious but worth stating, that all other aspects will fail if staff does."

Support. Byron provided the support of the chairmen, secretarial resources, instructional assistants, guidance personnel, and remedial teachers to assist in the classrooms. These resources were purchased through the differentiated staffing funds. Perhaps more important was the informal support teachers received from colleagues. A member of the women's group remembered the support from her department: "You couldn't come into our workroom and say I've got a problem without everybody leaping up and saying, 'well Jane here is how you can do it,' or 'here is an idea, try that, or have you read such and such.'"

Respect for Differences. The originating staff at Byron had many things in common—youth, idealism, and a work ethic. At the same time there was great diversity. One-third of the staff was female, which was a somewhat higher percentage than that in other schools at the time. There were four visible minority staff members in a system that at the time was white and middle class. A few staff members came with reputations as nonconformists in previous settings. This diversity was honored and encouraged. As a female teacher who was in her second year of teaching when she was transferred to Byron recollected, "There was a real feeling that every staff member was important and his or her point of view was taken into consideration. It was assumed they could take care of things in their classroom and could take on a new idea and follow it."

Another commented:

> You could "dare to be what you are." There was that element that you could be what you were, you did not have to leave yourself at the door, so you were what you were. It was not just walking in

> and knowing who you are, it was learning. Part of the whole discovery of yourself was what was professional and what was personal.

At the same time, this diversity created some competition within the framework of a cooperative enterprise. An experienced teacher, who came to Byron to restart his career, stated that "all staff were friends but there existed an intense competition among staff which stimulated more change." Still another teacher asserted that "we were listened to and had input into decisions and had to work in a cooperative way, but also [when conflict did occur] worked at conflict resolution. It seemed that people didn't just come out of those things just territorially, but there was a school view of things."

Another teacher who had come from another South school commented that "my previous school was very cliquey. At Byron, everything was new and with the new kinds of learning it meant that everyone was working with different people. There was a much bigger mix at Byron."

Openness. The staff room was a very positive place. Bond made few rules but he did insist that the only coffee pot was to be in the staff room. His rationale was that he wanted people to meet informally as a staff rather than congregate in department workrooms. He knew from his previous experience the problems of what has more recently been called secondary school "balkanization" (A. Hargreaves, 1994). The staff room was the focus of lively debate, the development of ideas, celebrations, and—with such a young staff—even a few romances. A teacher who came to Byron from Roxborough said that "there was less judgment and less categorizing and less bad mouthing of kids in the staff room than in any other school that I have been in and fewer divisions among the staff. The staff often disagreed, and there were often passionate disagreements, but there wasn't any nastiness." Another teacher stated, "We had a really talented and diverse staff, but it was also accepting of the differences of others." Virtually every respondent who was on the staff at Byron in the early years commented in one way or another on the openness of discussion, the willingness to share ideas and materials, and the acceptance of diverse opinions. They also commented on the joy, the humor, and the celebrations that characterized the culture in these early years.

Celebration and Humor. A principal at Byron in the 1980s declared: "Byron is a place of rituals and ceremonies and always has been, the staff covet them." Interestingly, many of the ceremonies involved interaction with students. People who were interviewed mentioned the combined student-teacher band, teacher involvement with intramural basketball, and so on. At the same time, the staff would adjourn almost en masse to the local pub on Friday night to replay the previous week. Byron parties in people's memories were always described as interesting and great fun. Sleigh rides, wine-tasting parties, corn roasts, and golf tournaments were part of the culture in the first few years. Bond loved a good party and rarely missed one. The relative youth of the staff meant that humor, high spirits, and enthusiasm were part of the culture. "We used to congregate more. There were a lot of type A personalities." The humor was never cynical, at least about the students, nor was it sexist or racist because of the strong presence of women and visible minority staff members. The importance of humor in a school culture has been well documented (Woods, 1979).

Overreaching and Entropy

As Garner recalled when he became Byron's principal in 1984:

> I had heard before, you know, the way they collaborated to a great extent. I think by the time I got there that was not happening to the extent that it was before. One of the things I really had to work hard on, was to really encourage staff in the same subject area to work together. I required grade levels to meet. Some departments weren't operating the way they should have.

Norms of Isolation and Separation. By the mid-1980s, the cultural norms of collaboration, shared goals, and risk-taking that had characterized Byron in the early years existed only in pockets among groups, and within some departments. At the whole-school level, however, a different set of norms had taken over. Goals were written every year but often ignored. Respondents talked of school policies on discipline that were not pursued by some, others of trying year after year to deal with the insurmountable "reputation" problem and failing. As one teacher reflected, "What did we do, I really don't remember. Except just talk amongst ourselves." A significant number of staff left the school to pursue creative opportunities elsewhere or were transferred by the system. Of those that stayed, some, like Blair Alden, admitted to just "giving up" and retreating into their subjects and departments. Others became active in subcultures, like the union group and the women's group. The Heads' Council was a subculture, and even it divided between those who had been at Byron in its "golden years" and those who had been appointed in the late 1970s and early 1980s. A teacher who joined the staff in the mid-1980s identified the major school subcultures:

> I think there has been a bit of a struggle to try and maintain a bit of the philosophy that was here in the 1970s but there has also been a group that wants to change that. We went through a tremendous transition about 5 or 10 years ago to become like other schools and I think there was a force back then which was pressing for that change. There was a group pressing to keep what Byron already had. These two groups have clashed from time to time.

The old optimism had disappeared, to be replaced by cynicism, disappointment, and divisiveness. The diminishing size of the school tended to have a negative effect on teacher learning. As one teacher who joined the Byron staff in 1971 explained, "In a small school your professional development does not occur within the school, you do not get the same sort of discussion back and forth, how do we modify this, how do you do that."

Norms of continuous improvement and risk-taking were replaced by fears of political or community reaction. Teachers commented on the "increased political scrutiny." As one long-term teacher stated, "Everything you do as a teacher is subject to political scrutiny." "It was much harder to have people work outside the normal school day," one of the women's group recalled. Garner stated that "by the time that I got there we even had difficulty getting people to volunteer for the staff development committee and the funds we did have for it weren't being allocated." As described previously, cooperation at the leadership levels was replaced by acrimony, dissension, and conflict. The staff that celebrated together in the 1970s had changed significantly. One veteran teacher reflected:

> I look back at the corn roasts we had, and you didn't beg people to come and we really had a great time. Now we don't even have a formal Christmas function and those things. I don't know if it is because we've got older and have kids in activities or it's a laid-back attitude—oh, I can't be bothered so you don't have that same bonding. We do things as a department not as a school.

How could a culture that was strongly collaborative in the mid-1970s become so fractured and fragile in a relatively short time? Respondents suggested three reasons in addition to the effects of leadership changes and changes in the school's external contexts: integration of new staff, recruitment of staff, and the rapid enrollment growth and decline.

Integration of New Staff. What emerged in the explosive growth period were two cultures on staff the originals and the newcomers. As one original stated:

> Those of us who started at the school came in with a real sense of what we were trying to accomplish. We talked to each other, to administration, so we had a real sense of culture. We went into school early because things were exciting and new. New people came in who didn't have that sense, and we didn't have the time to develop the same philosophy the school had and they felt isolated.

The women's group identified the same phenomenon:

> I think one of the things we didn't do well was we didn't pick up well with new teachers. We did not have any kind of mentoring program, whatever, to sort of support these people in all the ways they needed to be supported both in the classroom and out. We got too big too fast. We didn't talk to staff.

The group went on to comment on the nature of some of the new people:

> We got so large and it involved so many that they were hired but not trained well.
>
> We were hiring people for their personal qualities but at the same time I don't think we made the time to check them out.
>
> We made a lot of assumptions about what they could do.
>
> We did not check out professional skills. We assumed that their personal presentation was enough.

Recruitment. The careful recruiting of the Bond era crumbled under the weight of the number of people to be hired in a relatively short time span by people who were already overburdened. Quick interviews replaced careful selection. This resulted in a small but nonetheless significant number of new staff members whose actions contributed to the community's negative perceptions of the school.

A few teachers attracted by Byron's "radical" reputation were hired. One former department chair who moved to Roxborough reflected a significant view in the professional community when he claimed that "left wingers gave the school a bad name" and "mistakes were made and foolish things were done." Regardless of motivation, some of these new teachers did "some dumb, dumb things," which negatively affected Byron's image. A few teachers failed to check attendance, gave assignments that required little student effort, and taught courses that were of questionable academic rigor. Some of the people who were hired dressed in jeans, wore open-toed sandals, and used crude language in students' presence. Bond would have considered their behavior unprofessional and not tolerated it. Stories abounded among teachers, and of course among students and their parents, of teachers having students chant mantras in the classroom, not disciplining students who set a fire in the classroom, using coarse language with and to students, assigning make-work projects, and designing experiential courses of questionable academic validity. The stories have been elaborated on as the years have passed. The few teachers of questionable competence and professionalism hired during the great expansion of the mid-1970s did incalculable harm to the "perception and reputation" of Byron.

Growth and Decline. The tremendous growth in student enrollment in the last half of the 1970s created communications difficulties and, as described previously, processes that had been more interpersonal became systematized and bureaucratized. Balkanization occurred not only in relation to other schools but also within the school itself. Collaboration tended to be within departments because school size meant there might be four or five classes of the same grade and subject that required within-department collaboration. As the school population declined in numbers, departments competed for students because student enrollments in various courses protected teachers' jobs. Collaboration decreased not only across the school but also within departments because grades and subjects were often reduced to one or two classes, which precluded internal department collaboration. Rivalries sometimes occurred within departments among teachers with similar experience and qualifications as to who was best suited to stay. As one teacher explained, "It can become difficult for people with low seniority when you bring in someone with higher seniority, then it can become competitive, discussions go on behind people's back, what's going to happen to me." Coherence and team building within the school and within departments became increasingly difficult as teachers came and went in relatively short order. Teachers who knew their tenure at Byron would be short often found it difficult to do the extras that teachers have always done. The same teacher asked rhetorically, "How much interest were you going to put in to the designing of new courses and being innovative when you knew that after one year that you were going to be gone? It really has been in and out for many staff."

The previous discussion reflects the dissolution of staff collegiality and the retreat into balkanized and individualistic cultures. David Hargreaves's (1995) cultural model combines an orientation toward social control and social cohesion. In the early days under Bond, Byron's culture could be described as a combination of "hothouse" and "welfarist" cultures. It had high social cohesion and high social control, and people felt pressured to innovate by the shared expectations and by public scrutiny. The ambience of the school, however, was relaxed and caring, as in a "welfarist" culture. With the rapid expansion and change of leadership, Byron took on the claustrophobic, pressured, and controlled aspects of a hothouse culture and the increasingly welfarist tendency to low social control. By the early 1980s, as a result of declining enrollment and public pressure, Byron would approximate D. Hargreaves's (1995) description of an "anomic" or survivalist culture. This is a culture that has low social cohesion and low social control, in which people tend to feel isolated, alienated, and insecure.

Another approach to cultural analysis is that of Handy (1995b), which uses the metaphor of four Greek gods: Zeus, the club culture; Apollo, the role culture; Athena, the task culture; and Dionysius, the existential culture. In the early years, the South Board was dominated by a "Zeuslike" figure, Jim Sizemore, who ensured Byron's creation. Byron under Bond gave priority to the personal needs of the individual staff members and students, which is a Dionysian quality, structured within an Athenian task culture. As the school grew and less secure principals took over, there was a significant shift to an Apollonian role culture, which tended to replace interpersonal relationships with structures, and aspects of a Dionysian culture in which the school's size and lack of cohesion resulted in a great many teachers doing their own "existential thing" and discrediting the school. This Apollo culture persisted during the years of decline, as the school was obliged to conform to ministry mandates, board policies designed to ensure conformity, and collective agreements that determined the rules for determining surplus teachers. It was a culture characterized by roles, rules, and a lack of commitment to the kind of Athenian task culture that benefits students and makes teachers' work more productive and rewarding.

Each model provides a different focus for cultural analysis. Andy Hargreaves's model (1994) emphasizes the culture of the teaching staff. David Hargreaves (1995) provides a more encompassing organizational description, while Handy's "four gods" approach reflects a leadership-oriented model. Regardless of approach, the cultural pattern that emerges is consistent—from a unity of purpose to division and insecurity, from energy and innovation to entropy and retreat, from a culture that challenged contemporary educational meaning and structures to an environment of rules, roles, and conformity. In the early 1970s, Byron would fit Rosenholtz's (1989) description of a "moving" school. By the mid-1980s it could be considered a "struggling" school. This is a school that is ineffective but attempting to improve (Stoll & Fink, 1996). At no time did the school staff not have the collective "will" to improve, but the conditions that faced them both externally and internally were beyond their skills and energy (Louis & Miles, 1990).

Survival and Continuity

It would appear that Byron in the 1990s has found its comfortable niche. It is no longer the front-runner, the high-profile school, nor by the same token is it the recalcitrant school opposing even the most innocuous changes. As a teacher who joined Byron in the early 1980s explained:

> I would like to think that we are flexible and open. I don't necessarily think that we are trend-setters any more. I think there are other schools now. Looking at the Transition Years coming along, I don't see us in the forefront as doing dramatic new things. I see other schools if anything doing more than we are doing. We are taking a fairly conservative approach.

From a principal's perspective, Dennis Lawrence makes a similar point. We experience "the same kind of resistances that you might find in other schools." He added:

> People learn from their experience. I don't think there is anyone in the school who has been here since the school opened who feels badly about the programs the school has had. I think there are some people however, who feel badly that some things somehow got out of hand, and some programs were misinterpreted by the community, or discipline issues, or whatever issues might have been, were misunderstood by the community and are therefore quite cautious now when change is presented. They want to make sure, in fact good commonsense things, make sure that it's well thought through, that all the ramifications of changes are considered and that things are put into place to communicate the changes. There still are a few people who, as soon as a new idea is presented, the excitement of the new idea makes them want to run as far as they can with it.

A teacher who joined the staff in the mid-1980s commented that

> even in the Transition Years (destreaming grade 9) some of the people who were saying "let's be careful how we implement some of these notions" were people who were here from the first years, but because of prior experiences didn't want us to jump feet first into something that might later turn out not to be as positive as we felt initially and therefore perhaps, to be burned again with the same kind of stigma that Byron had at a period of time in its development.

Another teacher who came to Byron in the late 1980s from a large traditional school in the northern part of the region asserted that "it is no different from either of the schools I taught at before. People consider what has to be changed and they react according to the wisdom of the change."

A Culture of Caution. The evidence seems fairly clear that some of the old change rhetoric—what Goodson and Anstead (1993) called "collective memory"—survives, but Byron has lost the initiative to lead and is content to follow others. At a time when there is comparative stability for staff, when the community appears supportive and the old rivalry with Roxborough is significantly less intense, there is little desire to risk upsetting the status quo. Byron has blended into the mainstream of the continuity of education in South while retaining through its special programs a glimmer of its more open and unique past.

A Congenial Culture. Similarly, it would appear that Byron's traditional congeniality persists. Many respondents commented on this aspect of the school's culture. Betty Kelly observed:

> I came to Byron in 1984 and I had a 3-year-old daughter and a son who would have just been going to kindergarten. These are really intensive years for the parenting role and motherhood and all of that sort of thing. Byron has a tendency to cloister around people on staff and they help one another. There is informal support. They celebrate well and they cry together and out of that comes a real bonding. . . . Byron was really good for me because there was that support and that encouragement to keep going and recognition for what I did.

A female teacher observed:

> I came in the second semester to start at the last minute to cover a couple of geography classes. The one thing that still stands out in my mind is from day one, the staff sort of embraced you and took you in and you immediately became part of them, and there was that sharing and warmth and sense of belonging . . . and I think students sense that very same warmth and openness.

The evidence of congeniality is fairly consistent. People genuinely care about each other and about their students. The bond is particularly strong among the women. While congeniality pervades the total staff, it would appear that genuine collaboration occurs within departments or small work groups. There is evidence of a balkanized culture modified by some interdepartmental cooperation. The school at present has fewer than 700 students. Teachers often teach in more than one department. The reduced size of the total staff, plus the interdependency of cross-departmental teaching, makes schoolwide collaboration somewhat easier. What comes through strongly, however, is a staff that is reticent to take risks, does its job, and will cooperate with change initiatives, but in the present climate of retrenchment is quite content to enjoy the stability for as long as it lasts. Contentment, as opposed to the exhilaration of the early years, is one way to describe the present culture of Byron.

Byron today has more social controls than in the past and less social cohesion. In David Hargreaves's (1995) terms, Byron is tending toward a more formal type of school culture similar to that of Roxborough. Its teacher culture may be described as balkanized (A. Hargreaves, 1994) because professional and personal support tends to be based on departments. The content of Byron's culture also looks quite similar to that of other schools in South. Its commencements are quite elaborate, principals' pictures appear in the hallway, examinations punctuate the school year, and awards and trophies decorate the entrance to the school. Interestingly, however, when people were asked who the school heroes were, Ward Bond's name came up many times from people who had never met him. What Byron was has still not been forgotten.

CHAPTER 8

Teachers' Lives and Teachers' Work

If culture is the shared or collective "way we do things around here," the life-history approach to educational research provides still another analytical way to look at the "attrition of change" in Lord Byron—from the perspective of the changing lives and the nature of the work of its many teachers over time. Ball and Goodson (1985) outline the evolution of the research view of the teacher. They describe the research image of teachers in the 1960s as "shadowy figures" known only through large-scale surveys that focused on the teacher's role. In the late 1960s and the 1970s, researchers using case-study methods (D. H. Hargreaves, 1967; Lacey, 1970; Woods, 1979) examined schooling as a social process and began to look at teacher practice, particularly the ways in which teachers labeled and sorted pupils. "Research thus shifted from blaming the pupil to blaming the teacher" (Ball & Goodson, 1985, p. 7). A third generation of research examined contextual factors (Ball, 1981; Smith et al., 1987) that impinge on teachers' work and lives. Teachers were transformed from "villains" to "victims" or, to some, "dupes" of the system. Goodson (1981) opened another direction when he argued that teachers were active agents making their own histories and he has advocated more contextually sensitive research. Recent literature on the role of women in education (Acker, 1983; Shakeshaft, 1993), teacher life cycles (Huberman, 1992; Sikes, 1985), belief systems (Louden, 1991), and school culture and teachers' lives (A. Hargreaves, 1994; Nias et al., 1989; Rosenholtz, 1989) has provided insight into the connections between teachers' lives and their work. As A. Hargreaves (1991b) has written, however,

> if the research on teachers' lives has one flaw, it is the tendency to explain the relationship between teachers' lives and work in a one-sided way: with the life affecting the work but not vice versa. At its worst, this bias can lend (unintended) support to the deficit-based explanations of teachers' problems when they may actually have their roots in the conditions and management of the workplace. (p. 253)

A. Hargreaves (1995), however, has also cautioned against listening to *the* teacher's voice as though it were monolithic and the only voice worth listening to. In my interviews, therefore, I listened to a cross-section of voices from within the school and across the South system to determine the interaction between teachers' and principals' lives and their work. It became very clear as these interviews proceeded that participation in the Lord Byron experience had a powerful effect on teachers' lives and, conversely, the changing nature of teachers' lives and their professional contexts influenced their working lives. Since the two constructs of *work* and *lives* were interdependent and interactive, I treated them as one larger construct. The following discussion, therefore, focuses on concepts derived from the literature on teachers' lives and teachers' work that have particular relevance for Lord Byron.

THE LENS OF TEACHERS' LIVES AND WORK

Teacher Life Cycles

Life-cycle research (Huberman, 1992; Sikes, 1985) is particularly applicable to a longitudinal study of a school. Over 25 years, people aged; their personal circumstances changed. They changed jobs; they left the school; they sought promotion; they left the profession; their attitudes and values shifted. Sikes (1985) identifies five career phases:

- Phase one is the 21–28 age group. She calls this phase "entering the adult world." At this stage, new teachers are trying out teaching before making a career decision. Their immediate goal is to cope with the job. Huberman (1992) indicates that this phase is characterized by the teacher's preoccupation with self and whether he or she is up to the job. It is a phase in which the beginning teacher attempts to negotiate the difference between ideals and the daily reality of teaching. This survival theme coexists with the teacher's discovery of his or her own classroom, students, and program.
- Phase two involves the 28–33 age group. This is the "30 transition" when teachers decide whether teaching will be their career direction. It corresponds to what Huberman (1988) calls the "stabilizing phase" in which teachers become comfortable in their repertoire in the classroom and their commitment to the profession. This, he suggests, is more difficult for upper-secondary teachers, who tend to be better educated and keep their options open longer. Commitment to the profession, however, means affiliation with an occupational com-

munity. Teachers in this age group according to Sikes (1985) tend to become more interested in pedagogy as their links to their university days and their subjects become more remote.

• Phase three includes the 30–40 age group. As Sikes (1985) indicates, throughout the 30s the conjunction of experience and a relatively high level of physical and intellectual ability means that in terms of energy, involvement, ambition, and self-confidence many are at their peak (p. 48). Huberman (1992) describes this phase as one of experimentation and activism. Teachers at this stage try to increase their impact, face system limitations, and look for challenges. "The implicit theme here is the newly emerging concern with teachers growing stale in their profession, a malady one sees among older peers" (p. 125).

• Phase four, the 40–50/55 age group, is a phase in which teachers take stock of their careers. They tend to become more relaxed and self-accepting. Huberman (1992) suggests that they move from the frenetic pace of their earlier careers to a stage in which diminishing energy is counterbalanced by a greater sense of self-confidence, self-acceptance, and "serenity." It can also become an age of conservatism, nostalgia, and dogmatism. For some men it can be a difficult period. Prospects for promotion are gradually disappearing. Women, however, with their families well underway, often begin to apply for leadership positions. Teachers in this age group are "often authority figures, having taken on a role of maintainer of standards and guardian of school traditions" (Sikes, 1985, p. 52). Both Sikes and Huberman note a pattern of growing conservatism among some teachers as they move into their final career phase. The more positive want to focus on a grade level or a subject or a particular type of student rather than assuming major leadership roles in the school. They will support but not initiate change efforts. Others, disenchanted or disappointed with the direction of their careers or past change initiatives, will disengage and some will become active blocks to change efforts.

• Phase five is the 50/50-plus age group. Huberman (1992) suggests that toward the end of a career, disengagement occurs as teachers look to post-teaching pursuits. Many teachers continue serenely to focus on their teaching, confident of their own abilities and enjoying the rewards of working with young people. This age group, however, is one in which teacher "burnout" becomes a particular problem for schools as many older teachers experience less energy, less activism, less involvement, less idealism, more skepticism, more pessimism.

The implication of life-cycle research is that what motivates and inspires a young teacher to adopt innovative approaches to teaching will be significantly different from the motivation of a "50-something" teacher. Similarly, the challenges teachers found exhilarating at 30 may well be just plain exhausting at 55. The aging of a school staff can have a significant impact on an entire school's willingness, and indeed ability, to continue to be an innovative organization.

Gender Issues

Acker (1995) suggests that the term *career* needs redefinition for both men and women "to capture something of the fragile quality of the career as compromise or bargain at a moment in time" (p. 30). She suggests that life-cycle literature is generally deficient in describing the life cycle of female teachers and tends to explain the imbalances in women's leadership opportunities in terms of the demands of family and domestic concerns. She and others (Edwards, 1994; Shakeshaft, 1993) argue that women are caught in a paradox. They are often turned down for leadership positions because they do not have the required experience, while at the same time they are generally denied the opportunity to gain the requisite experience necessary to apply for formal leadership roles. Acker (1995) also observes that in secondary schools, men tend to be involved with the organizational aspects of the school and women in the counseling and care sides of the school. This, she asserts, gives men an advantage over women.

There is an argument that the counseling type of background combined with women's instructional leadership skills and their ability to develop an inclusionary school community provides them with superior preparation for educational leadership roles. Shakeshaft (1993) offers four answers to her rhetorical question: "If women are as good or better than men, why aren't there more of them as school administrators?" (p. 49). First she argues that the people who hire leaders systematically discriminate against women. "Most of the reason why women do not become school administrators can be explained by understanding that women are not valued as much as men and that bias results in negative attitudes and practices towards women aspiring to be school administrators" (p. 50). Edwards (1994) states that in a British context "the single most significant barrier to women in management was the existence of the men's club network and male prejudice" (p. 4). Both Edwards and Shakeshaft contend that women lack the networks and support systems to help in the search for promotion. Women still carry the burden of child care and homemaking. "The career break for child care reasons still poses a devastating career hurdle. . . . Schools have not proven flexible or women friendly organizations; they remain bureaucratically structured and geared to male career models" (Edwards, 1994, p. 4). Shakeshaft (1993) further indicates that females have lower self-confidence than males. Females will apply only for jobs for which they are qualified, whereas men will apply regardless of qualifications, which explains why there are always more male applicants, particularly at secondary levels. Moreover, females tend to internalize failure and feel that it is because they were not good enough whereas men will externalize failure. On average, it takes women four interviews to land a promotion, which, Shakeshaft (1987) states, is why many give up. The final reason Shakeshaft offers for the dearth of women in educational leadership roles is their alleged lack of aspiration to leadership positions. Studies, she contends, do not support this view, but it has become part of the "folklore." Women generally are not as high-profile as men and are given fewer opportunities to exercise informal leadership. "To further complicate matters, women have been taught that a womanly virtue is modesty; thus women are more likely to give others credit for the work they have done" (p. 52).

Intensification

Another area in which Acker (1995) challenges conventional thinking from a feminist point of view is the "intensification thesis." Intensification means extracting more work in the same amount of time in order to reduce labor costs and increase productivity. Mandated curricula, packaged lessons, standardized testing, among other practices, reduce teachers' professional discretion and have, according to some, resulted in the intensification of teachers' work (Apple, 1986), the deskilling of teachers (Apple & Teitelbaum, 1986), guilt (A. Hargreaves, 1994), and "burnout" (Byrne, 1994). Efforts to use school-based management as a vehicle to deliver government policies have met with teacher indifference and cynicism (Smyth, 1991) and divided teachers from their principals (Bishop & Mulford, 1996). Apple (1986) sees these efforts as part of an ongoing government strategy designed by men to proletarianize women. Teachers, women in particular, expend extra effort to effect change in a misguided notion that this "intensity" is what is required to be a professional. Acker (1995) challenges this interpretation. She suggests that government reforms do not just involve low-level trivial activities but rather require higher-level skills to rethink curriculum, pedagogy, and teacher collaboration. Acker contends that it is time "to stop generalizing about all (women) teachers and give them credit for being able to distinguish among 'good' and 'bad' forms of intensification" (p. 110). A. Hargreaves (1991b) offers a similar view when he suggests that the time and effort teachers "commit to their teaching and preparation comes not so much from grudging compliance with external demands as from dedication to doing a good job and providing effective care within a work context that is diffusely defined and has no clear criteria for successful completion" (p. 13). It would appear that feelings of intensification affect some teachers more than others. What some teachers may view as professional challenge others view as top-down pressure. Intensification seems to be tied more closely to the life and career cycles of more mature teachers who have assumed more responsibilities and are experiencing a decline in physical powers. A shared staff sense of the increased intensification of work may well be a symptom of the attrition of change in a school. Symptoms of intensification became evident when Byron teachers, when interviewed, stopped talking about the excitement and exhilaration of the school and instead used words like *exhaustion* and *burnout.*

Teacher Burnout

Feelings of intensification unrelieved by professional rewards can lead to teacher burnout. This is a topic of considerable contemporary interest, particularly in North America. Byrne's (1994) comprehensive survey of the literature on the topic indicates that burnout is a multidimensional construct comprised of three distinct but related facets: emotional exhaustion, depersonalization, and reduced personal accomplishment. She describes two personal factors that affect teachers' attitudes toward their roles. First, teachers who feel powerless to control events that affect their working lives are candidates for burnout. Among these needs are control and access to resources seen as necessary to ensure success for students. Firestone and Pennell (1993) list five different types of resources that act as "hygiene factors" (Herzberg, 1976) for teachers: an orderly environment, administrative support, adequate physical resources, adequate instructional resources, and reasonable workloads (pp. 508–509).

Byrne's (1994) research also indicates that

> it seems apparent that self-esteem is a critical and controlling factor in the predisposition of teachers to burnout. In addition to having an important and direct effect on perceptions of personal accomplishment, self-esteem appears to function as an essential mediator variable through which effects of environment-based organizational factors filter. (p. 667)

Teacher self-esteem or self-concept is a function of a teacher's self-perceptions (Purkey & Novak, 1984). Their perceptions of self are influenced by their responses to career cycles, gender expectations and aspirations, the changing nature of their work, and the pressures that in some create burnout. A number of studies described symptoms of burnout in new and innovative schools—for example, frustration with criticism (Fletcher et al., 1985; Moon, 1983), unappreciated work effort (Anderson & Stiegelbauer, 1990; Gold & Miles, 1981), and changed life-cycle pressures (Evans, 1983). In combination, these aspects of teachers' work and lives provide an insightful lens through which to view the conditions that affected teachers and other staff members at Lord Byron.

LORD BYRON AND ITS TEACHERS' LIVES AND WORK

An important aspect of the Byron story was its impact on the lives of its staff and conversely the influence of staff members' career and life cycles on Byron's development. To probe the interrelationship between teachers' lives and their work at Lord Byron, all respondents were asked to describe the nature of their work at Byron, how their work had changed over time, and how the Byron experience impacted on them both personally and professionally.

Years of Creativity and Experimentation

Other studies concerning the initiation of new schools (Hargreaves et al., 1992; Moon, 1983; Sarason, 1972) make the case that such schools require a tremendous amount of work by teachers. Byron was no exception. Virtually every interview subject who was on the Byron staff in the first 5 years commented on the scale of the task that confronted them. As one teacher said, "You had to be a workaholic." She described the workload this way:

> It was heavy. It was incredibly heavy. If you wanted something to teach for the next day you had to make it because there was nothing available. In designing courses and redesigning courses, every day you would come out and say what worked and what didn't work and can I progress with this tomorrow or do I have to change something for tomorrow. You were constantly writing program and it was exhausting but it was exhilarating. I found it a much heavier workload.

This theme of "exhaustion" but "exhilaration" pervaded teachers' comments. "I worked like mad writing programs for five grades. I worked harder than I have ever worked—all departments did." Another teacher recalled that "the early years were inspiring. There was a lot of altruism. People came to work because they thought they were doing something for humanity—more than a job, it was a mission." Another teacher declared, "I became a teacher at Byron. I wrote more, I created from the ground up. Our units are still floating around the county. I keep hearing bits and pieces of things we used to do."

The evidence collected suggests that the intensification thesis developed by Apple and others (Apple, 1986, Larson, 1980) did not apply to the Byron staff in the early 1970s. The combination of hard work and satisfaction suggests that people did not feel exploited. As one teacher indicated, "At Byron you tended to walk until you dropped—at least you had a sense of satisfaction out of it. Now you have the feeling what the hell have I done, there is not the satisfaction that goes with it." As long as teachers felt that the expenditure of time and energy enhanced students' learning and provided professional rewards, intensification would not be a problem. For many of the people I interviewed, their commitment to Lord Byron went beyond just professional commitment; it tended to influence—indeed, for some, to consume—their lives outside of school as well.

For most of my respondents who were at Byron during the creative, experimental years in the early 1970s, the experience was a turning point not only in their professional lives but also in their personal lives. An extended conversation among members of the women's group is illustrative:

> The kinds of relationships you build in that kind of pressure cooker situation were very difficult to repeat—a pressure cooker in that you shared so many things and the hours we were putting in and so on. There was very little time outside the school. Do you remember Friday nights at the "Pig" [the local pub]?
>
> I certainly do.
>
> We were in this together and I think you are referring to the spill-over into our individual personal lives. I just can't separate those. All through my 13 years, I cannot separate that experience from my development in every aspect as a principal. It is inseparable. It was so important in every way.
>
> You think of yourself as a teacher, you think of yourself as a woman, and it all just grows.

> My time was absolutely a turnaround for me personally. I wasn't being facetious when I said I came there and I didn't want to take on any visible roles. It really totally changed my approach. I never would have had the confidence to move ahead without the support of women. It was just absolutely without parallel. I also have to say the support of men, because when I think of the acceptance that I felt that I got from the men that I was working with.
>
> You learned that women needed to have feedback about what they did, not just how they looked. When we started getting lots of positive feedback about that kind of thing and when we started talking about people growing and learning and that kind of stuff, I think that was really important. I also felt that there was an expectation that if you were at Byron you would take something from Byron and take it somewhere else. You didn't have the right to stop where you were—that you had a responsibility to take it on—it was not optional.
>
> Right, after a while you just became that. You took it even if you were not trying to. You took it somewhere else because it was as much a part of your thinking and your way of relating to other professionals, men or women.

As the foregoing discussion suggests, women at Lord Byron found a voice, and a vision of a different role for women within education. By networking and inviting the support of influential men within Byron, many of the women of Lord Byron have been promoted within the South system and beyond.

The professional impact of Byron on its originating staff has been significant. Of the 76 Byron staff members in 1972, there were 49 men and 27 women. Only six staff members, four women and two men, left the profession prematurely. Among the staff members who continued in the profession, 65% of both the women and the men have gone on to leadership roles. Part of this pattern can be attributed to the age of teachers and selection criteria, as well as the supportive culture at Byron. Approximately 30% of the teachers at Byron would then be in phase one of Sikes's (1985) life-cycle scheme, the 21–28 age group, and in their first few years of teaching. Over 90% of them have continued in the profession. Only four Byron teachers were over the age of 40. All the department chairs were in phase three of Sikes's categorization, the 30–40 age group, which Huberman (1992) describes as an age of "activism and experimentation." Clearly, Bond had chosen staff members who were at their most energetic and productive career stages. The only teachers Bond did not select were those who were "force transferred" to Byron.

The relative youth of the staff and the level of commitment to the Byron concept had significant impact on teachers' personal lives. As one male teacher reflected, "We let it happen at Lord Byron, I was working long hours and barely saw my family." This resulted in a trend that gave Byron a reputation for changed personal relationships. Whether Byron's record in this regard was different from that of other schools is difficult to determine, but using the 1972 staff list, 12 people (six couples) on staff left one marriage to enter into a relationship with a colleague on the Byron staff. Perhaps the most cogent explanation was provided by a female teacher:

> People who did come to the school in the beginning came with a focus, they were hired on to the mission of the school. They were all young, strong minded, very creative, very leadership oriented people. When you get a group of people in circumstances together like that with that type of personality working long hours, and they all want to see change happen things are going to happen.

Most people interviewed suggested that the early years placed stress on personal relationships. For some, the school became life itself. A relationship that had been in some jeopardy when the teacher joined Byron was on occasion further damaged by the long hours, the emotional commitment to a task, and socialization with like-minded people. These conditions often exist in more conventional schools. Innovative schools, such as Byron in its years of creativity and experimentation, because of their "hothouse" cultures, do appear to place greater pressures on personal relationships than do other schools.

Overreaching and Entropy

External contextual factors may have accelerated the struggles, but changes in the staff itself over the 15 years from the school's inception also contributed to the attrition of change at Lord Byron.

The Graying of Byron. By 1985, only 14 of the 65 staff members at Lord Byron had been there in its first few years. All of the 14 were over 40 years of age and 7 were over 50. The average age of the staff was close to 40 years of age. The impact of declining enrollment resulted in a complement of very few teachers with less than 5 years of experience and a majority with over 10 years of experience. An experienced teacher who came to Byron as a department head commented that "the decline [in enrollment] meant that there was not a wide number of people to choose from, especially young people who could be dedicated to the school." He added that Byron "had come and gone by the time I got there." George Owens stated that the staff got "older and more tired." Owens reflected that becoming more conservative and more establishment is what happens as you get older, especially if you move into administration. In reflecting on his own career he said, "I was determined to subvert the smug middle class of Middleton" in 1970, but as principal "I tore down the smokers' shed" and attempted "to clean up the place." One long-time female teacher at Byron explained how time had affected many staff members:

> We don't run quite as fast and as far with it [new ideas] as we used to. It was moderated a little because we got older now and you get several things happening. First of all, the energy levels are dissipated by the fact that you have 8 million other responsibilities. When this staff was young, they didn't have kids and didn't have mortgages and they didn't have other domestic responsibilities. Their parents weren't aging, then they had more free time. The collegial relationship was more important so they had more time, it wasn't that they had more energy they had fewer demands outside the profession and also they had fewer experiences to make you a little cynical.

Most people at Byron in 1985 were now in phase-four or phase-five age ranges in which teachers were either "taking stock" of their careers or preparing for retirement (Sikes, 1985). Phase four is a life stage that is "almost as traumatic as adolescence" (p. 52). It is the age span in which children are becoming adolescents and parents are aging. As the previous teacher's comments reveal, it is often a particularly difficult time for women in teaching because women also tend to be the primary homemakers. It is also an age in which some men come to recognize that leadership opportunities are gradually diminishing and that they will probably spend the rest of their careers in the classroom. As both Sikes (1985) and Huberman (1988) suggest, while for some men this can be an age of contentment, others may turn bitter and cynical.

The 40-plus teachers are often the authority figures on staff and have "taken on the role of maintainer of standards and guardians of school tradition" (Sikes, 1985, p. 53). Three of the key in-school union leaders were in this group. As one of these leaders explained, we were an "interested union school. We were never rabid and tried to remain reasonable and supportive." Any militancy tended to be directed toward the system. "There was a lot of anger when differentiated staffing was forced out." Two of these three school leaders became president of the South Secondary School Teachers' Union. One used it as a step toward formal leadership in the system. The other stayed at Byron through the 1980s and provided "expert" leadership to staff members during the discussions about surplus teachers. His detailed knowledge of the contract and procedures resulted in a rather legalistic approach to the problem.

In 1985 there were 12 phase-five teachers, four of whom were department heads. As Sikes (1985) suggests, "senior teachers tend to be in senior posts as heads of departments or faculty and, particularly if they exercise a high degree of control, younger teachers can become frustrated and dissatisfied because they are unable to put their own ideas into practice" (p. 53). At Byron by 1985, we have a picture of an aging staff with some divisions, especially within the department heads group, between the older "keepers of the flame" and younger heads who were more in tune with trends within the province and within South, and ironically more conservative. The opportunities to change this balance of staff were negligible as long as enrollment declined. The principal in 1985, Patrick Garner, described his staff this way: "They certainly didn't have as much energy in all the things that they had been involved in before. Except when you got new staff. When you were able to hire a new head, and then all of a sudden that head would rejuvenate a department, but that's the same in any school." He went on to describe the situation he inherited in 1984:

> There was probably greater reluctance to accept change and to incorporate it into their style. I don't know if that was a function of the school or of the leadership. I do know it is a function of the staff getting older. I think they had been at this for a long time. They had sort of done their thing for many years and got tired. There are many staff members hired on to the Byron staff who were not necessarily hired to the school or to its changes, and I think that is a difference. Originally staff were hired to a concept and then later on the enrollment grew and people were put into Byron because they were surplus to other schools, or hired to fit the leadership of different principals which in some cases was quite different from the leadership style of the first principal.

Only one person on the staff in 1984 has gone on to a leadership role beyond the department level. That person was a female department head who is now a principal. As one observer commented, "the engines of innovation had left the school," "given up," or become frustrated or debilitated by "fighting ghosts" from the past. As one long-time teacher stated, "We got frustrated because the community didn't see it for what it was."

Exhaustion without Exhilaration. Most people who spoke about the workload in the late 1970s and early 1980s still commented on working hard but without the same degree of satisfaction as in the early 1970s. The exhaustion of trying to maintain the best of the Byron tradition in the face of what they saw was an indifferent—indeed, for some, a hostile—administration, board, and parent community just wore on them. People described others as experiencing symptoms of burnout but never admitted to me that they themselves had burned out. A total stranger might have been able to encourage more candor than I did, which is one of the disadvantages of a research project in which the interview subjects are friends and acquaintances of the researcher.

The Question of Burnout. Were Byron teachers burned out from years of striving in the face of adversity? The cumulative evidence suggests that the Byron staff experienced many of the symptoms. One advantage of a large school system like South, however, in which there was growth in some areas, is that teachers could move to other schools or alternative jobs. This proved to be a career-saver for some, and a safety valve for others. By relating Byron to Byrne's (1994) analysis of burnout, it will become clear that all the conditions for staff burnout existed at Byron in the early 1980s. Byrne discriminates between organizational and personal factors. She describes the following organizational factors that contribute to teacher burnout:

- *role conflicts that result from conflicting demands such as demands for both quality and equity in the classroom.* This certainly applied to Byron with its philosophy of equity and its need to compete with Roxborough's academic image.
- *role ambiguity, which is lack of clarity about the teachers' obligations, rights, status, and/or accountability—among these are the custodial and supervisory functions that are added to teaching assignments.* By the mid-1980s, Byron teachers were experiencing the changes brought about by provincial legislation. This meant that more students with learning difficulties and more students with English as

a second language were in teachers' classrooms. At Byron the stress of these changes was exacerbated by enrollment decline, leadership changes, and the teachers' deep feelings of resentment toward their educational and parent communities.

• *work overload, not only in terms of hours of involvement, but also the complexity of trying to meet so many, often conflicting, demands.* Most people who came as teachers and principals to Byron contend that the intensification of work (A. Hargreaves, 1994), if it existed at all, was similar to that experienced in every other school. While the workload was perhaps no heavier than in other schools, Byron teachers seemed to perceive their workload as more intense because they felt unappreciated and certainly misunderstood. The exhilaration that made hard work acceptable in the early years had disappeared. What one teacher had described as a mission had, by 1985, become just a job.

• *classroom climate such as discipline problems, student apathy, and student abuse of teachers "bears critically on teachers' attitudes toward teaching."* (Byrne, 1994, p. 649). As one teacher viewed the relationship with students at Byron: "Coming from the school that I taught at before, I have more behavioral problems in my classroom than I did at the other school so it is a different kind of work. I feel that I don't cover as much of the core content because I'm dealing with behavior. I don't have as much energy. It is more intense in the classroom than it used to be." Certainly attendance, credit completion, and student deportment in the school were issues for the community and an ongoing source of difficulty for the teachers.

• *decision-making that either ignores or permits minimal teacher input.* Confusion as to the decision-making processes continued through the 1980s into the 1990s at Byron, and teachers who had been used to being consulted felt that decisions were being made by either the administration or the heads without consultation and communication. Many tended to vent their frustration by creating a very active and vocal union in the school.

• *lack of social support from both administrators and peers.* As has been stated, this was a pervasive theme at Byron in the late 1970s and early 1980s. As one member of the women's group reflected:

> I probably left 3 years too late, and not because I was burned out, I'd had it. I had to take a year off. I couldn't deal with the pressure any more of working in a school where we talked about the perception and reputation. I couldn't deal with that any more. It just sapped all your energy. To me it was like swimming upstream all the time. It was exhausting and debilitating.

Byrne's (1994) personal factors that affect teachers' attitudes toward their roles seem to fit the Byron of the 1980s. The first is *powerlessness.* Certainly Byron teachers saw the structures in which they believed systematically stripped away by ministry and board decisions. From having abundant DSF money in the 1970s, staff saw resources dwindle dramatically. New secondary schools were built, and many Byron teachers moved to them. Those who stayed often felt their building's needs were neglected, and that others were getting a better deal. Enrollment declined; teachers were asked to teach subjects they had not taught previously or did not like to teach. Some saw courses they had pioneered in the 1970s, and on which they had worked industriously, eliminated from the school's program offerings because of low enrollment. Two department heads left the school in protest over this issue. One in fact moved to Roxborough as a classroom teacher rather than yield to thc inevitable contraction of his department's program.

The second of the personal factors described by Byrne (1994) is *self-esteem.* When teachers use terms like *debilitating, giving up, frustrating, fighting ghosts, betrayal, lack of support,* and *lack of appreciation,* this would suggest that the criticism, the loss of the many high-performing students to Roxborough, the annual scramble from 1977 to 1985 to decide what teachers must transfer to another school, had a profound effect on the self-esteem of teachers at Byron.

Survival and Continuity

Themes of congeniality and contentment permeate teachers' comments about their work and their lives in the 1990s. With the standardization of school organization as a result of ministry mandates and collective agreements between the board and the South teachers' union, Byron people recognize that the intensity of Byron's workload was similar to that of other schools but with some differences. As a veteran teacher observed,

> Teaching is the same in every school—it is open-ended. You can go till you drop. I think the only way the teaching load is any different here is that I think more teachers like what they do. Certainly teachers were happier with their jobs here, and you would hear that at social gatherings.

Another teacher elaborated on this theme: "I really don't see any difference between this school and the other schools. I see the same type of profile where some teachers do a lot, and some teachers do quite a bit and some teachers don't do quite enough. That's probably not too much different than other schools."

Patrick Garner thought that the workload at Byron is no different. He did suggest, however, that the work is different:

> It is part of the culture that there is an expectation that you will form some sort of personal bond with other staff members and with the kids. It is the way we operate around here. But I don't see it as inordinate stress. I think it is just, when you come there, you sort of gradually begin to do those things because other people are doing them and they seem to really work.

A teacher who has stayed at Byron for the past 24 years described the changing nature of his work, but also the adaptability of people at Byron:

> In the 70s there were still jobs for kids who didn't go on to university. I used a mastery approach in which students received either an A, B, or an Incomplete. It was a phenomenal amount of time I put in. It was nothing for me to be here at 6 o'clock at night working with kids and then go home and prepare for the next day. I kept my mark book from that era just to remind me of how hard I worked. The workload we are dealing with now are the social problems the kids bring into the classroom. Kids not knowing where they are going—heading toward. They are bringing into the classroom a lot of society's problems. I don't know whether those issues were as obvious to me back then. In 24 years the social issues have changed, society has changed. They look out there and they see no jobs and for a lot of them it is doom and gloom and they have no idea what to do. On an emotional level I am just as tired as I was back then. There has been a change in how I taught my courses trying to get every kid to complete [his or her work] and having stacks of different quizzes, and kids coming in to take tests or to catch up. Now I teach pretty "lock-step," all the kids do the same things at the same time and then we proceed on. The only place that that is different is the Satellite where they work at their own pace which brings me back to the 70s where kids are doing different things at different rates which makes your workload much different.

This teacher agreed to an assignment in the Satellite unit working with severely learning disabled students to ensure the continuation of a well-qualified but junior science teacher in the school. In commenting about this challenging assignment, this senior teacher acknowledged that his Byron work in the 1970s was important to his transition. "I think I have been able to adapt to that. If I had come from a traditional classroom and into that, I think I probably would have walked out after the first week, and having all these kids asking different questions. Without a doubt, the 70s helped me to adapt to that."

In some ways this theme of general contentment, and to a certain extent disengagement from the larger educational issues, reflects the aging of the staff and Sikes's (1985) fourth and fifth life-cycle stages. Of the 49 staff members in the 1995 school year, 32 were over 40 and 12 were over 50. Two of the nine department heads were also over 40 and 4 were over 50. At the time of this research the principal and the vice-principal were over 50 years of age. Only one staff member was in her first 5 years of teaching. In addition to the normal aging of a staff, enrollment declines in the previous 5 years have meant the continuing loss of younger staff members. Of the people from the 1985 to 1995 era that I interviewed, there appeared to be little of the resentment or cynicism that Huberman (1992) identified as the product of aging among some teachers. While the principals did identify some individuals who could be described as "just getting by" on a daily basis, the general tone of the teachers was one of dedication to their students, their subject areas, their departments. The kind of "pro-Byron" rhetoric that one heard in the early days has for the most part disappeared. At the same time, the people still at Byron appeared more positive than some of the former Byron people who had moved to other settings. Interestingly, while the ratio of males to females remains about the same as in the early years (one to three), six of the nine department heads at the time of the research are female as compared with none in the first 5 years of the school.

A Byron original who left after 3 years describes the situation for her and other teachers in the province in the 1990s:

> Teachers are going to give their best to the kids despite the system, not because of it but it means you try to deal with the kids and fight the system at the same time. I think teaching is not as much fun as it used to be simply because the creativity level has been taken out of it to a large extent. The whole focus of the province on what education means has changed so I think we are not turning out as well educated kids as we were, they are just not as knowledgeable.

The contrast between the collective attitude of the Byron teachers and the attitude of the teacher for whom the "fun" has disappeared may reflect the ability of Byron's staff to adapt to changing conditions over time. The student-first orientation at Byron has enabled it to adapt to the most significant change in education in Ontario during its history—the wide range of student abilities for which schools must now be responsible. Byron has always welcomed a diversity of students and has learned to deal with this range of abilities, while other schools struggle. What has also changed in the past few years is the stability and predictability of education in Ontario. Four changes in provincial governments within 10 years, successively more reactionary school boards in South, and the ongoing budget cuts in education in Ontario have created fear and apprehension in schools. The history of Byron has been fraught with instability and unpredictability, and over time the staff members have learned how to adapt to changing circumstances. It is probably true that they do not work harder or even more intensely than teachers in other schools, but there is some evidence that they do work smarter.

This chapter has particular relevance for contemporary educational policy, which tends to place tremendous stress on the people who have to carry out massive changes in schools—the teachers. This summary has shown how internal and external contextual factors have affected the work and lives of teachers. We have seen examples of "intensification," "deskilling," and "burnout." If relatively slow, almost evolutionary change can have these effects, then dramatic and revolutionary change will take a much larger toll on the work and lives of teachers (Gewirtz et al., 1995) and affect the quality of teaching in classrooms. Moreover, this chapter has dealt with gender issues and teachers' life cycles and suggested that gender and age influence people's responses to change and should be considered by policymakers (Acker, 1995). This chapter completes the examination of Lord Byron through the six frames or lenses of context, meaning, leadership, structure, culture, and the work and lives of teachers. Chapter 9 draws together the various strands of this study to provide a summary of its findings.

CHAPTER 9

Findings

In the Introduction to this book, I posed this question: Is there a "life cycle" to new and innovative schools that leads to the attrition of change? This examination of Lord Byron through six different but interrelated lenses suggests, strongly, that there was a very definite and definable pattern in Byron's evolution. From its creative and experimental origins, Byron evolved through a phase of overreaching and entropy to a third stage of survival and continuity.

WARNING SIGNS

If, as I have argued to this point, there is a life cycle for new and innovative schools, then what are the warning or danger signs of the attrition of change? To provide a summary and to avoid repetitiveness, the following briefly draws together the major factors leading to this attrition by using the conceptual framework that has pervaded this work.

Context. The following contextual factors contributed to the attrition of change:

- changes in the political climate at the central office meant that Byron lost its unique support; there was also the hostility of the educational community, the parent community, and the teachers' union;
- Byron had to compete for students and credibility with Roxborough, a well-regarded traditional school;
- rapid increases in enrollment led to less care in staff selection, problems of integrating large numbers of new staff and students, and pressures on structures designed for a smaller school;
- rapid decline meant the loss of younger teachers, innovative programs, and students to other schools;
- standardized staffing procedures built into the collective agreement meant the loss of younger teachers.

Meaning. The changing meaning of the Byron experience was affected by the following factors:

- the political and ideological climate in the province and the school district changed from one that supported and promoted innovation to one that constrained innovation and change;
- new staff members, not socialized to the Byron philosophy and therefore less committed to its success, especially those teachers "force transferred" to Byron during its growth years;
- the loss of the "critical mass" of innovators who had internalized the Byron ideal;
- the gap between the Byron conception of a "good" school (Lightfoot, 1983) and the public's conception of a "real" school (Metz, 1991).

Leadership. The following factors related to the selection, promotion, and locus of leadership contributed to the attrition of change:

- the early departure of the first principal;
- the change in leadership at the central office meant that Byron had lost its special status in the eyes of the senior administrators of South;
- the promotion of key school leaders out of the school;
- the difficulty of succession planning and the challenge of replacing Bond;
- the breakdown of the decision-making balance between the management, chairs (heads), and staff;
- fewer people on staff felt empowered because so many decisions had been removed from the school by the South Board and the province. When combined with the appointments of more directive principals, this factor resulted in the gradual attrition of the "leader of leaders" concept;
- the micropolitics of the school became more divisive because of contested decision-making procedures, "balkanized" departments, and declining enrollment.

Structure. These structural factors contributed to Byron's retreat from innovation:

- changes in ministry and board policies undermined important innovative structures; union hostility and the growing indifference of senior system managers compromised the innovative staffing patterns;

- the availability of flexible resources ended rather abruptly, forcing readjustment of school procedures;
- walls went up in the building, doors were added, and the physical openness that had facilitated staff and student interaction ended;
- structures like free time for all students did not hold up under the pressure of numbers;
- some innovations like experiential programs and community programming pushed too far, too fast and created serious image problems for the school;
- enrollment decline forced the abandonment of courses, and created inter- and intradepartmental rivalries.

Culture. The following factors reflect changes that took place in the cultural norms of the school over time and further contributed to the attrition of change:

- the shared schoolwide goals of the early years tended over time to inspire less commitment as teachers retreated into their departments and classrooms;
- the collective staff confidence in the school's purposes and activities wavered as a result of the criticism received from other professionals and from segments of the community;
- the collaboration of the creative years turned into "balkanization" and "individualism" (A. Hargreaves, 1994) in the years of enrollment decline;
- the continuous learning of the early years became less of a school focus and more of a department or individual activity, if it occurred at all;
- the changing political and philosophical climate eroded the willingness to innovate, to try, and to risk;
- the spirit of mutual support and help continued throughout Byron's history, particularly among the women, but the focus tended to be on personal more than professional support;
- the diversity of teaching approaches and organizational practices that characterized the early years turned into conformity to the cultural norms of the larger system as external pressures brought Byron "in line" with the expectations of the province and the school board;
- many staff members left the school for opportunities in less emotionally stressful environments;
- ceremonies and rituals such as commencements and competitive academic and sports activities, which had been eliminated or modified

in Byron's early days, were gradually made to conform to practices in other schools.

Teachers' Lives and Teachers' Work. The factors related to teachers' changing experience of work at Byron and the impact of the school on teachers' lives are:

- teachers at Byron worked very hard out of commitment and the exhilaration of the challenge, but in time this exhilaration turned to exhaustion;
- many teachers felt unsupported by senior administration, the school board, the community, and their professional colleagues;
- teachers at Byron believed they were working very hard and receiving little credit for their efforts; indeed, the criticism, which most felt was unfair and erroneous, led to the "intensification" of their work;
- teachers got older and assumed more familial obligations, and the school had to share their energies;
- the most innovative and creative staff were promoted, which left the followers to continue the tradition;
- governments at various levels assumed more and more control of education, which reduced areas of teachers' discretion and creativity;
- many teachers showed symptoms of burnout from years of experimentation and innovation and lack of respect for their efforts;
- declining enrollment in the late 1970s created an older staff that was less involved in student activities, and less inclined to provide leadership for change.

Many of these are factors over which the school had very little, if any, control. They were "givens" (Mortimore et al., 1988). There is no question that contextual factors were powerful and pervasive. For schools of the future, the severity of these forces will increase. What is important, therefore, is to learn from this experience of how a school like Lord Byron responded to these forces. By looking at Byron from these six different perspectives in an ecological way, it seems clear that preventing, or at least minimizing, the attrition of change requires attention to a complex interrelationship of many factors that influence purposes, structures, and cultures in schools. Some factors, like rapid growth or decline in student population, may exacerbate preexisting conditions that result in retrenchment and the attrition of change, but to suggest that these alone caused Byron's problems is too simplistic. The complexity of the factors described, and their connections and relationships, makes it virtually impossible to determine exact pathways of causation, and therefore impossible to *predict* with certainty that attending to this factor or that will ensure a school's continuing growth and development. The best that can be said is that schools that become aware of and attend to the factors I have listed will *be more likely* to retain their innovative edge and remain "moving" schools over time.

This study, and the cases of new and innovative schools documented throughout, suggests that the hopes and dreams of the initiators of "lighthouse" schools will prove disappointing in the long run. There does indeed appear to be a life cycle to new and innovative schools. With careful planning, a reasonably stable context, and a little good fortune, however, the stages of the attrition of change might be delayed by avoiding "overreaching and entropy." Simply stated, new schools such as Byron will, over time, look and sound like the other schools in the system. If innovative schools are not sustainable over time, the question remains: Do they have a positive impact on change in the rest of the system in which they are imbedded?

NEW SETTINGS AS A STRATEGY FOR CHANGE

In 1995, Lord Byron High School held a festive 25th anniversary. Students and staff returned in overwhelming numbers to celebrate their time at Byron. They shared a common bond of having participated in an experience that was unique in the educational history of Ontario and in South. They also shared a sense that this experience significantly influenced other settings in South, and perhaps in Ontario. The schools in the South system are more student-centered now, less bureaucratic and more flexible than they were in 1970. School leaders tend to be more democratic, open to change, and student-oriented than principals of that earlier time. Forty percent of the secondary principals and vice-principals are female. In 1970 there were no female secondary school principals and only one vice-principal. While it would be difficult to support the claim that these changes are directly attributable to Lord Byron, the continuing powerful influence of the men and women of South who spent significant parts of their careers at the school suggests that the Byron experience has influenced and continues to influence the South Board of Education. Of the 17 secondary principals in South in 1996, 14 had spent at least 3 years on the staff of Lord Byron. Of these 17, eight were part of the Byron staff during its "golden years" in the early 1970s.

The dispersal of these leaders over time suggests a dual meaning of the attrition of change. On one level, the loss of key people with leadership abilities was a factor that contributed to the wearing away of change in Byron. At a second level, however, as they moved to other settings within the South system, these leaders helped to break down barriers to change in other schools by another process of "attrition." It will be my purpose in this chapter, therefore, to document this influence of Byron on the South system, and then outline some of the implications of this study for policy development. This chapter concludes with some suggestions on possible applications of this study.

Perhaps the key question to be addressed in this study is how effective model schools are as catalysts for change in larger systems. Once again, the answer is that it depends on the context. However, this and other studies of new or changing schools can add insights that can help systems take advantage of opportunities to construct new schools so as to promote change in the larger system.

The originators of Byron envisaged the school as a catalyst for change in a newly created school district, the South Board of Education. As in the rest of the province, the 13 high schools in the board in 1970 were all typically 1960s Ontario schools. There is relatively little in the literature about the effectiveness of "lighthouse" or model schools as a vehicle for change. Those who have commented suggest the strategy has limited utility for promoting change in the larger system. In their study of Lincoln School in Ontario, Hargreaves and his colleagues (1993) suggest that model schools like Lincoln

> consciously break the paradigms of existing educational practice. At considerable risk to themselves, their staffs and their students, they create concrete examples of other ways of doing things. This paradigm-breaking function is the most important one that lighthouse schools perform. . . . Schools like Lincoln break the paradigms of practice by creating living images of possibility, practicality and hope. (pp. 126–127)

The evidence of Byron's impact on the South Board supports this paradigm-breaking concept. Byron made an immediate impression on the other schools in the system. Within 5 years of Byron's opening, all but Roxborough were semestered, and even Roxborough made an attempt to move to semestering in the late 1980s. Even now, as one teacher reported, when a new secondary school is planned it is an "automatic assumption" that it will be semestered. The fact that this was the only one of Byron's many structures that has been adopted almost as it was originally intended raises the question of why. Cuban (1992), in his study of kindergarten's longevity as a reform, suggests that its "ambiguity in purpose" enabled various interest groups to adopt it for often contradictory reasons. Semestering may fit this category. Byron leaders originally saw it as a way to alter time to allow for more individualized student programming. Unions saw it as a way to lighten teaching loads. Students saw it as helpful device to let them concentrate on a few subjects at one time, as well as to accelerate their high school programs. Principals viewed it as a timetabling device to offer more breadth of program and utilize staff more efficiently. Regardless of the reason, this timetabling approach remains the most obvious impact of Byron on the system. There were, however, other structures and practices that also traveled to other sites throughout the system, albeit with modifications.

A modified version of Byron's chairmanship structure was adopted by policy as the headship structure for all the schools in the district. As a result of this and subsequent policies, department heads in the South Board continue to play a greater leadership and supervisory role than do heads in many other school jurisdictions in Ontario. Department heads in South, for example, perform an important role in teacher appraisal. Byron's more humane approach to discipline is enshrined in board and school policies. Approaches to programming initiated at Byron continue to influence schools in the district. The mastery approach to science and mathematics operates in other schools, although not at Byron now. The multitext approach to English now characterizes most programs in the region, and because of George Owens's provincial role, has impacted the province. The focus on lifetime activities in physical education pioneered in Byron's early days is a feature of virtually every physical education department in the system. Schools designed after Byron provide flexibility in the use of space, locker bays, air conditioning for year-round use, and centrally located resource centers.

Byron has been more than just a paradigm-breaker in South. Over time it has contributed to a more student-centered secondary school philosophy in the South system. In its early days the Byron approach was the central topic of the system's leadership program, which trained many of the system leaders, both at the primary and secondary levels. Through his visits to schools, Sizemore challenged leaders to look at Byron as an alternative. This "challenging of conventional ideas" would appear to be Byron's most significant lasting legacy. Moreover, many Byron people themselves moved into leadership roles and became part of the staffs of other schools. As they did so they not only showed the system the possibilities for different organizational patterns, teaching approaches, and relationships with students, but also worked with other teachers and managers to make these "possibilities" a reality. It is through these former Byron staff member leaders that the Byron ideals have spread. My respondents spoke of an unwritten obligation, a mission, to carry the Byron message to other places. Just as I had to downplay my Byron roots when I became principal of my own school, Byron leaders who moved to other schools also tended to work toward the ideals of Byron while keeping their ties to their former school rather quiet. As some of these leaders moved beyond the school level to senior positions with the board, regional policies began to reflect the philosophy and policies of Byron. The inclusiveness of Byron is reflected in the special education programs initiated by Graham Clark. The significance of staff development in South as a key to educational change is attributable in large measure to Bill Wilson. Appraisal systems that focused on professional growth were championed by Ward Bond. It generally takes time for leaders to move into positions of influence within a school system. In my own case, it took 3 years from the day I left Byron to have a regional voice, and 8 years to be in a position to shape regional policies. This is one of the more important reasons that one must look at a model school over time to determine its influence on the larger system.

In natural or human systems, no part of the larger system is left unaffected by the changes that occur within it. As Wheatley (1994) states,

> the openness and creativity that influence a system's evolution will also affect the evolution of the environment. Self-organizing systems do not simply take in information, they change their environment as well. No part of the larger system is left unaffected by changes that occur someplace within it. (p. 97)

In some respects, Byron came to look more like other schools because other schools came to look more like Byron. As has been documented previously, the Byron "mafia" brought much of the "meaning" of Byron to other schools.

A unique contribution of Byron was to enhance the role of women in the system. In the words of a Byron staff member,

> the women's group at Byron is not focused here but it is all over the county now, because of those women, because of the peer support, and the advice and the information that they received are now principals and vice-principals and department heads and directors of education over the province. That came about because

> of this little nucleus of people who got together to talk about stuff. It was wonderful! wonderful! It certainly changed the face of secondary education in South.

As she explained, before the Byron Women's Group, the management of South was "an old-boys network." By 1995, South was considered one of the leaders in the province in establishing gender equity without an affirmative action policy. In fact, the attitude of many women was to reject such intervention because they felt they were promoted on their merits as opposed to meeting a quota. I suspect this is a manifestation of the original Byron women's attitude. These women saw a model of leadership at Lord Byron that was consistent with their values, and one in which they felt capable of competing with men. Beginning with the support they enjoyed at Byron, they applied for and in increasing numbers were appointed to positions of responsibility in other schools, in the school district, and at very high levels in the province.

What is less obvious is the impact that teachers from Byron have exerted on the other classrooms across the region. A number of respondents said that they felt it was part of their duty to carry the Byron approach to other settings. As a Byron teacher who continues to have extensive contacts with his former Byron colleagues stated,

> we have sprinkled the Byron staff through many schools and I think they take with them the philosophy and innovativeness. I see Leanne Hubbs who is now at Seven Maples and changes have occurred there. They had become a little stagnated for a period of time. Those are the people who still have the philosophy that change is important and we must continue to be innovative and carry out new designs. We can't just say, well it's worked well for the past 10 years so we'll just continue on for the next 10 years. Those are the things Byron has instilled in people and those people who have left the school carry with them. If you wanted to go up through the system you should go to Byron.

Carol Stewart, now a senior manager in South, described how she and a former Byron teacher became colleagues in 1975 at the rather traditional Oakridge High School. Carol retrospectively felt that this working relationship was a turning point in her own career. As Carol stated, the association

> proved to be one of the most important professional development experiences I've ever had. Joan brought with her an attitude of ex-

> perimentation with a view to the improvement of instruction that I had never experienced and she reveled in professional discourse as the bread of daily life . . . we would talk about what we had done in class that day, how it had gone, why it hadn't gone better . . . it was my first experience with that type of collaboration with a view to improving teaching.

This led to a joint project to improve teaching at the "general" level, which spread to the rest of the school. In association with two other teachers from other departments they developed an interdisciplinary approach to essay writing and published a document for students, which became widely used not only in the school but in the school system. The influence of a Byron teacher had led to collaboration, experimentation, and the first interdisciplinary work the more traditional school had experienced, and according to Carol influenced the way she operated in her subsequent career moves. Carol's experience was not unique. In obvious ways like semestering, and in the subtle changes that have taken place in school management and student programs over time, there is considerable evidence of Lord Byron's influence on teachers and teaching in other schools.

As a strategy for change, however, the system and its director, in the words of a retired secondary principal, "rammed the Byron model down our throats." Sizemore and others (Gold & Miles, 1981; Smith et al., 1987) hoped that other schools would adopt the successful aspects of the innovative school. This "shock and copy" strategy was typical of the times in Ontario and in South, and created a backlash of distrust, suspicion, anger, entrenchment, and jealousy—somewhat muted in Byron's early years but much more apparent as the school began to experience the "liabilities of newness." As one respondent who was a department head in another school in South in the 1970s recalled, "I felt we were doing a heck of a good job. Why is Byron getting all this attention?" Remarkably, some of these feelings still exist in the system. Byron, however, did change the rest of the system, not by shock or blueprint, but by the way it eroded traditional practices elsewhere through spawning influential teachers, leaders, men and women who slowly, over time, changed the system. In effect, Byron changed the system by long-term "attrition." The creation of new settings, therefore, can provide a venue for policy germination, opportunities for training in innovative practices, avenues for documentation and research, and a seed-bed for the long-term development of innovative educational leaders.

IMPLICATIONS FOR POLICY AND PRACTICE

"Good" Schools and "Real" Schools

Perhaps the dominant theme in the Lord Byron story is the school's struggle with its image. Throughout, I have suggested that an essential reason for the attrition of change within Byron was the disequilibrium between what the educators considered to be a "good" school and what influential elements of the parent community and the educational establishment in South considered to be a "real" school. This gap in perspective began with the early Innovations Committee and developed through the 1970s as successive principals and staff members attempted to sell the school's innovative concepts to the community. These attempts to persuade were made more difficult by a lack of scientific support for many of the experimental concepts. As George Owens suggested, "We were like paradigm pioneers." Attempts to convince the community of their philosophy of what constituted a good school tended to be based on appeals to the community's trust in the collective intuition, experience, and commitment of the Byron staff, without substantive proof that the new approaches were any better than more traditional patterns. As the 1970s progressed and problems at Byron became obvious, community support for Byron's image of schooling gradually withered. In the minds of many, Byron was an "artsy" school or a "Hall-Dennis school" or a special education school; it certainly was not a real school like Roxborough down the road. In effect, the professional image of the Byron staff of what a school should be had diverged significantly from the community's perception of schooling, and contributed to a disequilibrium in perceptions that almost destroyed the school.

Conversely, the perceptions of schooling of the staff and influential community members of Roxborough were quite similar. Ironically, there is significant evidence to suggest that in spite of its very positive reputation (Hargreaves et al., 1992), Roxborough was a "cruising" school (Stoll & Fink, 1998) that was resting on its laurels. Cruising schools may appear to be effective in terms of academic results but they have often developed little capacity for change and growth over time. A study that was replicated in South, to which I was privy in my role as a senior administrator, showed that over 30% of the students at Roxborough were not involved in the life of the school (King, 1986). While the school had high achievement, and excellence in many areas, the involved students were always the same students. In other words the football players, the choir members, and the theater performers were essentially drawn from the middle-class students. The school, however, was and is well supported by its community because the influential parents tend to be the ones whose students benefit from a school like Roxborough. This pattern of the middle class defining the change agenda for a school is not unique (Brouillette, 1996; Oakes, Wells, Yonezawa, & Ray, 1997). If Roxborough is typical, a school in which the staff's and the community's conceptions of a good school are very similar may not necessarily benefit *all* the students. The policy challenge, therefore, is to determine the appropriate degree of disequilibrium to ensure that a school continues to be "moving" (Rosenholtz, 1989) in terms of achievement for all students, while preventing the debilitating type of image problem faced by Byron on the one hand, and the complacency of a Roxborough on the other. The clear message is that the professional's concept of a good school must remain connected to, but not necessarily dependent on or a duplicate of, the community's concept of schooling. The professional staff must, however, provide leadership that is sensitive to the community's aims and aspirations for its young people. Contemporary evidence in South suggests that parents recognize the need for change, innovation, and experimentation, and are prepared to accept the professionals' leadership, but they expect changes to be based on more than just teachers' and managers' intuition and experience. Parents also expect professionals to explain the changes in language they can understand and to justify the changes based on valid research.

The relationships of Byron and similar schools to their communities contain another interesting paradox. Most of these schools were more open to their communities than were other contemporary schools, but their very openness led to widespread and often unfair criticism (Fletcher et al., 1985; Fullan et al., 1972; Gold & Miles, 1981). Stable schools like Roxborough, however, which let parents know only what the school wanted them to know, seldom faced concerted criticism. This apparent contradiction suggests a number of questions.

- How open should a school be to its community?
- At what point do the public's democratic rights intrude on the professional responsibilities of principals and teachers?
- Can innovation and public openness coexist in schools?

Generally, the change literature advocates openness with school communities (Fullan, 1991; Hargreaves, 1997; Stoll & Fink, 1996). Indeed, Ainley (1993) suggests that involvement of the public at early stages of a change encourages community assistance, support, and understanding. One would certainly be hard pressed to argue against this principle of community involvement in a change process on ethical grounds. The Byron case, however, suggests that community involvement in planning would probably have severely circumscribed the nature of the changes. This would seem to be particularly true when educators make up an influential part of the school's community (Gold & Miles, 1981).

Innovation and change tend to take place on the frontiers of what is considered acceptable. As Kuhn (1962) has stated:

> The man who embraces a new paradigm at an early stage must often do so in defiance of the evidence provided by the problem solving. He must . . . have faith that the new paradigm will succeed with the many large problems that confront it knowing only that the older paradigm has failed with a few. A decision of that kind can only be made on faith. (pp. 157–158)

Byron was more than a bounded change such as destreaming a grade level or developing an interdisciplinary curriculum. It was an attempt to change the prevailing educational paradigm quite dramatically. Bond and his "critical mass" of colleagues were paradigm pioneers. Pioneering, however, requires risk-taking. The pioneer must often act without a clear road map of the future. As Barker (1989) suggests, pioneering is more an act of the heart than an act of the head. It would seem from the experiences of Byron and many other innovative schools that both the educational and larger communities are generally unwilling or unable to accept pioneering that requires significant departures from the prevailing paradigm of schooling. Perhaps this is the reason that Sarason (1990) entitled his book *The Predictable Failure of Educational Reform.* In a sense, therefore, the politics of learning between school and community are in large measure determined by public opinion, which in educational matters tends to be inherently conservative. For change agents, however, the learning of politics is a necessity. They need to know how much and in what capacity various stakeholders should be involved in change processes. Perhaps there is a sliding scale of how open to be when pursuing change. Perhaps the desirable degree of public involvement depends on the radicalness of the changes—the more radical the change, the less open the initiators may have to be. At this point, however, future research will have to settle the issue. The challenge for practice and research is to find the optimum balance between the "politics of learning" and the "learning of politics" in different kinds of change situations.

The Attrition of Change: Its Dual Meaning

Looked at another way, however, the strategy of "model" schools can be considered a positive influence for change over time in the larger system. In many ways, the schools in South came to look and sound like Byron. One can see this growing influence in the student-centeredness of all schools, the pervasiveness of semestering, the strength of women's leadership in South, and the general acceptance by teachers in South of the importance of professional development and reflective practice. The system's acceptance of change as an integral part of practice has been well documented (Stoll & Fink, 1992, 1994, 1996). Over the years, Lord Byron has contributed significantly to the gradual attrition of barriers to change in the South Board—thus the second meaning of the attrition of change.

The Byron study indicates that the use of this "germination" strategy must be handled with discretion by avoiding overselling the innovations and by reducing the rhetoric of change. How well this strategy travels to different contexts requires further research. An examination of the impact of a school such as Countesthorpe on its Local Educational Authority and British secondary education in general would provide an interesting parallel to the present study and help to confirm or challenge some of the patterns identified in the Lord Byron study (Moon, 1983). Similarly, longitudinal ethnographic investigations of the American "break-the-mold" schools would contribute useful information on the "life-cycle" and "change-model" theories proposed here.

Leadership and Staffing Issues

Leadership at various levels played an important part in this and similar studies of new and innovative schools (Smith et al., 1987). At the system level, Byron experienced unique benefits and suffered undue criticism because of the initiating CEO's enthusiasm for its innovations. In addition, the choice of an outstanding charismatic leader for the school's first principal made his replacement very difficult. Loyalty to the person as opposed to the concept was a particular problem in both the Byron study and Smith and his colleagues' research (1987). These circumstances raise a number of questions of policy and practice. What type of person should be chosen as the first leader of a new and innovative school? What commitments should the formal school leaders make to ensure some stability in the first few years? Certainly Bond's early departure was a turning point. The question of succession planning, which was a problem in the Byron case and which is barely mentioned in the research literature, raises the issue of how system officials or school governors ensure some degree of continuity after the departure of the initiating leader(s).

A related policy problem results from the complex macro- and micro-political issues that confront school management teams. Few leaders in my experience have been trained to handle the politics of learning such as direct interference in the school's functioning by politicians and aggressive parents, or the challenge of dealing with competing and conflicting interest groups such as parents who want to include special education students in classes and other parents who want their children separated from less successful students. The ability to resolve or at least contain such political problems often determines school leaders' success and their schools' ability to function effectively. Few jurisdictions, at least in North America, provide training in the area. This leaves potentially capable leaders and their schools vulnerable to pressures from vocal and organized minorities.

The Byron case also raises the issue of the continuing relevance of a layer of department and/or year heads in secondary schools. There is evidence that this leadership structure contributes to balkanization and internal school rivalries (Siskin, 1994). Even at Byron, which tried to create a different leadership configuration, the chairmen's structure eventually evolved into an organizational layer that confused decision-making and detracted from a schoolwide focus.

In addition to the role of department or year heads, a school such as Byron also raises staffing questions related to recruitment, induction, the composition of a faculty, and differentiated staffing. The most important appraisal of a teacher often occurs the day he or she is hired. It is very difficult in most jurisdictions to remove a teacher once that teacher has received a contract. Bond spent a great deal of time ensuring that he assembled the people needed to achieve the kind of school he envisaged. Subsequently, rapid growth meant that hiring became rather frenetic and induction programs became increasingly haphazard. Equally problematic were the procedures in place to respond to the surplus teachers produced by the declining enrollment that followed. Teacher contracts in Ontario and many other jurisdictions usually specify that the last person hired is the first person declared surplus to a school. From an individual point of view this would appear to be the fairest solution to a difficult problem. It results, however, in school staffs in which career stages, gender, and expertise of the teaching staff can often become quite unbalanced. Byron, for example, has in twenty-five years gone from a very young staff to one of the oldest in the region. Certainly in South, procedures at the secondary level to facilitate transfers to other schools might have some merit.

An associated policy issue relates to the differentiation of staff.

Byron demonstrated the advantages of alternative staffing patterns, but the unions in Ontario are understandably opposed to the hiring of paraprofessionals unless they are added on to existing teaching staff. Some politicians in Ontario have advocated alternative staffing as a way to save money by hiring people who would be paid less than teachers. This pattern has been used in hospitals in Ontario to reduce the number of nurses and replace them with lower-paid nurses' assistants. If, as in the Byron situation, differentiation is used to assist the teaching-learning process, it can be a useful innovation. Conversely, differentiation as a teacher-cutting exercise will probably result in such resentment from teachers that few benefits will accrue to students. Lord Byron has demonstrated that alternative ways to look at the staffing of schools are possible, and may even be desirable if they are used to improve teaching and learning and not as a cynical governmental exercise in cost-cutting.

The Role of the System

Smith and his colleagues (1987) have described how Kensington school existed within a "nested system." Throughout this study I have connected Lord Byron to the South system, and in turn to the province of Ontario. There is an increasing effort in Canada and other countries to allow market forces to determine educational policies (Barlow & Robertson, 1994; Gewirtz et al., 1995; Robertson, 1996; Whitty, 1997). Governments, through various policy initiatives like direct funding to schools, changes in taxing responsibilities, and direct and overt restructuring of school districts, have often limited the role of the local educational authorities. Such intermediary levels of governance are usually viewed as impediments to governments' change agendas. School districts are depicted as unnecessarily bureaucratic and inefficient. While there are no doubt districts that fit this description, the Lord Byron story suggests an alternative picture indicating that school districts can and do play an important role in trying to ensure a quality education for all children, not just those of the influential middle class. The South Board and Jim Sizemore created the opportunity for the creation of Lord Byron, which attempted to respond to the needs of all students. Throughout the difficult times, the board through its administrative support ensured the continuing viability of Lord Byron. The selection of principals in the mid-1980s, the addition of regional programs, and the efforts to balance enrollments between Roxborough and Byron are examples of the system's intervention to protect the quality of programs for all students. In a pure market approach, Roxborough would have accepted the most academically suitable students, which would have left Byron as a repository for lower socioeconomic, non-academic, and special education students (Whitty, 1997). As a result of the board's intervention, however, Byron maintained a comprehensive student population that enabled it to offer a breadth of programs to meet a wide variety of student needs. While the market might promote quality for some schools, although even this is doubtful (Whitty et al., 1998), the Lord Byron experience suggests that governments should reassess the role of the district in maintaining equitable education for all students. In their rush to eliminate the intrusive effects of local government bureaucracy, national and regional governments may also end up removing invaluable forms of coordination and support.

Practitioner Research

As I suggested in the Introduction to this book, I am in what Handy (1995a) has called my "Third Age." In increasing numbers, former school and system managers like me are opting for early retirement. Many possess rich insights into the macro-policies and practices of schools and systems. Some have the potential to combine their extensive practical experience and their newly found time to carry on significant intellectual activity. The present study is an example of this conjunction. Studies of this type, however, are quite unlike other forms of practitioner research. They are not "action" research because they do not focus on the investigator's personal actions—nor are they exclusively life histories, or studies undertaken by "outsiders" to a setting. Rather, if successful, they are thoughtful historical ethnographies about the schools and systems in which the researcher has played a part. While teacher research practitioners can provide rich understandings of the micro levels of schools and systems, they are often unknowing of the larger "nested systems" (Smith et al., 1987). Educators with an extensive management background can, therefore, contribute insights into the complex interconnections and interrelationships among the various levels of schools and systems that others may not see or understand. As a senior administrator and as this study illustrates, I dealt on a daily basis with the relationships among linked settings—the province, the district, the schools, and the community, among others. Practitioner research of the nature of the present study, therefore, has the potential to provide unique insights into the linkages between and among these macro and micro settings and to open significant new directions in our understanding of educational policies, practices, and the processes of change (A. Hargreaves, 1985).

Multiple Lenses

Finally, the conceptual framework that was introduced in Chapter 1 and used to structure Chapters 3 through 8 provides an approach that ensures that issues, problems, or in this case a school are looked at through multiple lenses or frames. By collecting and analyzing data in this manner, the researcher is obliged to see the complexity and interconnectedness of issues. In a sense, one is obliged to see school change in an ecological way (Morgan, 1997; Sirotnik, 1998). This multidimensional look at Lord Byron over its history, therefore, precludes simple explanations and trite prescriptions. It also provides a framework that might help schools to analyze their own change processes and develop problem-solving strategies and their capacity for change over time.

CONCLUSION

The literature on change has grown significantly in recent years. Most of it, however, attends to strategies to change ineffective or in Rosenholtz's (1989) term "stuck" schools into effective or "moving" schools. Such organizations are characterized as learning organizations that can respond to the vicissitude of a rapidly changing context (Garratt, 1987a; Senge, 1990; Stacey, 1995). Very little, however, has been written on how innovative or moving schools can maintain their momentum in the face of an increasingly complex, diverse, unpredictable, and often unforgiving world. While this book does not address this issue directly, it has shown how one school struggled to maintain its essential meaning while confronted by forces over which it had little or no control. In the process, this study provides a number of possible "warning lights," which, depending on a school's context, may help moving schools to stay the course and school systems to use the opportunity to construct new schools as a vehicle for bringing about long-term innovation and change across the system.

The stories of new and innovative schools referred to throughout have the stuff of classic tragedy—heroic leaders laid low by often unfair criticism, exciting visions of new educational worlds blinded by people's timidity and fears, and promising organizations and institutions destroyed or significantly diminished by internal and external discord. Lord Byron has many of these qualities—a gradual attrition of its innovative ethos after the departure of its revered leader, aggressive opposition from the people it was trying to serve, and internal divisions and conflicts precipitated by forces over which the school had little control. Unlike many other stories of innovative schools, however, this study views the school over an extended period of time, and also focuses on the school's relationship to its district context. Looked at from this perspective, we have a more romantic picture of a school with a powerful vision of educational change, which produced a generation of leaders who carried the school's message to more traditional settings and used their Byron experience to initiate processes to speed the attrition of barriers to change in these other settings. While the internal manifestations of the Byron experiment have eroded over time, the power of its essential meaning can be seen in every secondary school in the South Board of Education, as each day they attempt to respond to the diverse needs and interests of *all* their students.

Notes

Introduction

1. Lord Byron is not the real name of the school. I have attempted throughout this book to protect the school, the school district, and the identities of participants in the Lord Byron story by using pseudonyms.

2. Lord Byron serves a middle- to lower-middle-class, mostly white, geographical area in a largely residential district in Ontario, Canada. This demographic pattern has remained relatively unchanged over the past 29 years. Many residents of Middleton, where Lord Byron is located, commute for employment to large neighboring cities. Students were and continue to be assigned to their neighborhood school based on attendance areas. Optional attendance was and is allowed by the school district after the student had been in his or her home school for at least one year. Optional attendance proceeds through an application and approval process.

3. Over the course of Lord Byron's history, therefore, from a research perspective I might be considered both an "insider" and an "outsider." The insider's doctrine, according to Merton (1970), stated simply, is that "you have to be one to understand one" (p. 15). An insider, according to this view has a "monopolistic or privileged access to knowledge," and an outsider is "wholly excluded from it, by virtue of one's group membership or social position." This view suggests that outsiders have not been socialized in the group and "cannot have the direct, intuitive sensitivity that alone makes empathetic understanding possible" (p. 15). Conversely, "outsiders" hold that "knowledge about groups, unprejudiced by membership in them, is accessible only to the outsider" (p. 31). As Merton suggests, neither has an exclusive claim to certainty. Both roles bring advantages and disadvantages that, as Hammersley (1981) points out, the researcher must anticipate and accommodate. As the research progressed, therefore, I paid very close attention to the real possibilities of bias and distortion created by my unique "insider-outsider" relationship to Lord Byron and attempted to the best of my ability to anticipate and respond.

Chapter 2

1. All unattributed references are taken from interviews conducted between 1992 and 1996.

2. To graduate with a Secondary School Graduation Diploma a student

had to complete 27 credits. A credit was a course of 110 hours. In addition, to receive an Honours Secondary School Graduation Diploma a student must complete six higher-level credits, which led to university entrance. Until recently Ontario has offered 13 years of public education. The 13th year led to university. After completion of "grade 13," students need to complete only 3 years in university to receive a BA. These requirements are in the process of change as this is written. Ontario has reduced its program to 12 years.

3. Until 1967, Ontario students in grade 13 (the final year of secondary school) were required to write examinations administered by the Ontario Ministry of Education. These centrally marked examinations were considered too expensive to continue and therefore terminated. As a result, individual schools continue to determine the grades for graduating students. Therefore universities and colleges had to develop their own admission standards to replace the provincial examination results. Needless to say, they liked the former system.

4. This assertion is based on the comprehensive reviews conducted by both external and internal teams of evaluators in 1975 and 1980, as well as the rather thorough annual review processes in the South Board of Education (Fink & Stoll, 1997). Surveys of parents, teachers, and students were extremely positive. Moreover, optional attendance requests into Byron far exceeded requests to leave in the first 8 years of the school's history.

5. Two major factors affected school enrollment in the South Board—increase or decline in the student population of a school's attendance area, and optional attendance. Until the late 1970s both factors augmented Byron's enrollment. Beginning in 1978, construction of new homes slowed down and student enrollment began to decline. As enrollments declined, certain programs became difficult to sustain and some students transferred to other schools to register in the programs not available at their local school.

6. In the early 1980s, the government of Ontario eliminated separate provincially operated facilities for mentally challenged young people and required local school districts to accommodate and program for them. Moreover, the province terminated funds to educate severely learning disabled students in private schools in other provinces and in states of the United States. Local school boards were mandated to provide educational services for these students. Both of these programs continue to be accommodated at Lord Byron.

Chapter 3

1. The Bensonville district had applied for and received a substantial grant to initiate a large-scale school-improvement project. The teachers' union supported it initially but eventually withdrew its support. In addition, rivalries within the district among communities doomed the attempt to failure.

2. Cottonwood was a district in a western state in the United States. When the Cottonwood trustees (school board members) tried to equalize boundaries to protect the enrollment and the program offerings of a school with a significant percentage of minorities, the white middle-class parents used their political sophistication and influence to pressure the school board to rule in ways

that advantaged students who were already advantaged. This pattern is not unique (Oakes et al., 1997).

Chapter 4

1. As indicated in Chapter 2 (page 32), Byron augmented its traditional open-door policy for students who found school difficult by accepting two regional programs for special education students. The "Life Skills" program for mentally challenged students and the Satellite for seriously learning disabled students were considered by special education professionals in the region to be extremely successful, and attributed much of their success to Lord Byron's inviting ethos. Success in special education programming, however, adds little to a school's reputation in contemporary society.

Chapter 6

1. Comprehensive schools are schools that enroll all the students, regardless of ability, from an attendance area. A vocational school is one that is designed to provide students with trades skills. A staff-development school is one that is designed to support the professional development of teachers, or to serve as a center for educational research. A university "laboratory" school would be an example. Work experience refers to programs in which students work in shops, factories, or community agencies for periods of time as an extension of their school program. Cooperative programs are usually jointly run between the community and the school system. Students traditionally spend large blocks of time in community activities. Regardless of the organizational design, these are examples of schools occurring in different types of spaces.

References

Acker, S. (1983). Women and teaching: The semi-detached sociology of a semi-profession. In L. Barton & S. Walker (Eds.), *Gender, race and schooling* (pp. 123–139). Lewes: Falmer Press.

Acker, S. (1995). Gender and teachers work. In M. Apple (Ed.), *Review of research in education, 21* (pp. 99–162). Washington, DC: American Educational Research Association.

Adelman, N., & Pringle, B. (1995). Education reform and the use of time. *Phi Delta Kappan, 77*(1), 27–29.

Ainley, J. (1993). Parents in the transition years. In A. Hargreaves, K. Leithwood, & D. Gerin-Lajoie, *Years of transition: Times for change* (pp. 294–315). Toronto: Ministry of Education and Training.

Anderson, S., & Stiegelbauer, S. (1990). *Project excellence: A case study of a student centered school.* Toronto: Queen's Printer of Ontario.

Apple, M. (1986). *Teachers and texts.* New York: Routledge and Kegan Paul.

Apple, M., & Teitelbaum, K. (1986). Are teachers losing control of their skills and curriculum? *Journal of Curriculum Studies, 18*(2), 177–184.

Ball, S. (1981). *Beachside comprehensive: A case-study of secondary schooling.* Cambridge: Cambridge University Press.

Ball, S. (1987). *Micropolitics of the school.* London: Methuen/Routledge and Kegan Press.

Ball, S. (1993). Self doubt and soft data: Social and technological rajectories in ethnographic fieldwork. In M. Hammersley (Ed.), *Educational research: Current issues* (pp. 32–88). London: Paul Chapman Publishing.

Ball, S., & Goodson, I. (1985). Understanding teachers: Concepts and contexts. In S. Ball & I. Goodson (Eds.), *Teachers' lives and careers* (pp. 1–26). London: Falmer Press.

Ball, S. G. (1984). Beachside reconsidered: Reflections on a methodological apprenticeship. In R. G. Burgess, *The research process in educational settings: Ten case studies* (pp. 69–96). London: Falmer Press.

Ball, S. J., & Bowe, R. (1992). Subject departments and the implementation of national curriculum policy: An overview of the issues. *Journal of Curriculum Studies, 24*(2), 97–115.

Barber, M. (1995). *The dark side of the moon: TES/Greenwich education lecture.* London, Times Educational Supplement.

Barker, J. (1989). *Discovering the future: The business of paradigms.* St. Paul, MN: ILI Press.

Barlow, M., & Robertson, H. (1994). *Class warfare.* Toronto: Key Porter.
Barth, R. (1990). *Improving schools from within: Teachers, parents and principals can make the difference.* San Francisco: Jossey-Bass.
Bascia, N. (1994). *Unions in teachers' lives: Social, intellectual, and practical concerns.* New York: Teachers College Press.
Bennet, C. (1985). Paints, pots and promotion? Art teachers' attitudes towards their careers. In S. Ball & I. Goodson (Eds.), *Teachers' lives and careers* (pp. 120–137). London: Falmer Press.
Bennis, W., & Nanus, B. (1985). *Leaders.* New York: Harper and Row.
Berliner, D. (1990). What's all the fuss about instructional time? In M. Ben-Peretz & R. Bromme (Eds.), *The nature of time in schools* (pp. 3–35). New York: Teachers College Press.
Bishop, P., & Mulford, W. (1996). Empowerment in four Australian primary schools. They don't really care. *International Journal of Educational Reform, 5*(2), 193–204.
Blase, J. (1988). The teachers' political orientation vis a vis the principal: The micropolitics of the school. *Politics of Education Association Yearbook, 1988,* 113–126.
Blase, J. (1998). The micropolitics of educational change. In A. Hargreaves, A. Lieberman, M. Fullan, & D. Hopkins (Eds.), *International handbook of educational change* (pp. 544–557). Dordrecht, The Netherlands: Kluwer Press.
Block, P. (1991). *The empowered manager: Positive political skills at work.* San Francisco: Jossey Bass.
Block, P. (1993). *Stewardship: Choosing service over self interest.* San Francisco: Berrett Kohler.
Boleman, L., & Deal, T. (1997). *Reframing organizations: Artistry, choice and leadership* (2nd ed.). San Francisco: Jossey-Bass.
Boyd, W. (1998). Markets, choices, and educational change. In A. Hargreaves, A. Lieberman, M. Fullan, & D. Hopkins (Eds.), *International handbook of educational change* (pp. 349–374). Dordrecht, The Netherlands: Kluwer Press.
Bracey, G. W. (1991). Why can't they be like we were? *Phi Delta Kappan, 73*(2), 104–120.
Bracey, G. W. (1992). The second Bracey report on the condition of public education. *Phi Delta Kappan, 74*(2), 104–117.
Brouillette, L. (1996). *A geology of school reform: The successive restructuring of a school district.* Albany: State University of New York Press.
Burgess, R. (1983). *Experiencing comprehensive education: A study of Bishop McGregor School.* London: Methuen.
Burns, J. M. (1978). *Leadership.* New York: Harper and Row.
Byrne, B. M. (1994). Burnout testing for the validity, replication, and invarience of causal structure across the elementary, intermediate, and secondary teachers. *American Educational Research Journal, 31*(3), 645–673.
Central Council for Advisory Education. (1967). *Plowden report: Children and their primary schools.* London: H.M.S.O.

Cohen, D. K. (1995). What is the systems in systemic reform? *Educational Researcher, 24*(9), 11–17, 31.

Coleman, P., & LaRocque, L. (1990). *Struggling to be good enough: Administrative practices and school districts.* New York: Falmer.

Conley, S. (1991). Review of research on teacher participation in school decision making. In G. Grant (Ed.), *Review of research in education* (Vol. 17, pp. 225–226). Washington, DC: American Educational Research Association.

Corbett, D., & Wilson, B. (1995). Make a difference with, not for, students: A plea to researchers and reformers. *Educational Researcher, 24*(5), 12–17.

Covey, S. (1989). *The 7 habits of highly effective people: Powerful lessons in personal change.* New York: Simon & Schuster.

Crittenden, B. (Ed.). (1969). *Means and ends in education: Comments on living and learning.* Toronto: Ontario Institute for Studies in Education.

Crump, S. J. (1993). *School-centered leadership.* Sydney, Australia: Thomas Nelson.

Cuban, L. (1988). A fundamental puzzle of school reform. *Phi Delta Kappan, 70*(5), 341–344.

Cuban, L. (1992). Why some reforms last. *American Journal of Education, 100*(2), 166–193.

Curtis, B., Livingstone, D. W., & Smaller, H. (1992). *Stacking the deck: The streaming of working class kids in Ontario schools.* Toronto: Our Schools/ Ourselves Education Foundation.

Davies, B., & Ellison, L. (1997). *Strategic marketing for schools.* London: Pitman.

Day, C., & Bakioglu, A. (1996). Development and disenchantment in the professional lives of headteachers. In I. F. Goodson & A. Hargreaves (Eds.), *Teachers' professional lives* (pp. 205–207). London: Falmer.

Deal, T. (1987). The culture of schools. In L. Sheive & M. Schoenheit (Eds.), *Leadership: Examining the elusive* (pp. 3–15). Washington, DC: Association for Supervision and Curriculum Development.

Deal, T. E., & Kennedy, A. (1982). *Corporate cultures: The rites and rituals of corporate life.* New York: Addison Wesley.

Deal, T. E., & Kennedy, A. (1983). Culture and school performance. *Educational Leadership, 40*(5), 140–141.

Deal, T. E., & Peterson, K. (1994). *The leadership paradox: Balancing logic and artistry in schools.* San Francisco: Jossey-Bass.

Delpit, T. L. (1988). The silenced dialogue: Power and pedagogy in educating other people's children. *Harvard Educational Review, 58*(3), 280–298.

Donohoe, T. (1993). Finding the way: Structure, time, and culture in school improvement. *Phi Delta Kappan, 75*(4), 298–305.

Doremus, R. R. (1981a). Whatever happened to: John Adams High School? *Phi Delta Kappan, 63*(3), 199–202.

Doremus, R. R. (1981b). Whatever happened to: Nova High School? *Phi Delta Kappan, 63*(4), 274–276.

Doremus, R. R. (1981c). Whatever happened to: Melbourne High School? *Phi Delta Kappan, 63*(7), 480–482.

Doremus, R. R. (1982). Whatever happened to: Wayland High School? *Phi Delta Kappan, 63*(5), 347–348.

Doyle, W., & Ponder, G. A. (1977). The practicality ethic in teacher decision-making. *Interchange, 8*(3), 1–12.

Edmonds, R. (1979). Effective schools for urban poor. *Educational Leadership, 37*(1), 15–27.

Edwards, P. A., & Jones Young, L. S. (1992). Beyond parents: Family, community, and student involvement. *Phi Delta Kappan, 72*(1), 72–80.

Edwards, S. (1994). *Leading a learning organisation: Gender issues in secondary headships.* Paper presented at the annual meeting of the British Educational Management and Administration Society, Manchester.

Elmore, R. (1995). Structural reform in educational practice. *Educational Researcher, 24*(9), 23–26.

Epstein, J. L. (1995). School/family/partnerships: Caring for the children we share. *Phi Delta Kappan, 76*(9), 701–712.

Evans, B. (1983). Countesthorpe College, Leicester. In B. Moon (Ed.), *Comprehensive schools: Challenge and change* (pp. 5–32). Windsor, U.K.: Nelson Publishing.

Fink, D. (1992a). Invitational leadership. In J. Novak (Ed.), *Advances in invitational theory* (pp. 139–156). San Francisco: Caddo Gap Press.

Fink, D. (1992b). The sixth "p"—politics. *Journal of Invitational Theory and Practice, 1*(1), 21–30.

Fink, D. (1997). *The attrition of change.* Unpublished doctoral dissertation, Open University, Milton Keynes.

Fink, D. (1998). Confronting complexity: A framework for action. *Improving Schools, 1*(3), 54–58.

Fink, D., & Stoll, L. (1997). Weaving school and teacher development together. In T. Townsend (Ed.), *Restructuring and quality: Issues for tomorrow's schools* (pp. 182–198). New York: Routledge.

Fink, D., & Stoll, L. (1998). Educational change: Easier said than done. In A. Hargreaves, A. Lieberman, M. Fullan, & D. Hopkins (Eds.), *International handbook of educational change* (pp. 297–321). Dordrecht, The Netherlands: Kluwer.

Firestone, W. A., & Pennell, J. R. (1993). Teacher commitment, working conditions, and differential incentive policies. *Review of Educational Research, 63*(4), 489–525.

Fletcher, C., Caron, M., & Williams, W. (1985). *Schools on trial.* Milton Keynes, U.K.: Open University Press.

Fullan, M. (1982). *The meaning of educational change.* Toronto: O.I.S.E. Press.

Fullan, M., & Eastabrook, G. (1977). *Bayridge secondary school: A case study of the planning and implementation of educational change.* Toronto: O.I.S.E.

Fullan, M., Eastabrook, G., Spinner, D., & Loubser, J. J. (1972). *Thornlea: A case study of an innovative secondary school.* Toronto: O.I.S.E.

Fullan, M. G. (1990). Beyond implementation. *Curriculum Implementation, 20*(2), 137–139.

Fullan, M. G. (1991). *The new meaning of educational change.* New York: Teachers College Press.

Fullan, M. G. (1993). *Change forces: Probing the depths of educational reform.* London: Falmer Press.

Fullan, M. G. (1997). Broadening the concept of teacher leadership. In National Staff Development Council (Ed.), *New Directions* (pp. 38–48). Oxford, OH: National Staff Development Council.

Fullan, M. (1998). The meaning of educational change: A quarter century of learning. In A. Hargreaves, A. Lieberman, M. Fullan, & D. Hopkins (Eds.), *International handbook of educational change.* Dordrecht, The Netherlands: Kluwer.

Garratt, B. (1987). *The learning organization.* Glasgow: Wm Collins Press.

Gewirtz, S., Ball, S. J., & Bowe, R. (1995). *Markets, choice and equity in education.* Buckingham: Open University Press.

Giddens, A. (1984). *The constitution of society.* Cambridge: Polity Press.

Goetz, J. (1988). Review of membership roles in field research. *The International Journal of Qualitative Studies in Education, 1*(3), 291–294.

Gold, B. A., & Miles, M. B. (1981). *Whose school is it anyway: Parent-teacher conflict over an innovative school.* New York: Praeger.

Goodson, I. (1981). Life history and the study of schooling. *Interchange, 11*(4), 62–76.

Goodson, I. (1983). *School subjects and curriculum change.* London: Croom Helm.

Goodson, I. F. (1992). Studying teachers' lives: An emergent field of inquiry. In I. F. Goodson (Ed.), *Studying teachers' lives* (pp. 1–17). New York: Teachers College Press.

Goodson, I. F., & Anstead, C. J. (1993). *Through the school house door: Working papers.* London, Ontario: Garmond Press.

Goodson, I. F., & Walker, R. (1991). *Biography, identity and schooling: Episodes in educational research.* London: Falmer Press.

Grant, G. (1988). *The world we created at Hamilton High.* Cambridge, MA.: Harvard University Press.

Grossman, P. L., & Stodolsky, S. (1993). *Adapting to diverse learners: Teacher beliefs in context.* Paper presented at the annual meeting of the American Educational Research Association, Atlanta.

Grossman, P. L., & Stodolsky, S. (1994). Considerations of content and the circumstances of secondary school teaching. In L. Darling-Hammond (Ed.), *Review of research in education* (Vol. 20, pp. 197–221). Washington, DC: American Educational Research Association.

Gunter, H. (1995). Jurassic management: Chaos and management development in educational institutions. *Journal of Educational Administration, 33*(4), 5–20.

Gustavson, C. G. (1955). *A preface to history.* Toronto: McGraw-Hill.

Hallinger, P., & Murphy, J. (1986). The social context of effective schools. *American Journal of Education, 94*(3), 328–355.

Hammersley, M. (1981). The outsider's advantage: A reply to McNamara. *British Educational Journal, 7*(2), 167–171.

Handy, C. (1995a). *The age of unreason.* London: Arrow Books.

Handy, C. (1995b). *Gods of management.* London: Arrow Books.

Hargreaves, A. (1984). Contrastive rhetoric and extremist talk. In A. Hargreaves & P. Woods (Eds.), *Classrooms and staffrooms*. Milton Keynes: Open University Press.
Hargreaves, A. (1985). The micro-macro problem in the sociology of education. In R. G. Burgess (Ed.), *Issues in Educational Research* (pp. 303–329). London: Falmer Press.
Hargreaves, A. (1986). *Two cultures of schooling*. Lewes: Falmer Press.
Hargreaves, A. (1991a). Curriculum reform and the teacher. *The Curriculum Journal, 2*(3), 249–258.
Hargreaves, A. (1991b). *Prepare to meet thy mood: Teacher preparation time and the intensification thesis*. Paper presented at the annual conference of the American Educational Research Association, Chicago.
Hargreaves, A. (1994). *Changing teachers, changing times*. London. Cassell.
Hargreaves, A. (1997). Rethinking educational change: Going deeper and wider in the quest for success. In A. Hargreaves (Ed.), *Rethinking educational change with heart and mind: The 1997 ASCD yearbook* (pp. 1–26). Alexandria, VA: A.S.C.D.
Hargreaves, A., Earl, L., & Ryan, J. (1996). *Schooling for change*. London: Falmer Press.
Hargreaves, A., & Fullan, M. (1998). *What's worth fighting for out there*. Toronto: Ontario Public School Teachers' Federation.
Hargreaves, A., Fullan, M., Wignall, R., Stager, M., & Macmillan, R. (1992). *Secondary school work cultures and educational change*. Toronto: Ministry of Education.
Hargreaves, A., Leithwood, K., & Gerin-Lajoie, D. (1993). *Years of transition: Times for change*. Toronto: Ministry of Education and Training.
Hargreaves, A., Lieberman, A., Fullan, M., & Hopkins, D. (1998). *International handbook of educational change*. Dordrecht, The Netherlands: Kluwer Press.
Hargreaves, A., Shaw, P., & Fink, D. (1997). *Research questions for the seven frames*. Toronto: Authors.
Hargreaves, D. H. (1967). *Social relations in a secondary school*. London: Routledge and Kegan Paul.
Hargreaves, D. H. (1995). School culture, school effectiveness and school improvement. *School Effectiveness and School Improvement, 6*(1), 23–46.
Harris, A. (1998). Differential effectiveness in secondary schools: Strategies for change and development. *The Journal of Educational Management and Administration, 26*(3), 269–278.
Harvey, D. (1989). *The condition of post modernity*. Oxford: Basil Blackwell.
Herzberg, F. (1976). *The managerial choice: To be efficient and to be human*. Homewood, IL: Dow Jones-Irwin.
Hopkins, D., Aincow, M., & West, M. (1994). *School improvement in an era of change*. London: Cassell.
House, E. R. (1979). Technology versus craft. A ten year perspective on innovation. *Journal of Curriculum Studies, 11*(1), 1–15.
Huberman, A. M. (1988). Teacher careers and school improvement. *Journal of Curriculum Studies, 20*(2), 119–132.

Huberman, M. (1992). Teacher development and instructional mastery. In A. Hargreaves & M. Fullan (Eds.), *Understanding teacher development* (pp. 122–142). London: Cassell.
Huberman, M. (1993). *The lives of teachers.* London: Cassell.
Huberman, M., & Miles, M. (1984). *Innovation up close.* New York: Plenum.
Janis, I. (1972). *Victims of groupthink.* Boston, MA: Houghton Mifflin.
Johnson, S. M. (1984). *Teacher unions in schools.* Philadelphia: Temple University Press.
Joyce, B. R., & Murphy, C. (1990). Epilogue: The curious complexities of cultural change. In B. R. Joyce (Ed.), *Changing school culture through staff development* (pp. 247–250). Alexandria, VA: Association for Supervision and Curriculum Development.
Joyce, B. R., & Showers, B. (1988). *Student achievement through staff development.* New York: Longman.
Kanter, R. M. (1983). *Change masters.* New York: Simon & Schuster.
Kerchner, C. T., & Koppich, K. D. (1993). *A union of professionals: Labor relations and educational reform.* New York: Teachers College Press.
King, A. J. (1986). *The adolescent experience.* Toronto: Ontario Secondary School Teachers' Federation.
King, A. J. C., Warren, W. K., & Peart, M. J. (1988). *The teaching experience.* Toronto: Ontario Secondary School Teachers' Federation.
Kohn, A. (1998). Only for my kid. How privileged parents undermine school reform. *Phi Delta Kappan, 79*(8), 568–577.
Kuhn, T. (1962). *The structure of scientific revolutions.* Chicago: University of Chicago Press.
Lacey, C. (1970). *Hightown grammar: The school as a social system.* Manchester: Manchester University Press.
Lacey, C. (1977). *The socialization of teachers.* London: Methuen.
Larson, S. M. (1980). Proletarianization and educated labour. *Theory and Society, 9*(1), 131–175.
Leithwood, K. A. (1992). The move toward transformational leadership. *Educational Leadership, 49*(5), 8–12.
Leithwood, K. A. (1993). *Contributions of transformational leadership toward school restructuring.* Address to the University Council for Educational Administration, Houston, Texas.
Lieberman, A., & Grolnick, M. (1998). Educational reform networks: Changes in the forms of reform. In A. Hargreaves, A. Lieberman, M. Fullan, & D. Hopkins (Eds.), *International handbook of educational change* (pp. 710–729). Dordrecht, The Netherlands: Kluwer Press.
Lightfoot, S. (1983). *The good high school.* New York: Basic.
Little, J. W. (1982). Norms of collegiality and experimentation: Workplace conditions of school success. *American Educational Research Journal, 19*(3), 325–340.
Little, J. W. (1987). Teachers as colleagues. In V. Koehler (Ed.), *Educators handbook. A research perspective* (pp. 491–518). New York: Longmans.
Little, J. W. (1993). Professional communities in comprehensive high schools. The two worlds of academic and vocational. In M. McLaughlin & J. W.

Little (Eds.), *Cultures and contexts of teaching* (pp. 137–163). New York: Teachers College Press.

Lortie, D.C. (1975). *School teacher: A sociological study.* Chicago University of Chicago Press.

Louden, W. (1991). *Understanding teaching.* London Cassell.

Louis, K., Toole, J., & Hargreaves, A. (1998). Rethinking school improvement. In K. Louis, J. Toole, & A. Hargreaves (Eds.), *Handbook in research in education administration* (pp. 251–276). New York: Longman.

Louis, K. S. (1990). The role of the school district in school improvement. In M. Holmes, K. Leithwood, & D. Musella (Eds.), *Educational policy for effective schools* (pp. 145–167). Toronto: O.I.S.E. Press.

Louis, K. S., & Miles, M. B. (1990). *Improving the urban high school: What works and why?* New York: Teachers College Press.

Martel, G. (1995). *A new education politics.* Toronto: James Lorimer and Company.

McDonnell, L. M., & Pascal, A. H. (1988). *Teachers' unions and educational reform.* Washington, DC: Rand Corporation.

McLaughlin, M. (1990). The Rand Change Agent Study. Macro perspectives and micro realities. *Educational Researcher, 19*(9), 11–15.

McLaughlin, M. (1993). What matters most in teachers' workplace context? In M. McLaughlin & J. W. Little (Eds.), *Cultures and contexts of teaching* (pp. 79–103). New York: Teachers College Press.

McLaughlin, M. W., & Talbert, J. E. (1993). *Contexts that matter for teaching and learning.* Palo Alto: Center for Research on the Context of Secondary School Teaching.

Merton, R. K. (1970). Insiders and outsiders: A chapter in the sociology of knowledge. *American Journal of Sociology, 78*(1), 9–47.

Metz, M. H. (1991). Real school: A universal drama amid disparate experience. In D. E. Mitchell & M. E. Goetz (Eds.), *Education politics for the new century* (pp. 75–91). New York: Falmer Press.

Miles, M. (1998). Finding keys to school change. In A. Hargreaves, A. Lieberman, M. Fullan, & D. Hopkins (Eds.), *International handbook of educational change* (pp. 37–69). Dordrecht, The Netherlands: Kluwer Press.

Miles, M. B., & Huberman, A. M. (1984). *Innovations up close: How school improvement works.* New York: Plenum Press.

Mirel, J. (1994). School reform unplugged. The Bensonville New American Schools Project. *American Educational Research Journal, 31*(3), 481–518.

Mitchell, D. E., & Kerchner, C. T. (1983). Labour relations and teacher policy. In L. S. Shulman & G. Sykes (Eds.), *Handbook of teaching and policy* (pp. 214–238). New York: Longman.

Moon, B. (1983). *Comprehensive schools: Challenge and change.* Windsor, UK: Nelson Publishing.

Morgan, G. (1997). *Images of organizations.* London: Sage.

Morgan, G., & Morgan, K. (1992). *Beyond the glitterspeak.* Toronto: Ontario Teachers' Federation.

Mortimore, P. (1991). The nature and findings on school effectiveness in the primary sector. In S. Riddell & S. Brown (Eds.), *School effectiveness research: Its message for school improvement.* Edinburgh: HMSO.

Mortimore, P. (1995). *Effective schools: Current impact and future potential.* The Director's Inaugural Lecture. London: Institute of Education.

Mortimore, P., Sammons, P., Stoll, L., Lewis, D., & Ecob, R. (1988). *School matters: The junior years.* Somerset, UK: Open University Press.

Mortimore, P., & Whitty, G. (1997). Can school improvement overcome the effects of disadvantage? In *Pursuing Excellence in Education* (pp. 1–17). London: Institute of Education.

National Commission on Education. (1996). *Success against the odds.* London: Routledge.

Neil, A. S. (1960). *Summerhill: A radical approach to child rearing.* New York: Hart Publishing.

Neil, A. S. (1966). *Freedom not license.* New York: Hart Publishing.

Newmann, F. M., & Wehlage, G. (1995). *Successful school restructuring.* Alexandria, VA: Association for Supervision and Curriculum Development.

Nias, J., Southworth, G., & Yeomans, R. (1989). *Staff relationships in the primary school.* London: Cassell.

Oakes, J., Wells, A. S., Yonezawa, S., & Ray, K. (1997). Change agentry and the quest for equity: Lessons from detracking schools. In A. Hargreaves (Ed.), *Rethinking educational change with heart and mind: The 1997 ASCD yearbook* (pp. 43–72). Alexandria, VA: Association for Supervision and Curriculum Development.

Odden, A. (1996). New American schools: Improving schools productivity in the United States. *Management in Education, 10*(5), 10–12.

Ontario Department of Education. (1968). *Living and learning: Report of the provincial committee on aims and objectives of education in the schools of Ontario.* Toronto: Newton Publishing Company.

Ontario Department of Education. (1971). *High School 1: Curricular HS1.* Toronto: Ontario Department of Education.

Ontario Royal Commission on Learning. (1994). *For the love of learning: Report of the Royal Commission on Learning.* Toronto: Queen's Printer for Ontario.

Purkey, W. W., & Novak, J. (1984). *Inviting school success* (2nd ed.). Belmont CA: Wadsworth.

Reynolds, D. (1996). Turning around ineffective schools: Some evidence and some speculations. In J. Gray, D. Reynolds, C. Fitz-Gibbon, & D. Jesson (Eds.), *Merging traditions: The future of research on school effectiveness and school improvement* (pp. 150–162). London: Cassell.

Reynolds, D., Creemers, B. P. M., Nesselrodt, P. S., Schaffer, E. C., Stringfield, S., & Teddlie, C. (1994). *Advances in school effectiveness research and practice.* Oxford: Elsevier Science Ltd.

Reynolds, D., Hopkins, D., & Stoll, L. (1993). Linking school effectiveness knowledge and school improvement practice. Towards a synergy. *School Effectiveness and School Improvement, 4*(1), 37–58.

Reynolds, D., & Packer, A. (1992). School effectiveness and school improvement in the 1990s. In D. Reynolds & P. Cuttance (Eds.), *School effectiveness: Research policy and practice* (pp. 171–187). London: Cassell.

Riley, K. (1998). *Whose school is it anyway.* London: Falmer Press.

Robertson, S. (1996). Teachers' work, restructuring and post fordism: Constructing the new professionalism. In I. F. Goodson & A. Hargreaves (Eds.), *Teachers' professional lives* (pp. 11–44). London: Falmer Press.

Rosenau, P. M. (1992). *Post-modernism and the social sciences: Insights, inroads, and intrusions.* Princeton, NJ: Princeton University Press.

Rosenholtz, S. J. (1989). *Teacher workplace: The social organization of schools.* New York: Longman.

Rudduck, J. (1991). *Innovation and change.* Milton Keynes, UK: Open University Press.

Rudduck, J., Day, J., & Wallace, G. (1997). Student perspectives on school improvement. In A. Hargreaves (Ed.), *Rethinking educational change with heart and mind: The 1997 ASCD yearbook* (pp. 73–91). Alexandria, VA: Association for Supervision and Curriculum Development.

Rutter, M., Maughan, B., Mortimore, P., & Ousten, J. (1979). *Fifteen thousand hours: Secondary schools and their effects on children.* London: Open Books.

Sammons, P., Mortimore, P., & Hillman, J. (1995). *Key characteristics of effective schools: A review of school effectiveness research.* London: Office for Standards in Education.

Sammons, P., Mortimore, P., & Thomas, S. (1996). Do schools perform consistently across outcomes and areas? In J. Gray, D. Reynolds, C. Fitzgibbons, & D. Jesson (Eds.), *Merging traditions: The future of research of school and school improvement* (pp. 3–29). London: Cassell.

Sarason, S. (1971). *The culture of the school and the problem of change.* Boston: Allyn & Bacon.

Sarason, S. (1972). *The creation of settings and the future societies.* San Francisco: Jossey-Bass.

Sarason, S. (1990). *The predictable failure of educational reform.* San Francisco: Jossey-Bass.

Sarason, S. (1996). *Revisiting the culture of the school and the problem of change.* New York: Teachers College Press.

Schein, E. H. (1985). *Organizational culture and leadership.* San Francisco: Jossey-Bass.

Senge, P. (1990). *The fifth discipline: The art and practice of the learning organization.* New York: Doubleday.

Sergiovanni, T. (1992a). *Moral leadership.* San Francisco: Jossey-Bass.

Sergiovanni, T. (1992b). *Schools as moral communities.* San Francisco: Jossey-Bass.

Shakeshaft, C. (1987). *Women in educational administration.* Newbury Park, NJ: Sage.

Shakeshaft, C. (1993). Women in educational management in the United States. In J. Ouston (Ed.), *Women in educational management* (pp. 45–63). London: Longmans.

Sikes, P. (1985). The life cycles of the teacher. In S. Ball & I. Goodson (Eds.), *Teachers' lives and careers* (pp. 27–60). London: Falmer Press.

Sirotnik, K. A. (1998). Ecological images of change: Limits and possibilities. In A. Hargreaves, A. Lieberman, M. Fullan, & D. Hopkins (Eds.), *International handbook of educational change* (pp. 181–197). Dordrecht, The Netherlands: Kluwer Press.

Siskin, L. (1994). *Realms of knowledge: Academic departments in secondary schools.* London: Falmer Press.

Smith, L. M., Dwyer, D.C., Prunty, J. J., & Kleine, P. F. (1987). *The fate of an innovative school.* London: Falmer Press.

Smith, L. M., & Keith, P. (1971). *Anatomy of educational innovation.* New York: Wiley.

Smith, W. F., & Andrews, R. L. (1989). *Instructional leadership: How principals make a difference.* Alexandria, VA: Association for Supervision and Curriculum Development.

Smyth, J. (1991). International perspectives on teacher collegiality: A labour process discussion based on the concept of teachers' work. *British Journal of Sociology in Education, 12*(3), 323–346.

Soja, E. (1989). *Postmodern geographies: The reassertion of space in critical social theory.* New York: Verso.

Stacey, R. (1995). *Managing chaos.* London: Kogan Page.

Stamp, R. (1982). *The schools of Ontario.* Toronto: Queen's Printers of Ontario.

Starratt, R. J. (1993). *The drama of leadership.* London: Falmer Press.

Stevenson, H. W. (1992, December). Learning from Asian schools. *Scientific American,* p. 76.

Stodolsky, S. S. (1993). A framework for subject matter comparisons in high schools. *Teaching and Teacher Education, 9,* 333–346.

Stoll, L., & Fink, D. (1992). Effective school change: The Halton approach. *School Effectiveness and School Improvement, 3*(1), 19–41.

Stoll, L., & Fink, D. (1994). Voices from the field. *School Effectiveness and School Improvements, 5*(2), 149–177.

Stoll, L., & Fink, D. (1996). *Changing our schools. Linking school effectiveness and school improvement.* Buckingham, UK: Open University Press.

Stoll, L., & Fink, D. (1998). The cruising school: The unidentified ineffective school. In L. Stoll & K. Myers (Eds.), *Schools in difficulty: No quick fixes* (pp. 186–206). Chichester: Falmer Press.

Stoll, L., & Myers, K. (Eds.). (1998). *Schools in difficulty: No quick fixes.* London: Falmer Press.

Stringfield, S., Ross, S., & Smith L. (Eds.). (1996). *Bold plans for school restructuring: The new American schools design.* Mahwah, NJ: Lawrence Earlbaum Associates.

Sweetland, S. R. (1997). Human capital theory: Foundations of a field of inquiry. *Review of Educational Research, 66*(3), 341–359.

Talbert, J. E. (1993). Constructing a school-wide professional community: The negotiated order of a performing arts school. In M. McLaughlin & J. W. Little (Eds.), *Cultures and contexts of teaching* (pp. 164–184). New York: Teachers College Press.

Teddlie, C., & Stringfield, S. (1993). *Schools make a difference. Lessons learned from a 10 year study of school effects.* New York: Teachers College Press.

Telford, H. (1996). *Transforming schools through collaborative leadership.* London Falmer Press.
Toffler, A. (1990). *Powershift.* New York: Bantam Books.
Tyack, D., & Tobin, W. (1994). The Grammar of schooling: Why has it been so hard to change? *American Educational Research Journal, 31*(3), 453–479.
U.S. National Education Commission on Time and Learning. (1994). *Prisoners of time.* Washington, DC: U.S. Government.
Van Velzen, W., Miles, M., Ekholm, M., Hameyer, U., & Robin, D. (1985). *Making school improvement work.* Leuven, Belgium: Acco Publishers.
Walter and Duncan Gordon Charitable Foundation. (1995). *The seeds of change: The Manitoba school improvement program.* Toronto: Author.
Watts, G. D., & Castle, S. (1993). The time dilemma in school restructuring. *Phi Delta Kappan, 75*(4), 306–309.
Watts, J. (Ed.). (1977). *The Countesthorpe experience.* London: George Allen and Unwin Ltd.
Wells, A., Carnochan, S., Slayton, J., & Allen, R. (1998). Globalization and educational change. In A. Hargreaves, A. Lieberman, M. Fullan, & D. Hopkins (Eds.), *International handbook of educational change* (pp. 297–321). Dordrecht, The Netherlands: Kluwer Press.
Wheatley, M. (1994). *Leadership and the new science.* San Francisco: Berrett-Koehler.
Whitty, G. (1997). Creating quasi-markets in education: A review of recent research on parental choice and school autonomy in three countries. In M. W. Apple (Ed.), *Review of research in education* (pp. 3–47). Washington, DC: American Educational Research Association.
Whitty, G. (1998). *New labour, education and disadvantage.* Paper delivered at the Department of Applied Social Studies, University of Oxford, February 24.
Whitty, G., Power, S., & Halpin, D. (1998). *Devolution and choice in education. The school, the state and the market.* Buckingham, UK: Open University Press.
Wohlstetter, P. (1995). Getting school-based management right: What works and what doesn't. *Phi Delta Kappan, 77*(1) 22–26.
Woods, P. (1979). *The school divided.* London: Routledge and Kegan Paul.
Woods, P. (1986). *Inside school: Ethnography in educational research* London: Routledge and Kegan Paul.
Yaakobi, D., & Sharan, S. (1985). Teacher beliefs and practices: The discipline carries the message. *Journal of Education for Teaching, 11,* 187–199.

Index

About the Author

Dean Fink is an international educational development consultant. He is a former superintendent and principal in Ontario, Canada. In his career he has taught at all levels of education from primary grades to the Ph.D. level. He holds postgraduate degrees in both history and educational administration from the University of Toronto and the Open University in the United Kingdom. In the past 6 years, Dr. Fink has made presentations or conducted workshops in 27 different countries including Canada, the United States, the United Kingdom, Australia, New Zealand, Israel, Russia, Ukraine, Ireland, Sweden, Denmark, Turkey, and the Baltic states. Dean has presented keynote addresses to a number of national and international conferences. He has also published numerous articles on topics related to school effectiveness, leadership, and change in schools, as well as co-authoring *Changing Our Schools* (Open University Press, 1996) with Louise Stoll of the University of Bath. His next book with Louise Stoll and Lorna Earl, *It's About Learning and It's About Time,* will be published by Falmer Press. Dr. Fink is an associate of the International Centre for Educational Change at the Ontario Institute for Studies in Education, where he is involved with the Peel/University partnership project on the Change Frames and the Change Over Time project funded by the Spencer Foundation. He is a fellow of the University of Hull, England, and Queens University–Belfast and a research associate of the Centre for Teacher and School Development of the University of Nottingham.